*Praise for*

LIGHT IN BANDAGED PLACES

"*Light in Bandaged Places* is a brave, beautiful book about over-coming betrayal and sexual abuse by a trusted teacher. Liz Kinchen's healing journey is an inspiration that will resonate with those searching for answers within progressive Christianity and Buddhist teachings. This insightful memoir is full of painful yet poignant stories that illustrate the author's quest to find authentic love and her true spiritual home."

—Vanessa Linsey, author of *Metta Mom,*
*A Mindful Guide to Managing Your Mood and Your Brood*

"When her connection with her middle school teacher—one that felt safe and mutually-respectful—crosses boundaries into groom-ing and adulterous behavior, Liz must overcome the confusion and deceitfulness of this early and intimate relationship as she navigates her passage into adulthood. *Light in Bandaged Places* offers its readers a courageous examination of the long-lasting effects of trauma during vulnerable teen years."

—Anne Reeder Heck, author of *A Fierce Belief in Miracles*

"This memoir is a vulnerable account of the sexual abuse Kinchen, the author, suffered at the hands of a trusted middle school teacher. . . . This is an important book for anyone who is suffering with brokenness from the silent shame and feelings of unworthi-ness. Through her honesty, she shines a light of hope as she goes through the process of bandaging the wounds of betrayal; she sparks a conversation that allowed her to heal her own darkness that will open doors for others too. Powerful and moving."

—Meg Nocero, award-winning author of *Butterfly Awakens:*
*A Memoir of Transformation Through Grief, The Magical Guide to Bliss,*
and *Sparkle & Shine*

"Kinchen offers us a meticulously written, honest, and unflinching account of her path from early-on betrayal through her impressively mined history of love to a courageous, exultant emergence. This beautifully rendered memoir invites us into the journey of an intrepid woman's aching need to not only reclaim her story but, just as importantly, to revive her faith in the holiness of one's lived truth. It is larger than one person's recovery; it serves as a benediction for all of us seeking wholeness."
—Nina Carmel, MSW, RYT, CMT, founding director of The Therapy
     Center for Mind and Body, guiding teacher of The Awareness
     Training Program, psychotherapist, and meditation teacher

"Liz's book is an inspirational story of abuse and overcoming childhood trauma. Her story is that of many survivors who may not see the full extent of sexual abuse till they are older. As she tells her story of childhood, teen years, and adulthood, her book draws you into her story—feeling the pain that she endured, and the confusion, and celebrating her growth. As a fellow survivor, I was reminded of the power of survivors, their incredible gifts and their resiliency. A must-read for survivors and their families."
     —Elizabeth Sullivan, founder of EmpowerSurvivors

"Written with generous vulnerability and uncommon grace, Liz Kinchen's memoir *Light in Bandaged Places* is an unflinching exploration of self-discovery, faith, resilience, and love. Kinchen's hopeful honesty serves as an invitation to us all to allow light into our own broken places and find strength in the mending."
     —Julie Carrick Dalton, author of *The Last Beekeeper*

"A deeply personal look at how a predator's actions reverberate throughout someone's entire lifetime innumerable ways. Liz Kinchen's beautifully constructed memoir shines a light on the insidious nature of sexual abuse by a trusted adult. Her thoughtful examination also provides hope for survivors searching for authentic healing."
     —Melinda G. McCall, DVM, author of *Driving Home Naked*

"Liz shares from deep in her soul the doubts and almost unbearable pain of survivorship from a menacing child predator. While uniquely her own, her story offers light for many others seeking to swim back to the surface after abuse disguised as 'love.' The journey to become whole again—to emerge stronger, wiser, and more resilient after suffering—is a universal tale. Read this to feel the strength, power, and courage."

—Shirley Eichenberger-Archer, MA,
author of *Pilates Fusion: Well-being for Body, Mind & Spirit*

"*Light in Bandaged Places* is a moving, introspective, and honest memoir. The first half of the book is the story of abuse by a trusted teacher. In the second half, Kinchen takes us on her journey of healing, from childhood trauma to wholeness. The story is beautifully interwoven with reflections on complex family relationships. Kinchen's writing is raw, brave, and full of hope."

—Kathy Elkind, author of *To Walk It Is to See It:*
*1 Couple, 98 Days, 1400 Miles on Europe's GR5*

# LIGHT

# IN

# BANDAGED

# PLACES

## Healing *in the* Wake
## *of* Young Betrayal

LIZ KINCHEN

SHE WRITES PRESS

Published 2023
Printed in the United States of America
Print ISBN: 978-1-64742-535-7
Ebook ISBN: 978-1-64742-536-4
Library of Congress Control Number: 2023902533

For information, address:
She Writes Press
1569 Solano Ave #546
Berkeley, CA 94707

Interior Design by Stacey Aaronson

She Writes Press is a division of SparkPoint Studio, LLC.

Dedicated to my husband, Jason—the true love of my life;
my three beautiful children, Max, David, and Savannah;
and all of the angels in my life who brought me this far.
You saved me, and you continue to save me every day.
I am forever grateful.

*Amazing grace, how sweet the sound*
*That saved a wretch like me.*
*I once was lost, but now I am found,*
*Was blind, but now I see.*

—JOHN NEWTON

## author's note

I have tried to recreate events, activities, and conversations from my memories of them. Nothing has been intentionally misrepresented. To protect privacy, I have changed the names of individuals and places in some instances and changed or blended some identifying characteristics and details, including physical properties, occupations, and places of residence. Dialogue is constructed from my best memory, journals, and input from others. Many significant people and relationships that matter to me didn't make it into this story—maybe I'll catch you in my next book! My intent is to tell my story for the potential benefit of others who have touched similar experiences; it is not to harm anyone. This is for all the girls and the women they grow into.

## cover art

Kintsugi, based in Zen Buddhism, is the ancient Japanese art of using precious metals such as gold to bond together pieces of broken pottery. The cracks are highlighted, drawing attention to, rather than away from, the breaks. Symbolizing healing and resilience, the broken object accepts that its imperfect past makes it more robust, more beautiful, and more precious than before it was broken. The broken, imperfect, and painful parts of ourselves radiate light, gold, and beauty.

*Don't turn away. Keep your gaze on the bandaged place.*
*That's where the light enters you.*

—JELAL AL DIN RUMI,
translation by Coleman Barks

# TABLE OF CONTENTS

*Confirmation—Age 13*

*High School Graduation—Age 18*

*one*

---

## ISOLATION AND SILENCE

MY PARENTS BELIEVED GOD WOULD TAKE CARE OF ALL THINGS, including me, when I was lost and confused or needed someone to notice me. Although it was never spoken out loud, the way it worked was that God was to play the role of parent in my young life, and my parents pretty much left the job up to Him.

If someone asked what religion I grew up with, I explained my father was a minister in the strict Missouri Synod branch of Lutheran Protestantism. More accurately, the religion of isolation and the dogma of silence raised me. This was not the gracious silence of a Quaker meeting, with intentional quiet to hear God better. My silence was nonintentional, an artifact of being born into a family with little overt emotional attachment to each other, thus little conversation, contact, concern, or comfort. I knew none of these. I suppose God raised me, which sounds like it should be a pretty great prospect, but to me, He was at best elusive or punishing, or both. This is how the Lutheran Church portrayed Him to me all my young life.

My religion of isolation taught me to avoid feeling disappointed or hurt by not seeking or expecting much from people, believing I had little or no worth, and keeping myself invisible. I learned not to engage emotionally with people or life. Still, I carried inside me the possibility of a gentler, loving God, but I had to find that version of God on my own.

It was summertime on Long Island, and I had no place to be, nothing I had to do. I was like a feral child, roaming around the rambling house and yard in my bare feet, which were black from wearing no shoes for long and lazy days. My skin was dark, too, from endless days outdoors in the sun. By the end of summer, I was a bronzed shade of honey-laced mocha, which looked almost strange on a white girl. I often drifted over to the fence near the red storage barn to coax some more raspberries from the straggly bushes. Every sun-warmed luscious berry went into my watering mouth.

"Come on, Lisa!" I urged. "Let's run fast, faster than yesterday!"

I reached back to give her a fond but firm slap on the rump as we pranced around the yard, dodging among bushes, feet clacking when we crossed the asphalt parking lot next to our church. Lisa was my imaginary horse. I switched between imagining I was riding my horse and being the horse. I desperately wished I was a horse. Or rode a real horse. Even more, I desperately wished I had a twin sister who knew all my thoughts and liked all the same things I did. So, when Lisa wasn't my horse, she was my twin sister. We did everything together, and she filled that empty space inside. Together we were complete. We were perfect.

Tired of running around outside, Lisa and I flopped on the bed, pulled a random Nancy Drew book from the stack of books on the floor, and read for a while.

"I think Bess is a scaredy-cat," Lisa frowned.

"She's just not as brave as Nancy," I countered. "But she's such a good friend, don't you think? So loyal. And Nancy loves her."

"Yeah, you're right. They make a good team—like us! Let's go back outside and set up the high jump."

Clomping down the stairs, we passed Pete's room. Behind his closed door we heard him strumming his guitar, as usual. He hardly ever came out of that darkened room, and when he did, a strange musty sweet smell spilled into the hallway.

Outside, the white rope waited for us on the ground between two trees spaced perfectly apart.

"You get that end, and I'll get this end," I called to Lisa, reaching up to tie my end to the branch just within my reach.

"I bet I can jump higher than you today!" Lisa teased, taking a running start.

"Not this time! Watch me!"

We used the scissor-cut, approaching the rope sideways and throwing first one leg over, then our bodies, until we reached a scary and impossible height. Sure enough, neither of us made it over. But we didn't mind; we switched to working on our embroidery project, picking up the cloth and threads which waited there on the hammock where we last left them. While we stitched, we made up a play in our heads. We never actually showed anyone; even though there were seven in my family, everyone was too busy or somewhere else. Andy, four years younger than me, never wanted to play, talk, or do much of anything. Pete's main interaction with me was to hide in my closet after I went to bed and terrify me by leaping out just as my eyes were closing. Judy, seven years older, was always out somewhere with her friends, and my oldest sister, Pat, lived a few towns away with her husband and baby. Mom was at work at the mall, and Daddy just did his own things in his home office or at the church. Even when any of us were in a room together, to me, it felt like I was alone.

So, hanging around at home, it was Lisa and me.

I lived my whole childhood, from 1955 until I left for college in 1973, in that old white house next to the church, so I got to know its every nook and cranny. It sat on four acres of land, along with our barn-like shed, stuffed with unused and unidentifiable items, like ancient lawnmowers and rakes, car parts, and lots of sagging boxes of papers and files. Between our house and the church, a large square parking lot was filled with cars on Sunday mornings, but the rest of the week it sat empty, allowing me space to hit tennis balls against the church's white concrete wall. I often watched Daddy hit golf balls from one end of our long yard to the other. I heard the *thwack, thwack, thwack* as the ball ricocheted among the leafy branches of the tall oak trees, then dropped with a plop onto the packed earth below.

"Go run and find the balls, Lizzie. But don't move them or pick them up. I'll meet you down there and you stand next to each one to show me where they are."

I scampered off, happy to play this ball-finder role for him. "You hit five but I can only find four," I called as he made his way to the trees.

"Don't worry, it's probably stuck in the branches of a tree. It'll come down eventually, but be on the lookout so it doesn't fall on your head!"

Sometimes he hit the golf balls in our living room, gently knocking them across the carpet with a quiet *quock* sound. No ball retrieval was necessary indoors, but he didn't mind that I watched. Every day he sat in his office smoking, and every afternoon he rested on the green vinyl couch at one end of the living room.

All of it was my playground, including the inside of the church building. There was a big, empty fellowship hall where my brothers and I sometimes ran around. For me, the altar of the fellowship hall was the Coke machine in the corner. For a dime, it would loudly dispense a pale green glass bottle of ice-cold Coca-Cola. The day Pete raced across the empty hall on a furniture dolly and broke his two front teeth, we had just knelt at that altar rail and sipped its icy sweetness.

Nearly every day after school during my elementary years, I walked from my house across the parking lot to the church. The rich, earthy smell of mimeograph ink wafted from the church office while the machine rhythmically spat out its paper offerings, which became the Sunday service bulletin. Many days, I skipped past the office and climbed the steps to the choir loft in the sanctuary. I took organ lessons and used the enormous electric pipe organ in the church to practice. My teacher was the church music director, which my parents considered a privilege. He was a kind man, but I dreaded those lessons, shamed by my lack of talent. I practiced out of a strong sense of obligation.

The sanctuary was a scary place to me, so dim and still I feared I might hear God quietly breathing. It was neat and tidy, the hymnals neatly tucked in their racks behind every staunch pew. Its orderliness was peaceful to me, so unlike my disheveled home, but I always felt like I did not belong there. I had permission to practice the organ, but part of me was always ready to bolt if I got spooked by an unexpected noise. Lisa wasn't usually with me when I was in the church. If she was there, she was quiet, too.

When the sun went down in the late winter afternoons, no light came in through the stained-glass windows, and the large space became cloaked in cold and darkness. I tiptoed to the choir loft and sat on the smooth, polished wood bench in front of the electric organ. I rolled open the cover to reveal the double keyboards and turned the electric switch on. I jumped when it immediately came alive, humming and buzzing with electricity and creaking as all the pipes warmed up. My feet could barely reach the row of pedals beneath the console, but I perched on the edge of the bench and played them tentatively, their deep tones vibrating throughout the sacred space.

I was afraid of the organ, but I liked learning the sound of each instrument it could tone, from the brash strings to the smooth reeds. When I practiced my pieces, I made sure to keep the volume low in case anyone stopped by the office; the thought of anyone listening to me was mortifying. I knew my timid playing held no creativity or enthusiasm.

I guess it's hard to embrace one's instrument when you are frightened of it and the space it's in.

This fear of being in the church's sanctuary was how I felt about God in general. I was fearful and uncomfortable, small and deficient in my relationship with Him. Of course, I went to church and Sunday School every week. How could I not, with Daddy being the minister? I sang in the choir even though I could not carry a tune; I only mouthed the words. I did every activity a child was supposed to do in church. I was an acolyte, a teacher's helper, and I became confirmed at age thirteen when

I was supposed to. I memorized the catechism, could recite all the books of the Bible in order, and I prayed to God at dinner and before bed. But, through it all, I was scared of Him.

I didn't think God was anywhere except in the sanctuary at church, so when I wasn't practicing my organ lessons, I freely roamed about the other rooms. I wrote on the dusty classroom chalkboards, peeked into boxes of arts and crafts supplies, climbed up on the stage, and explored every bathroom and closet. These were hours and years spent alone and in quiet, as the church was empty except for evening meetings and Sunday services, when people wearing their finest filled the sanctuary. The rest of the time, the building was mine; when it was empty, I belonged there.

Odd to think that although the church was "God's home," to me God occupied a distant and authoritarian place in the sanctuary, just as Pastor Fink, my father, occupied a distant place in my house across the parking lot—and in my life. My father's connection with God lent him authority in my mind, not any parenting he did. Rather than God or anyone else except Lisa, the church building itself was my friend and companion, and it filled the landscape of these years of my life.

I didn't know it then, but soon I would find a special friend to keep me company. I had one more year of elementary school to finish before I would meet him.

Every morning before school, I kept watch at the dining room window and waited for the school bus to pull into the church parking lot. Mom waited with me in her bathrobe, looking tired already.

"Have you got your lunch, dear?" Mom asked. This is what

she asked every morning. It was the only thing she asked, as we kept our otherwise silent vigil, as if having that lunch could fortify me from all harm.

"Yes, I've got it, Mom."

She hadn't even started on last night's dinner dishes, still dirty and cluttered on the kitchen table. The brown cuckoo clock on the wall, with its two long chains and heavy pinecones on the ends, ticked steadily in the quiet room. I had my coat on, my bookbag packed, my trusty bag lunch of the bologna-and-butter sandwich on Wonder bread, and Twinkies. When the bus finally made its laborious wide turn in the empty parking lot and pulled to a squeaky stop, I scurried out the door.

"Bye, Mom," I called over my shoulder as I ran down the flagstone walkway, barely seeing her goodbye wave.

I climbed into the bus and joined the four or five other children already collected in their seats, waiting to complete the journey to our school several towns away.

I mumbled hello to them as I got on, but once I settled into my seat, we were all silent. We lived in different neighborhoods and towns and were in different grades in school. Three Black girls rode the bus with me; two were twins with matching neatly braided hair. I envied their twinness. Their long hair contrasted with my own short bowl cut that I desperately wanted to grow out. The third girl, Angela, was pretty and always had beautiful new clothes at the beginning of each school year, which I also envied. The twins sat together, of course, but the rest of us sat in separate seats. I invoked Lisa to sit next to me on these rides. In a few years, race tensions would mount across the country, and hallway violence became the norm in our schools, but now it was shyness that kept us apart.

We headed off to Nassau Lutheran School, where we all received a strict education in the dogma of the most conservative version of the Lutheran Church in America, just like Daddy's church. School wasn't scary like church, but it wasn't much fun, either, and I gravitated toward the shadows.

The hallways of this school were dreary and dimly lit, perhaps to restrain any excitement we kids might have wanted to express while passing in the halls. Across the street was a fire station, and when the whistle blew, no one could speak or be heard. We just waited it out, covering our ears. The siren did come in handy when we had those Cold War drills that sent us cowering under our desks, hands covering our heads.

Every night for homework, we had to memorize a Bible verse and recite it the next day. I was a conscientious student and did well in school. I conducted myself well, too, always quiet and unassuming, never sullying the halls or classrooms with any childhood exuberance. Only one time was there an exception to this unremarkable record of behavior, when the teacher called me up to the front of the class. She told me to hold out both hands in front of me, palm side down, and I knew what was coming next: the metal ruler.

I don't know what I had done wrong—maybe I had sinned by memorizing the wrong Bible verse? For ten strikes, I had to receive the blow of the solid, cold ruler on the top of my knuckles without pulling away. I am sure that whatever it was I did wrong, I never did it again.

Even though I was a reasonably athletic child and tried all the sports they taught in gym class, I was usually among the last to be chosen for teams. I liked gymnastics best because it didn't involve a team I could let down.

One spring day, our school held a field day competition at another school. I was on a relay team with several schoolmates;

one of them was Angela from my bus, who was not just a pretty girl but the best girl athlete in my grade. I was nervous and wanted to do well because I was on her team; I was determined to give it my all. Our relay team spread out around the open field, each girl at her station. When the baton came to me, I shot out like a rocket toward the next girl. But then, sheer panic overcame me when I realized I wasn't entirely sure where the next girl was. Many girls were on the field; everything was a blur. Which girl was mine? I slowed down, then stopped, scanning the field for someone wearing our blue gym uniform, and decided I had found her up the hill. I sped out toward her.

"What are you doing?" shouted my teammates from down the hill. "Here, here. We're over here! Run this way! Give it to *her!*"

They waved their arms, pointing to a girl down the hill who was jumping up and down, arm extended and screaming, "Give it to me, here. Come on!"

Mortified, I ran toward her and slapped the dreaded baton into her outstretched hand. Tears streamed down my cheeks despite my desperate attempt to hold them in. Of course, we lost. On the bus ride home, Angela turned her back to me, refusing to look at me or talk to me. She continued to do so for several days afterward. I didn't know how I could have messed up so badly.

It turned out I had the visual acuity of a bat. We discovered this impairment several weeks later when Mom took me to the eye doctor. I had no idea the world was supposed to look sharp and clear. Fog and haziness were all I knew. After failing many tests at the stuffy optometrist's office, I consoled myself by choosing a stylish pair of sparkly pink glasses with pointed tips. I noticed I could now see really well.

Using my newfound vision to scan the *New York Times* magazine section one day, I came across an article that mentioned marijuana. I had no idea what that word meant and couldn't figure it out from the article's context, but I got the sense marijuana might be something bad or forbidden. Buttressed perhaps by my new glasses, I gathered up my courage to broach the subject with my mother.

After dinner one night, when everyone left the table, leaving my mother, as usual, to put away the food and do all the dishes, I squeaked out my question, "Mom, what is marijuana?"

She whirled around from the sink. "Why are you asking me about that?" Her voice was surprisingly sharp.

"I read an article about it in the newspaper and didn't understand it," I mumbled, taken aback by her tone. Knowing Mom didn't like anything controversial, I expected tension in this conversation, not hostility.

"That is something you should know nothing about. Don't think about it, and don't ask about it again! Just forget about it."

"Sorry," I said, and slunk away to my room. The humiliation crushed my heart. So much for my courage. Although I still wondered what marijuana was, I promised myself never to ask my mother a question like that again. Certainly not her, and maybe not anyone. I'd just figure things out on my own. And I'd behave better.

## two

# FINALLY, FRIENDS

IN SEVENTH GRADE, I SWITCHED FROM NASSAU LUTHERAN
School to the local public junior high. Right away, I saw Mr.
Johnson from afar, although I didn't have any classes with him
that year. He was a popular, well-liked teacher. When I
switched schools, they placed me in the B-track along with the
kids who got Bs and Cs. Although I was a straight-A student,
someone thought this would make the transition easier for me.
It did not. They moved me to the A-track in eighth grade, and
then life really began for me. That's when Mr. Johnson became
my teacher. Everyone wanted to be in his English class, and I
was!

Mr. Johnson was so tall, he appeared to always lean down
slightly, but he wasn't scary. His eyes sparkled, and his face
seemed kind and safe when he smiled. He was young and didn't
act formal or old-fashioned like my other teachers. Students
knew he was cool, with that crazy, curly, brown hair and mus-
tache. Mr. Johnson had an easy-going and calm manner; his
sentences were smooth, and he spoke clearly. He didn't talk
down to us, and he acted like everything was serious but not too
serious. But mostly, I believed he was on my side.

Usually, in all my classes, I sat in the last seat along the wall of every classroom. The middle or front of the classroom, unanchored and too visible, was disorienting to me; I may as well be thrown, alone, into the middle of the ocean. I sought my comfort zone of anonymity and invisibility, and my teachers either didn't notice or didn't mind. Except one. Mr. Johnson let me keep my seat along the wall in the back but, after a day or two, asked if I could see and hear well enough.

"Yes, I am fine, thanks," I assured him, not wanting him to force me to move.

"Just let me know if you decide you want to move up closer." His deep voice sounded friendly and warm, so I didn't worry that he was unhappy with my seat choice; he just wanted to be helpful.

The day we read *Evangeline* turned out to be an important day for me. It was the first time I saw a poem that long, and although I tried to follow it, the words and verses were a muddle. I worked to stay with it, though, out of a combination of duty and fear—a duo that was my constant companion throughout junior and senior high. These two kept me focused, gave me purpose, and provided an anchor in the middle of the ocean that was my childhood. I bobbed in the waves out on the ocean, my dependable legs treading water steadily and constantly, keeping my little head just above the waterline. My determination to do well in school kept me within sight of the shoreline, affording me some respite from my unconscious loneliness.

Mr. Johnson called on us one by one down the long rows of seats, and we marched our way through the long poem, each student taking their turn reading the next verse. I put forth a silent prayer that God would spare me from having to read out loud. A few seats in front of me, a girl named Judy Weil read her verse of *Evangeline* with clarity, feeling, and drama, which seemed old for her age. That put me on edge. Was this how we were expected to read aloud? There was no comment from Mr. Johnson about any of our renditions; he just nodded toward each of us. Now with only four kids ahead of me, my panic rose from my gut, higher and higher until it overtook my chest and lodged itself in my throat. I wanted to melt under my desk and die. I desperately hoped I wouldn't pee. The humiliation of that thought made me squeeze my legs together and ratcheted up the shaking coursing through my body. I chewed on the ends of my hair, now conveniently long and available for this use. Lightheaded, I prayed for the bell to ring or for some other deliverance to save me from the pending mortification. None came.

Mr. Johnson nodded at me and smiled, and I had no choice. I cleared my croaky throat, peering down at the words swimming on the page, and began to read. As I feared, my words came out pinched and shaky, and I tried to hide it all behind my book. I couldn't wait to get to the end of each long line, barely having enough breath left to get me through.

It didn't take long before Mr. Johnson coaxed, "Could you speak up a little louder so we can hear you in the front?" Forcing a little more pressure past my parched throat, I pushed out the rest of the verse.

As the next reader began, shame overtook me. I knew I must have sounded like I was about to cry through the whole long verse. I had to hold back the tears as I imagined the ridicule and judgment of my classmates and teacher. I hated the attention. No doubt they thought I was some sort of weird crybaby, and my ability to imagine any of them as my friends faded into darkness.

When the bell finally rang, I lowered my eyes to avoid the inevitable stares of my classmates. I dragged myself toward the door and out into the relative safety and anonymity of the hallways. Then I sensed a slight tug on my arm.

"Just a minute!" a voice called.

I had no choice but to turn and face my accuser. Judy Weil looked into my eyes and smiled, her long, curly, red hair springing around her shoulders.

"What's your name?" Judy asked. "I really liked how you read today in class!"

I immediately thought she was mocking me, so I just glanced at her and said nothing. My mind was in a swirl. What was she talking about? How could anyone say that about my reading? Either she was making fun of me, or she was strange. Either way, I wanted nothing to do with her.

Judy persisted, sincere. "No, really, I liked your reading. You read with real feeling. Nobody else did that. What is your name?"

"My name is Liz," I murmured. I didn't even like how my name sounded.

"Liz, I want you to come over to my house after school today. Do you think you can?" Judy was positively bouncy.

I thought either she actually meant what she said, or she was carrying her mockery a little far. Not knowing what else to say and feeling pressured by the unexpectedness of it as well as the urgency of getting to my next class, I said, "I guess so. I don't know where you live."

"Wait for me by the lockers after school, and I'll find you. We can walk home. I'm so glad you can come. See you later!" Judy called as we both walked our separate ways.

My heart beat faster as I considered going to the house of someone I didn't know. What would we talk about? What would it be like at her house? How long would I have to stay? Was it all a joke? Did she mean to taunt me about my reading once she got me to her house? Part of me dreaded the experience. But some small part of me felt noticed and maybe even sought after, with the possibility of a new friendship. Despite my doubts and fears, a little corner of my heart ventured a smile.

Judy did find me at the lockers later that day, and on the walk to her house, she was talkative and lively. She wondered why she hadn't seen me before. I told her about Nassau Lutheran School, and that in seventh grade I was in the B-track with a completely different set of kids. Judy understood then that I probably didn't know anyone in my classes, and I think it must have doubled her resolve to befriend me.

Like my house, hers was big. However, unlike mine, her house was in a development where all the houses on the street were the same: Long Island–style split levels. These homes had dozens of families with children who went to her local elementary school together. I imagined the boys in a stickball game in the front yards after dinner on summer nights and the girls playing hopscotch drawn in chalk on the sidewalk, like on TV.

Judy bounced into her house and sang out, "Hi, Mom! I'm home! I've brought a friend with me. Come and meet her!"

She flung her books and lunchbox at the foot of the stairs with confidence and grace, like she did this every day knowing her house was happy to see her. She was bouncy and sensitive at the same time.

Her mother came up from a lower level to greet me. "Hello. My name is Darle Weil." She shook my hand. "Welcome to our house. What is your name?"

"Liz," I whispered, not having much more to add but impressed with her immediate warm smile.

"Well, welcome, Liz. Do you girls want a snack? I just made some oatmeal cookies. Evelyn, Margie, and Danny will be home a little later, after their voice lessons."

Her mother spoke with a slight accent, which I couldn't place; it made her words clear and lyrical. She wore her salt-and-pepper hair in a loose bun on the top of her head; I wondered how it stayed up there. Her face was friendly and relaxed, her eyes sparkled, and she held herself with a subtle poise, as though she knew every part of her mattered.

After we ate the warm cookies with milk, Mrs. Weil suggested Judy show me around their house. We went down the few steps leading to the den of their home, which was a well-used room with books, games, and things sprinkled about, yet it was clean. It seemed to carry itself as though everything about it had importance.

We made our way upstairs to Judy's room, which she told me she shared with her sister, Evelyn. She asked me if I liked listening to music, to which I replied with some degree of confidence, "Yeah, I do. I like Bob Dylan and Joan Baez and Judy Collins. How about you?"

"Oh, yes. They're my favorites. That's great—we like the same music! I just got this album by Don McLean. Do you know him? There's a song I want you to hear."

I didn't know Don McLean, but I listened carefully when Judy placed some headphones on my head. She let the whole song play so I could hear it all, and she watched me as I listened to a song about a man who lost his way but was hopeful that he'd return to the one he loved—my kind of lyrics. Judy played a few more songs for me, and then told me about a neighborhood where her family and some other people from a place called the Ethical Humanist Society worked on weekends. There was a shelter or youth center in disrepair, and they were painting and fixing it up so kids who lived in that tough neighborhood could use it. I had never heard of anyone doing that—certainly not anyone I knew—and I was impressed again. *What kind of family does that together?* I wondered to myself.

"Maybe you can go with us sometime," Judy offered.

"Sure," I said with some doubt in my voice that I wished was not there. It was just so different from anything I'd ever done. It seemed a little beyond my grasp.

Several days later, Judy invited me to stay for dinner. I was worried about this because I rarely ate at anyone else's house, plus I was a fussy eater. But my curiosity was stronger than my fear, and I agreed.

I was surprised and then dismayed when a garden salad— the first course (a first course?)—appeared on the table before each of us. I could eat a garden salad with no problem, but as I inspected more closely, I saw my salad had dressing on it. I had never eaten salad with dressing before, and a weight crept into my chest. I always thought salad dressing was for adults. At the Weil dinner table, each person was given their own plate, already filled with dressed salad. In contrast, my mother would set a large bowl set in the middle of the table from which we could help ourselves—or not. There I was staring down at this unknown, and undoubtedly inedible, plate that was all mine.

Then the talking began. Everyone talked. The four kids talked about their day in school. They talked about current events and their opinions about the news. At one point, Mr. Weil asked me what I thought about the two candidates running for president. I barely knew the candidates' names, so I had little to add to this part of the dinner conversation. Mr. Weil switched to asking me about my family and myself, and I did pretty well with those questions, all the while pushing lettuce around the plate, searching for any pieces that might have escaped the dressing. There were none. I ventured a small bite, which confirmed my steadfast belief I did not like salad dressing; it stung my mouth. My strategy was to continue pushing the salad around politely until something else happened.

I waited for the rest of the meal to be brought to the table. But it was not forthcoming. After a while, everyone had finished their salad except me, who still faced a full, even if scattered, plate. Eventually, the conversation quieted, and people began to look at me and my plate.

Mr. Weil cleared his throat a little, saying, "You see, in our home, we have a rule that no one at the table receives their next course until everyone has finished what is on their plate. This way, we are all eating together."

My stomach clenched. They couldn't mean it! Surely, they weren't going to force me to eat something I didn't want to eat. I wanted to push myself, yet I knew I couldn't do it. Shame burned hot around my eyes. This all served to confirm what I already knew: I didn't belong there.

"Oh," was all I could say.

No one else spoke until Mrs. Weil queried with curiosity, "Don't you like the salad, dear?"

"I do like salad, but I've just never had it with dressing be-fore," I offered quietly.

"Oh, I see. Well, then it looks like you've given it a try and didn't like it. We'll move on."

Danny piped up, "That's not fair! She has to eat it! We all have to."

Silence and a frown from Mr. Weil. Was he frowning at me?

I peeked with trepidation at Mrs. Weil and then at Judy, my two allies at the table. I wanted to shrink under the table. This meal was a disaster. I knew I should never have said yes to stay for dinner. I had no business doing something like that.

"She should have her dessert tokens taken away!" Danny didn't want anyone to remove the dreaded plate without a fight for his rights. I had no idea what dessert tokens were, but I got the impression that in the Weil household, you had to follow some rules to get them. I wondered what further unknown rules I was destined to violate before I could go home.

Then, Mr. Weil said, "Liz is our guest, Danny. And she doesn't have to earn dessert tokens. Maybe in her house, they do things differently. You just pay attention to your own dinner, and don't worry about other people. You know what is expected of you."

The tense moment passed, perhaps for everyone but me. Next appeared a plate, again served to each person at the table, filled with meat, rice, and string beans. There was gravy on the meat. I hated gravy. And I never ate cooked vegetables of any kind except beets warmed up from the can. Ever. The pit in my stomach expanded, allowing no room for anything that I might be able to force down my throat. Now we were discussing plants and what needed to be put into the ground before the winter came. They asked which kind of flower each person liked the best. Another topic I could contribute almost nothing to; no one had ever asked me what my favorite flower was, so I was unprepared for the question. I picked at the rice and pushed the gravy off the meat to hide some string beans. By the time everyone else was done, I again sensed the eyes around the table moving in my direction.

Again, the Weil parents took pity, this time not bothering to query whether I liked the food. My plate, with its accusatory evidence, was mercifully whisked away by Mrs. Weil. When everyone's plate was cleared, and a luscious chocolate cake appeared, Mrs. Weil cut individual slices.

"Liz, can I serve you a piece of cake? I just made this today. It's a favorite in this house."

"No, thank you," I demurred, aware of the aforementioned tokens, of which I deserved none.

"I want to share my slice with Liz," Judy chimed, smiling and keeping the peace. I gratefully accepted.

Finally, the dinner was over. Every Weil child had their own set of chores; one cleared the plates, one the glasses, one wiped down the table, and Judy loaded up the dishwasher. I did anything I could to be useful and to not interfere too badly with the assignments, lest I inadvertently break a table-clearing rule. Judy and her dad drove me home, and I thanked them again for inviting me to dinner.

"We'll do it again real soon!" Judy declared with certainty and an optimism I wished I could have shared.

I went into my house, relieved to be in an environment I knew, where no one expected anything of me, and I would not have to engage in lively conversation about topics I did not know enough about. I went up to my room, shut the door, and was alone with my deep embarrassment. Despite my humiliation, I was amazed at what I had witnessed in the Weil household. I didn't know families could be like that. They had rules, but the rules kind of made sense. And what a variety of food! Even if I didn't want to eat it, how great that they had different courses, served each person their own plate, and had homemade cake for dessert. It was great that all the kids helped clean up, and no one complained. It was great they talked so much. It was great the parents asked a lot and knew a lot about their children's days at school. It was great Judy seemed to like me, despite my naivety and shyness and my being so thoroughly different from all of them. All these thoughts swirled around in my head and my heart, and I didn't know what to make of it all.

Perhaps I was inspired by Judy's organized and tidy household, but I began to notice my own unkempt, if not downright dirty, home through a new lens. The thought of bringing a friend to my house for a visit filled me with horror. One day I decided to take action. I detested the bathrooms the most (and indeed they were quite detestable). I made a deal with my mother; if she bought me a pair of rubber gloves and all the supplies needed, I would take over the responsibility of cleaning the little bathroom closest to my bedroom. She would no longer have to worry about it. I was generously assuming it might have figured prominently in her list of worries.

She vaguely agreed to my offer. "If you feel you want to, dear."

I eagerly began my new duties, relieved to have some control.

In the late winter, Mr. Johnson organized an organic gardening club and taught us how to pot seeds. Although I hated to sign up for things after school because I'd have to talk with kids I didn't know, I wanted to work in a garden. I thought I'd try to grow an organic garden behind my garage at home and had a lot to learn. I loved the musky smell of tomato plants and the large yellow flowers hiding beneath the giant cucumber leaves. I began to look forward to Mr. Johnson's class and to working in the garden. I liked him. Lots of kids did, especially the girls. He helped me feel better about being in a new school, where I still didn't know many people and had made only a couple of friends besides Judy. Bonnie, Sophie, and Joan were Organic Farm Club members and also in some of my classes. Like me, they were conscientious students who got good grades, and they slowly invited me into their world. Mr. Johnson went out of his way to encourage my interest in the club and often asked me to stay after the other kids left to help him clean up.

One day near the end of the school year, Mr. Johnson surprised us all. "I have some news, guys, that I'm pretty sad about. Next year I'll be teaching at another school, closer to my home. I'll need you to take care of this garden and keep it growing. Watch those weeds!"

We all groaned.

An anchor was yanked away from someplace inside me.

"But you are all welcome and encouraged to write to me. I'll write back, I promise! I'll want to know how you're doing in your classes, and you can keep me up to date on what you're growing in the garden."

After everyone else left that day, I lingered behind as I usually did. Mr. Johnson and I sat on the wooden bench surrounded by pots and hoses.

"You know, I'm really sad about you leaving," I said, glancing down. "I hope you like your new school." I might have sounded calm, but inside, my heart raced and my hands were hot and buzzing. The prospect of not having Mr. Johnson around each day hit me hard. I felt lost and almost scared, and that scared me, too.

"It will be fine for me with a much shorter commute, which is better for my family. Our kids start kindergarten and first grade this year, so working closer to home is good. But I'm also sad about leaving, and I want you to know that I meant what I said. I want you to write to me. I will miss you, too. Especially you."

*Yes!* I thought. *I'm not making it up. He does like me. Tell me more. Tell me I matter to you!*

"You are a really special young lady. Look," he said, taking a pencil and paper from his shirt pocket. "Here's my address. Write to me. Once you do, I'll write back. I have your address. But here is another way we can keep in touch, at least over the summer. I'll be teaching summer school at the high school here in town. You can visit me there if you want, when my class gets out at noon. Come by any time. I often go to the beach when class gets out. You and your friends could come."

That was *great* news! My hope lifted. I could easily visit him at the high school, and I definitely would. I'd be around all summer, and it was just a mile walk down the turnpike to the high school. "That's a great idea! I'll do that sometime. When do your classes start?"

I tumbled out of the greenhouse and went to find Bonnie, Sophie, Joan, and Judy. We all agreed to visit him.

"Sure! Sounds cool," said Bonnie and Joan immediately.

Sophie agreed. "Yeah, I think I can do that."

Judy said she'd have to check with her parents about their summer plans, but she never came with us.

The first day of the summer session, Bonnie, Sophie, Joan, and I went to see him. We hung out in his classroom for a while, drawing with chalk on his blackboard, talking, and laughing. Then we girls walked over to Bonnie's house for lunch. Bonnie was easy-going and always opened her house to us; she was always ready for adventure.

Mr. Johnson had told us to come back again and bring our bathing suits. We'd head out to Jones Beach for the afternoon. I loved that idea and couldn't wait. Sophie was usually busy, which left Bonnie, Joan, me, and Mr. Johnson. We swam in the salty waves and sunned ourselves. We girls covered our bikini-clad bodies with baby oil to get darker tans. Mr. Johnson stopped at Carvel on the way home and bought us ice cream. That cold, soft chocolate would glide along my tongue and slip down my throat. It was perfect. Those trips to the beach in the hot days of summer were fun, and we thought we were pretty cool to be going there with Mr. Johnson.

One day, no one else could go. I thought I shouldn't go, either, but Mr. Johnson said it was okay and he'd take just me. Excellent! I was only a little nervous about having to talk to only him all day. But I thought he would probably come up with things to say. On the car ride, he asked, "So what books are you reading this summer?" He already knew I loved to read.

"*Dr. Zhivago*," I replied with enthusiasm.

"Excellent book. Tell me what you like about it."

"I'm learning a lot about Russia and the war, although it's confusing sometimes. Lots of names to keep straight."

He laughed. "Yeah, it's not a light read. Good that you're tackling it, though. I admire that." The radio was playing, "The Times They Are A-Changin'" by Bob Dylan.

"I love Dylan," I interjected.

"He's a modern-day prophet." Mr. Johnson nodded his head, then asked, "What do you think about what's happening in Vietnam?"

There he caught me up short.

"I don't know. It seems pretty bad." I gazed out of the car window, and he changed the subject to vegetable gardening. He was easy to be with and talk to, and I felt comfortable with him, even a little bit chosen. We went to the beach, just the two of us, many times that summer. I had more conversations with him than with anyone besides my girlfriends. In some funny way, I sensed he was my friend, even though he was my teacher. I adored him and loved being with him. I dreaded the end of summer.

One afternoon I skipped into the house after a beach day with Mr. Johnson and noticed my father was not in his usual spot, asleep on the green couch in the living room, but awake and watching television. He called out in a clear voice as I walked in.

"Come in here, Lizzie. I want you to see this." I heard scratchy men's voices saying things that were unintelligible and saw on the screen the image of a barren landscape.

"History is being made right this minute," he said, communicative for once.

"What is that? What are they doing? Who are they?" I was full of questions.

Dad gently shushed me and explained. "We sent two men to the moon, and they have just landed."

I sat down with him, and we continued watching together in silence. I did not fully comprehend what I was seeing, but I clearly understood it was very important to my father, important enough to keep him off the couch and alert that afternoon.

And he was sharing it with me. I was happy just for that. These days, when he wasn't out visiting people in the hospital, he was smoking Chesterfields and drinking in his office or asleep on the couch.

I was sad when school started up again. Although it wasn't hard for me, I hated it anyway because I had to fit in with all the kids. I carried a dull pang in the pit of my stomach when I walked into the building, passed kids in the halls, or sat at the lunch table. Everyone seemed to know each other. I didn't even want to be like them. I was not popular, loud, or chatty, and I never was interested in anything they talked about. They were having fun, and I wasn't. They belonged, and I didn't.

I missed Mr. Johnson a lot, even though we wrote letters back and forth. My ninth-grade English teacher was a little strange. I wrote a term paper in English on Folk Rock (both Bob Dylan and Joan Baez were my heroes) that the teacher said deserved "the accolades of publication," whatever that meant. He also told me I had "the grace of a gazelle." I wasn't sure if that was a compliment or an insult, until I looked up what a gazelle was. I guess it was a compliment, but I thought it was an odd thing to tell me. He was odd, with a big ring on his pinky finger and not at all like Mr. Johnson.

*three*

———

# THE TIMES THEY ARE A-CHANGIN'

IN HIS LETTERS, MR. JOHNSON ALWAYS TOLD ME HE MISSED ME. One day, as I left the biology classroom, I saw him walk toward me, like he had been waiting. Excitement flooded my body.

"Hey, how are you? Why are you here today? Don't you have to teach at your school?"

He smiled back at me. "No, today is a day we have off, so I thought I'd visit my friends." We walked the short distance to my next class, but before he left me there, he leaned down and said, close to my ear, "I'll be stopping by the Organic Farm Club after school today. Will I see you there?"

"Yes, definitely," I said. "See you then!"

I skipped through the rest of my day. *He still likes me*, I thought, my heart beating hard. Finally, the last bell rang, and I hurried down to the farm. The whole club was there, and we showed him the new plants. He seemed impressed. Our time with him was way too short. He pulled me aside and said, "My next visit will be in about a month. I'll write to tell you the exact date. Maybe the two of us can hang out a while after school that day."

He had said this to just me. I beamed.

I was not, as a child or a preteen, highly aware of the world around me. I watched a number of television shows, like *Bonanza* and *I Dream of Jeannie*, but rarely the news. I read only the comic pages of the newspaper. Perhaps this was true of most children. I had a vague sense of some danger emanating from a place called Russia or the USSR, which I knew from reading *Dr. Zhivago* was far away, very cold, and now threatening.

I recognized the name Martin Luther King, and I knew he was an important, good man, a leader of the Civil Rights movement. One afternoon while I was in my bedroom doing adolescent preening and watching myself in the mirror while I danced to music on the radio, a news report interrupted my activities.

"This just in. The Rev. Martin Luther King Jr. was shot and killed by an assassin late today as he stood on a balcony in Memphis, Tennessee. Dr. King had planned to lead another civil rights march in Memphis next Monday."

I recognized this was a serious and tragic event, but I was confused. I thought the person shot was the son of Martin Luther King because they kept calling him Martin Luther King Jr. I pictured a little boy shot down. Yet the news report said he had been giving a speech at the time and talked about him as though he were an adult. *Am I stupid not to know this?* I was so much in my own world that I couldn't tell if this report was about a child or a famous national leader. A childhood of political illiteracy rendered me bewildered and uncertain.

When Mom got home from work later that afternoon, I asked her about it, but she was unaware of the news. We went to the television, and the continued news coverage confirmed that the appropriate response to this event was both sadness and shock, and that the whole country was changed forever. History was unfolding in front of me. My worldly ignorance received a crash course that afternoon, moving me up a notch or two toward some semblance of social consciousness.

My exposure to Judy Weil and her family, their social-justice causes, and their household conversations helped foster my awareness of the incredible things going on in the world during those years. As remarkable as I found Judy's family to be, there was one thing about them that puzzled me. Being members of the Ethical Humanist Society, they were avowed atheists. This was shocking to me. Being immersed in a religious environment—between my father's role as minister, the church's prominence in our lives, and my religious elementary school—God was very present. To go out of one's way to reject the existence of God was alarming; I was frightened for them. The irony about my worry for the souls of the Weil family and my shock at their audacity to reject God was that I continued to struggle with my own relationship with God.

As an emerging adolescent, I had many questions about life, religion, God, morality, how the world worked, and what I believed. I thought confirmation class was the perfect, exact place to bring such questions. I tested the water one day and stepped out of the exemplary pastor's daughter mold to voice some of my concerns. My father's young assistant pastor led the class.

Sitting around the table with a dozen other teens in one of the church's classrooms, I braved a question.

"Pastor Altvater, how can it be fair that all the heathens in places like China, who never heard of Jesus, will all go to hell? And what about the babies who die before getting baptized? How can it be fair that they go to hell, too?" The injustice of it bothered me.

"Well now, Lizzie, these are important questions. But frankly, I am surprised to hear you ask them. We all know the only way to get to heaven is to believe in Jesus Christ and accept Him as your Lord and Savior. This is why it's so important to spread the Gospel to everyone around the world and to baptize every baby as soon as possible."

A sting of anger flashed through me. I knew that answer. Couldn't he see I was asking for more than that? How is it okay with God that innocent people get sent to hell when they could not accept Jesus as their Savior because they had never heard of Him?

I let that pass for a few minutes while we recited the Ten Commandments from memory. Then I decided to try again.

"Pastor, I have another question. Sorry to be asking these questions, but I really want to understand better. Bad things, like cancer, happen to people who are faithful and good and believe in Jesus. Why does that happen? And why do people who are mean or evil often get away with great lives? For that matter, why does God let bad things happen in the world, like Hitler? Or murder? Sometimes God doesn't seem fair." I tried to keep my voice steady, but I was swallowing my words. The room went quiet, and my eyes stared at the table. I knew I was the only kid in the class who asked stuff like this—or asked anything at all. But I thought this young pastor was somewhat cool, so I thought it was safe enough to ask. Plus, I wanted to know the answer.

"Elizabeth," he said with a stern voice. "These questions reflect a lack of faith on your part. Again, I am surprised—

shocked—that you, of all people, are questioning what God says and does. God knows exactly what He is doing, and it isn't for us to doubt or question His motives or ways. He knows what is best for us and tells us in the Bible how we are to live our lives and what we are to believe. I suggest you go home, read over the catechism and the Bible, and think about your faith. Above all, pray for more faith." He then continued with the next part of his lesson.

Beneath my shame, I was deeply disappointed in his handling of my questions. His comments resulted in closing my heart to the faith of my childhood. Although I got confirmed (I had passed the written exam, so he had to confirm me) and continued to go to church until I moved away from home, I hesitated to call myself a Christian after that. Nonetheless, not being an enthusiastic Christian was quite different from being an atheist, like Judy and her family. I still wanted there to be a God. I believed there was some kind of a God, even if I didn't understand or like the teachings of His church.

The summer after ninth grade, Mr. Johnson taught summer school at the high school again. He explained it was a great way for a teacher to earn some extra money. He had two young children at home, and this helped since his wife didn't work.

Bonnie, Joan, Sophie, and I were Mr. Johnson's beach crew. We loved to be taken to the beach by this man who was so fun and easy to be with. The few times Joan couldn't join us on a beach trip, she acted kind of glum. Because I always could go, I thought she might have been mad at me for that. Joan was quieter than Bonnie and Sophie, and I didn't spend much one-on-one time with her, so I wasn't sure what she thought. But we never discussed it, so it remained in my imagination.

I knew Mr. Johnson saw me more than anyone else and that I was his favorite. He told me I was an extraordinary person—smart, kind, sensitive, and growing into a lovely young woman. These words from him went straight into my heart and lingered there like a glowing ember.

On one of the days when I was the only one who could go to the beach, he asked, "So tell me about you and boys. Do you have a special guy?"

"No, not really. There is one boy from my church, but he's a little older than I am, a couple years, I think. He's kind of interested in me, but I'm not so sure how much I like him." I found myself wanting to play down this interest, even though what I said was true enough.

Mr. Johnson said, "Well, be careful. Boys are going to like you, and you want to be sure about them. You know, you can ask me anything you want about dating and guys. After all, I've been there!"

"That's good to know. Thanks. But I don't have any questions right now." I was a little embarrassed at the idea of discussing boys with Mr. Johnson.

"In fact," he said, turning toward me, "maybe it's time for you to start calling me Mark, instead of Mr. Johnson. I feel like we're friends by now. What do you think?"

My eyes darted away, but I forced them back to him. "Hmm," I said, at a loss, the awkwardness and thrill swirling together in my chest. I laughed a little. "I can try, but it is a little strange."

"You can try it out right now." He smiled. "Just say, 'Okay, Mark.'"

I took a nervous breath and smiled. "Okay . . . Mark." Definitely awkward. But also, *Wow! First name!* Something shifted and I felt closer to him, more chosen.

Mark also told me he was coming back to our school system in the fall. He'd be teaching at the high school, where I was starting tenth grade, and he was going to run the Organic Farming Club again. I could see him often in the building and at the farm.

A new chapter in our friendship began. He was no longer far away, likely to eventually fade out of my life. He was there, every day, not hard to find. I could settle into security, knowing I hadn't lost him.

The times they were a-changin' indeed. In the spring of 1970, the Kent State killings nearly shut our school down for the day. Racial tensions ran high in the news and in my school, caus- ing periodic school closures. My sisters Judy and Pat allowed me to go with them, against our parents' wishes, to a Vietnam protest march in DC. It was, for our country and society, a sea change, and I was growing up in it. Despite my sheltered, uninvolved, detached household, my life swirled in this cauldron.

I began to dress with the times: miniskirts so short that when I stood up, I could cup the hem in my hands; fishnet pantyhose; long beads; bell bottoms; and go-go boots. I made most of my own clothes and could control what I wore.

Music was exploding. I sat in Judy Weil's large basement room with her various friends from the Ethical Humanist Soci- ety, listening to *Abbey Road* for the first time. The music was mind-blowing. Ironically, Judy's ragtag group of friends (Judy would never participate in such things) dropped acid and smoked grass, and she watched over them, giving them a safe haven in which to experience these times. As usual, I stayed on the outskirts but was witness to them. Shy, inexperienced, and fearful, I wanted nothing to do with drugs of any kind, but even substance-free, I could hear the genius of that music. It transported a whole generation.

*four*

---

## AND SO IT BEGINS

AS THE WORLD OUTSIDE ROILED AND RUMBLED, INSIDE MY house, the roiling was internal. Everything appeared copasetic and predictable, but we still practiced our religion of isolation. My mother rose early to see that my brother Andy and I got up on time. She worked a full day selling clothes at a large department store in the mall, skipping her lunch break so she could get out by 4:00 p.m. and fight the frenzied shoppers and rush-hour traffic. After stopping at the grocery store, she entered the house armed with many paper bags of food and supplies. She dropped the bags onto any bare surface that could receive them. There were not many available surfaces in our kitchen at any time of the day or night. The bags competed with the dirty dishes, cans, and jars taken out of the cupboards and left where they had last been set down, used silverware, newspapers, mail, schoolbooks, lunch boxes, magazines, keys, and clothes. All vied for any identifiable inch of space. After releasing the bags, she then made herself a cup of instant coffee, a piece of toast with jam, and sat down amidst the rubble to enjoy the only food she'd eaten since early that morning.

After her refreshment, she then tackled the evening meal preparation, taking out of the grocery bags only the items she needed for that night's dinner and the perishables, which eventually found their way into the overcrowded refrigerator. Undeterred by this chaos, she cooked while my brothers and I busied ourselves elsewhere with homework, listening to music, talking on the phone, or daydreaming in the yard. When everything was ready—the meatloaf, instant mashed potato buds, boiled canned green beans (which I never ate), and ketchup, she told me to ring the dinner bell. I rang the large bronze bell that hung on the front porch, summoning my siblings from outside or inside the house. Then I laboriously roused my father from his deep slumber on the green vinyl couch in the living room. After a few pokes and shakes from me, he shuffled to his place at the head of the table. When all were present and sitting, we said grace together.

"God is great, God is good; let us thank Him for our food. Amen." We recited the same blessing every night.

My spot was behind the table, against the wall of the kitchen. I would scoot myself back there and sit on a stack of old newspapers. Sometimes this stack was quite high, and I had an excellent vantage point over the dinner table. My brother Pete sat at one end of the table, which was particularly convenient for him during his "health food" years. He was able to pop up regularly and attend to his unique dinner concoctions: wheat-free toast, wheat germ mash, sprouts, protein shakes, and any number of mysterious-looking, odd-smelling brews. He sat with us during dinner but didn't eat any of the same food.

I cannot remember anything out of the ordinary about Andy or his presence at the table. He ate his dinner quietly. Mom sat next to Andy, seated closer to the stove, so she also could pop up regularly to fetch things the rest of us needed—coffee, more milk, salt, a napkin, a clean fork, dessert. It was all hers to procure and present. Dad sat at the other end of the table across from Pete. He ate with some gusto, not having eaten anything all day. At some point during my later childhood years, I realized all his consumption during the day was liquid and amber in color.

Dad had a couple of quirks at the dinner table, which stand out in my memory. He wasn't afraid, like I was, to eat the fatty part of the meat. If we had meat like ham or steak, he saved the fatty parts for last and savored them. I, on the other hand, carved them away with great care and put them at the far corner of my plate so as not to contaminate any other food. Often, I slid my fat over to Dad's plate when he showed interest . . . our little bonding moment. Although Dad was distant and often did not remember my age or the names of my few friends, he was gentle. He never raised his voice.

There was some talking at the table, but not a conversation. It centered around Mom asking, "Did you get enough to eat? Would you like some coffee now? Andy, pass the potatoes to your father. Shall I get you a new fork?"

After a meager few minutes of popping and fetching and starting and stopping, we were all done. Well, all of us except Mom, whose plate was often barely touched by the time the rest of us were done, returning to our previous activities elsewhere in the house. Some nights she finished her room-temperature dinner by herself. The escaping diners left their dirty dishes on the table for Mom to clean up, so I sometimes stayed to do these chores, although she always told me I didn't have to. Often, she had an evening meeting or choir rehearsal at the church, and before leaving, she'd say, "Leave those. I'll do them when I get back."

On late evenings, the three of us often watched the 11:00

news—Dad in his armchair, Mom in hers, me on the brown shag-carpeted floor. About five minutes into the newscast, both parents' heads were tilted back against their chairs, eyes closed. Loud breathing turned to snoring. In Dad's case, the alcohol in his system once again lulled him into his quiet escape. In Mom's case, sheer exhaustion offered her peace.

For a while, I watched the news, hearing names like Saigon, Pol Pot, and Phnom Penh. My mind drifted as my eyes saw the familiar images of green jungles and wounded bodies.

Even after my march on DC to protest the Vietnam War, I didn't follow it in detail; it was more like background against the more compelling drama and dilemma of my world of friendships and relationships, particularly with Mark Johnson.

When my older sister Judy left for college, I moved out of my little bedroom and into her larger room. Mom let me pick out new wallpaper: bright yellow sunflowers boldly dancing in their twelve-inch glory against a backdrop of dizzying, small, black-and-white checker squares. It was mod. It was hip. It was early 1970, and I'd just turned fifteen. I replaced my *Sound of Music* soundtrack with *The Sounds of Silence* by Simon and Garfunkel and listened to it incessantly. Over time, I added the Beatles' *Abbey Road* and The Band and Joni Mitchell to my collection. During those years, a highlight of my musical life was going to hear Pete Seeger live at the Nassau Coliseum. Judy Weil took me. My excited anticipation was dwarfed by the utter thrill of hearing and seeing him live. We hung our arms and legs over the balcony bar and allowed his stories to take us away. He talked to us and sang about civil rights and lives of hardship, heroism, and hope. I cried as five thousand voices sang along with his raspy, homey voice to the words of "We Shall Overcome." I was swept away. I felt alive with the passion of wanting to *do* something good in the world, whatever that could be for someone like me. I was at home among this faceless crowd of strangers who cared about things; I belonged with them.

When I told Mark about the Pete Seeger concert, he nodded, smiled, and agreed that to see him live in concert was a privilege. He called Pete Seeger "a great man." Mark understood!

As tenth grade progressed, I had more confidence in my relationship with Mark. I spent most afternoons with him after school, at least on the days he didn't have to get home to his family. We had an easy routine. It was his idea, and it worked beautifully. After school, I took the bus home, put my things in the house, and then started to walk down my quiet, shaded street. All the houses sat behind large hedges or high fences protecting their privacy. Mark picked me up as I walked along, and we parked the car in a quiet lot that was part of an old school no longer in use, and we talked. It was comfortable and friendly. We talked about school, politics, books, gardening . . . anything.

Mark was an attractive man by anyone's standards, and I knew it. He was probably six foot four, lean, bright, and friendly. Mark's deep, gentle voice and affable, mild manner made him very appealing, and he was popular among both teachers and students. Mark was modern; there was youthfulness about him, despite his deep voice and strong physical presence. I was undeniably drawn to him, and these feelings grew stronger every day. I thought about him all the time; everything else in my life paled next to my feelings for him. They weren't sexual feelings, but they were very exciting. I yearned for his attention, to be someone special to him. I was not whole without him.

During these afternoons of parking after school, our relationship had the chance to flower. One fall afternoon, as I walked along the road, I wondered what I'd say if a car stopped and asked me where I was going, a young girl walking alone along a quiet road that led to nowhere in particular. I imagined a man or woman leaning out of the car window, saying, "Hey, do you need a ride somewhere?"

I decided I would say, "I'm fine, just out for a walk. I don't need a ride. Thanks."

Then, when Mark pulled up, I climbed into his car with a sense of relief. Although I was excited and happy to see him, as I always was, I noticed a dull, distant feeling of guilt. I quickly pushed it away and allowed my mind to become empty. Or maybe it's more accurate to say "fuzzy." No one knew Mark and I met up like this, and he said it was better that way. It was our secret.

Once in the deserted parking lot, Mark turned off the engine. He shifted slightly in his seat to see me better. He had his usual take-out cup of coffee that he picked up from the diner in town.

"Want some?" He offered the cup.

"Sure. Okay." I took a sip. I wasn't that familiar with coffee and thought I wouldn't like it, but the sweet, hot, creamy liquid was delicious. I wanted more!

"Can you bring me my own cup next time?" I asked.

"Sure, I can bring a second cup sometimes, but not always. The waitress at the diner knows me, and she might start to ask who the second cup is for. Better not to get anyone thinking." He glanced my way and chuckled a little. We were co-conspirators.

As we chatted about the day, Mark lit up a Virginia Slim and rolled down the window to blow the smoke out. I loved how he held the cigarette between his teeth while he got his matches out. I liked the initial woodsy smell of the cigarette when he first lit it; I found it comforting. Same with the coffee. It smelled and tasted comforting. I adored the way Mark smelled—strong, fresh, and clean, but not too smelly like most men's colognes. To me, he smelled like his voice sounded: calm, deep, pleasant, and safe. I loved it. I was happy and at home in his presence, chatting together while I watched him smoke and drink coffee.

When the cigarette and coffee were gone, Mark reached for his pack of mint Chiclet gum in his glove box. I loved how this smelled, too, fresh and clean.

"Would you like some gum?" he asked, resting his forearm on my thigh as he reached across me to open the glove compartment. A thrill shot through me as his muscles moved against my leg. "Is it okay if I put my arm here?" he asked.

I took a quick inbreath. "Yeah, it's okay." My voice was soft. *Is this okay?* I wondered vaguely. It didn't matter to me if his action was okay or not. His touch electrified me. It sealed our specialness.

"It's just that I feel so close to you; I'd like us to be able to show affection toward each other. What do you think. Would that be okay with you?"

I nodded.

"For example, you could put your hand on my leg, here, and see how that feels." He took my hand and gently placed it on his thigh. His leg felt secure and warm. I pressed down a little harder, and I could feel his muscles, strong beneath the khaki cloth. "How is that?" he asked, watching my face. "How does that feel?"

"It's good," I managed to say, a wobbly smile at the corners of my mouth, and a sense of thrill because Mark asked me to do this, and I had the "right" to touch him. He reached over and touched my face with his fingers and smiled.

"You are so beautiful. You grow up more every day, and you look even more beautiful every day. And that's hard to do!" he added with a quiet laugh. Then he leaned closer to me and kissed me lightly—so lightly—on my lips. I shivered from the dizziness. I smelled his minty breath, and I wanted more. We kissed like that for some moments, slow and gentle, taking small breaks. When his tongue slightly grazed my lips, heat shot through me. But I reached my limit. I needed to catch my breath, and I pushed back a little, now embarrassed, self-conscious, and a little confused.

"Are you okay? Did I do anything wrong? Is this all right?"

I nodded and said, "Yes, I just need a little break. I'm okay. It's okay. It's just new."

"It is new. Let's just take it slowly."

Mark put on the radio, and we listened to music without talking, my hand tucked between the seat and his leg. I was so confused and excited. I decided to push my uncertainty away for now and think more about it later. Right now, I still wanted to be with him. Right now, I considered myself the luckiest fifteen-year-old in the world.

"It's okay. Let's do that some more." I smiled. The electricity sparked between us. My ears buzzed, my mind was a little fuzzy, and there was heat. Mark pulled me a little closer to him and touched my face and neck. His hands were warm and big as they slid over my thin shoulders. He hugged me closer, navigating around the gear shift, his hand resting on my collarbone while we kissed. I liked it, but I was losing control of what was happening. This was a foreign zone, and I didn't know the rules or what Mark expected of me.

—

He murmured between kisses, "You can touch me; put your hand on my leg like before. I love your touch."

I could do that.

When his hand slid down and touched my breasts, first one, then the other, I was immediately self-conscious. *Are they big enough? Is my bra too clunky and bumpy? Does he think I am a child?* Part of me hoped he would continue, even while numbness spread through my body and my mind. He reached under my shirt and my bra and lifted it up. He covered my breast with his hand, not pausing this time to ask if I was okay. He seemed to like this; he got more involved, more focused. He made small groaning sounds and breathed in my ear.

"Do you know how beautiful you are and how happy I am to be with you?" He moved my hand farther up his leg to the front of his lap. I could feel his hardness there, and he pressed my hand down on him and groaned some more. He whispered, "You do that, just for a second," and took his hand away. I was embarrassed, and I worried I wasn't doing it right. This was all new territory. But I pressed and rubbed a little, and he seemed to like it.

After a long moment, Mark stopped and exhaled slowly and pulled back a little. I moved my hand away. I was relieved but wondered if I had done something wrong.

He said, "I need to take a little break. You are too exciting for me. You are one powerful young lady, to have this effect on me. You know you are very special to me, and I love you. I love you more than any teenage boy will ever love you."

*Wow,* I thought. *All this touching, and he says he loves me!* I was not used to saying those words, "I love you," to anyone, and I was uncomfortable saying them, but thought I must now. *This must be what love feels like,* I imagined. But I couldn't say it back.

Not then. I just said in reply, "Wow. This is a lot. Not too much, just a lot. I mean, I like it. A lot!"

I wanted to reassure him. Maybe reassure myself.

"Yes," he replied. "This *is* a lot. It's a lot for me, too. When you go home, just remember this. I love you. Okay?"

"Okay," I said, adjusting my clothes.

We sat quietly for a few minutes. Even though I was disoriented by what we did and said, this was a happy moment because Mark loved me.

After another song finished playing on the radio, Mark said, "I hate to have to say this, but I'm going to have to hit the road soon."

"I know," I replied. I knew he had a long drive home—close to an hour. A few minutes later, Mark adjusted himself into his seat behind the wheel and turned on the car. He shifted the meddlesome gear shift, backed out of our spot, and drove me to the place where he picked me up. It seemed a lifetime ago. Before I got out of the car, which had to be quick because he was pulled over to the side of the road, he smiled at me, and I smiled at him, and he winked.

"I'll see you tomorrow after school. Have a good evening and have sweet dreams. I love you."

"Have sweet dreams, too," I said and closed the door.

Mark drove off, and I waved as he went. Retracing my steps from earlier, I walked up my driveway. I was relieved no one would be waiting for me with any questions. I went up to my room and started to do homework until dinnertime. At first, it was hard to shut off my thoughts and memory of what had happened, but soon I did. I had to; I had to push it all down and focus on homework and dinner. My body had a lingering humming sensation, but my mind was perfused with numbness. No one around the table asked me about my day, so it was easy to keep my feelings in a box deep inside myself.

So began a regular rhythm of driving to our spot, chatting, touching, kissing, and fondling, which left us breathless, until it was time for him to drive home to his family and time for me to return to mine. I was fifteen.

Later that fall, one glorious Indian summer day, we spread a blanket out under a tree in our secluded spot. To my surprise, Mark packed some cheese and crackers and brought some wine in a thermos . . . Pink Catawba. It was cold and sweet and made me pleasantly lightheaded. We set up our blanket and nibbled on his snacks and wine.

Mark stretched out beside me, and said, "Come on down here, lay next to me." Mark began slowly running his hands over my body. Being this close and not constrained by the car was new to me. I wondered, *Do I really want to be here? Yes!* And a very small voice asked, *Do I? Yes, yes, yes, I do, because look at this man. Tall, good looking. Over thirty years old!*

His voice was so smooth, and he made me feel I belonged there with him. I trusted him completely because he cared about me. He told me he loved me. He chose *me* to love this way. He told me he knew no one in my life would ever love me as much as he did. I was so lucky to have him to be with, to learn things from. I wished I could spend all my time with him. His loving me was proof I was as wonderful as he said I was. Part of me believed him.

I only wished I wasn't so shy and uncomfortable about sex. I didn't know what I was supposed to feel or do. That's why it was so great that he was much older and experienced. At least I'd learn about it. I flashed on how humiliating it would be if someone saw us—someone we knew! The thought of it made me weak. I'd rather die.

"Hey, do you ever worry that someone will see us?"

There was some dismay in his voice. "Yeah, I do worry about that. That's why we need to keep being careful and stay aware of what's around us. I think we are okay here, though. There's no one around at all."

Still, my thoughts continued. I couldn't begin to think about my parents knowing about us . . . or his wife! I did feel guilty about what his wife would think or feel, but Mark didn't talk about that with me, so I didn't dwell on it. Instead, I focused on Mark, who was kissing me and caressing me. Then he placed the whole length of his body on top of mine, which I liked but only briefly because I couldn't breathe. His hardness showed me he loved me. He started to move on me, and doubt and fear took over. What was I supposed to do now?

"Press up," he whispered in my ear.

I did, but only because he told me to. I didn't really want to. I wondered what he would ask me to do next. Whatever it was, I knew I'd do it because I didn't want to make him stop loving me.

"You are a very sexy young lady, you know," he said then. "And I love you. And love is good."

Although I was awkward with those words, I was able to say them back. "I love you, too," I breathed.

After a bit, Mark moved to my side, and we lay there in stillness. "I could stay here with you forever, but I'm afraid I need to get ready to go." Mark sighed.

"I know," I replied, again wondering what happened when he went home.

We packed up, and Mark drove me back. I was full of elation and bewilderment.

We continued our afternoons like that throughout tenth grade. Mark began to regularly suggest we find a way to spend a night together, to express our love completely. From somewhere deep within my numbness, I found I was hesitant to take that step. This commenced a long period of confusion and despair for me over what to do. I knew it was wrong to have sex with a married man. It was adultery! Sometimes I worried someone was going to get hurt. I imagined it would be his wife. I prayed a lot during that time, begging God to tell me what I should do, and hoping He forgave me the trespasses I was already committing. Even though I had serious doubts about the Christian religion, I still believed in God, and fear of His wrath and punishment burrowed in my bones. I spent weekend afternoons wandering in my yard. I weighed the pros and cons, considered how much sin I dared commit, and wondered how much choice I actually had. If Mark was to be in my life, this is what needed to happen next. He never said "do this or else we're over," but in my mind, everything pointed to it. I knew I wanted Mark in my life; I was less interested in the sex part, but I believed it would cement him to me.

My deliberations didn't get me anywhere. My brain became cotton-headed, and I couldn't think clearly about it.

Mark didn't talk much about his wife, Emily. I could tell his marriage had problems just by the way he referred to her and his home life. He did speak with warmth and love about his children, a boy and a girl, who were both under eight years old.

Often Mark would say, "The happiest time of my day is when we're together. Lots of people would say we shouldn't be together or love each other, but they don't know anything about what we have. They don't know how special our relationship is; they wouldn't get it. Love is what matters. Love like ours is a beautiful thing, a rare thing. Love matters more than what people may think. People are so narrow-minded. We know we love each other, and it's no one else's business."

"Still," he cautioned me, "since people in the world won't understand or approve of our loving each other, we have to keep it to ourselves. It's best if no one knows so that no one can interfere. At school, they would definitely not understand and might not want me to teach there if they knew about our love."

What he said made perfect sense to me. Besides, who was I going to tell? The only people I could imagine telling were my girlfriends Bonnie, Sophie, and Joan. But I certainly couldn't tell them because they might be jealous or feel left behind. For their own sakes, I could never tell them. Telling Judy was not an option; she was maternal, and I think she would have been dismayed about what I was doing with Mark. Or she might confirm some of the feelings of guilt I constantly dealt with but couldn't walk away from.

My oldest sister Pat was out of the house, living nearby with her husband and kids. I sometimes went over there to help her out, like a mother's helper, but we rarely talked about anything, certainly not about me. My sister Judy, seven years older than me, was friendly to me but mostly involved in her own world; we never had sisterly chats. My sisters often said I was sixteen going on sixty because I was so serious. Whenever they said it, I shrunk inside like a wilted flower. I guess I was too serious to see its humor, or maybe it wasn't said to be funny.

I never talked with Pete or Andy. How could they help me, anyway? My parents? They knew nothing about me and showed little interest in knowing me. My guilt and their religious judgment sealed that door shut.

So keeping our relationship a secret wasn't hard for me. It was just between Mark and me, where it belonged.

*five*

---

## SWEET SIXTEEN

ONE JANUARY AFTERNOON, ON MY SIXTEENTH BIRTHDAY, I felt blue because no one had said much more than a distracted "Happy birthday" before I ran to get the school bus that morning. Plus, I was not going to see Mark because he had teacher conferences in the afternoon.

I was in the car with my sister, Judy. We had just stopped by the house of a friend of hers who offered me some clothes she no longer needed, thinking they'd fit me. On the ride home, I sighed heavily. To my surprise, Judy noticed.

"What's the matter? Are you bummed that the clothes ended up being too big?"

"No, that's fine. It was really sweet of her to offer. Thanks for taking me over there."

"Then what?"

"It's nothing. I'm fine." I knew it was pointless to explain my sadness.

We rode the rest of the way in silence. Dragging myself out of the passenger seat, like the sulky teenager I was in that moment, I headed for the house and started up the stairs to my room—my refuge in my din of loneliness—when Judy called out, "Oh, wait a second. I want to show you something in the living room."

What could possibly be of interest in our tired living room?

Obediently, I shuffled over to the closed door and reached for the knob. Judy was right behind me.

"What's so important in here?" I fussed. "I have homework to get to before dinner."

I opened the door and stepped into the room, which was dim, given that it was wintertime on Long Island. Flipping on the light switch, I saw the room was filled with balloons and streamers, amid shouts of "Surprise!" and "Happy Sweet Sixteen, Liz!"

I was speechless. Completely and absolutely speechless. This was a surprise birthday party? Who did this . . . for *me*? Who in my family even knew the names of my friends, or how to contact them?

I stumbled into the room, dazed in my astonishment.

"Are you surprised?" asked Judy, right behind me. Her voice was hopeful.

"Oh my God, I *am* so surprised!" was all I could squeak out. I didn't know what or how to feel. "Who did this?" I asked, as my girlfriends gathered around me.

"Your mom planned this," Sophie confessed.

*Mom did this?* My overworked, overwhelmed, distant mother had planned and executed a surprise birthday party for me. She had kept it a secret and orchestrated a perfect surprise party in our own house. The house of constant clutter was now neat and clean and set up for a party. I was delighted. To be given a surprise party was, for me, an undeniable statement that I existed.

By nature, my mother was a kind and gentle woman. As a mother, she was reserved and withheld . . . certainly in her parenting style of me.

I can't speak for my siblings; perhaps they had different parents. Because I was the fourth of five kids, it's possible that she just became tired, and since I was an easy and independent child, it makes sense that she mostly overlooked me. I am sure she loved me, but she mainly left me to look after myself.

Her life during the years of my childhood was not easy for her. She had to work to help supplement the near-poverty level wages my father earned as a minister—this while she still had three or four children at home. She also bore the weight of being the minister's wife, and was expected to be the proper support for him, have a wifely demeanor, partici- pate in church activities, run the household, raise suitable children, and live a faithful life. All this under the shadow of the secret she diligently defended: her husband, the minister, was an alcoholic.

I imagine in the 1960s and '70s she was bound by the norms and expectations for women, mothers, and wives of ministers, and she tried to fulfill those roles. Who she was underneath is difficult to know, at least during this phase of her life.

But the day of my surprise party, the way I saw my mother shifted. This sliver of being noticed by her awakened a sliver in me to want to notice her.

## six

## ASKING FOR FORGIVENESS,
## JUST IN CASE

WHEN THE WEATHER WARMED UP, MARK'S WIFE TOOK THEIR children to her parents' house in Rhode Island for the weekend. Mark had his house to himself. All we needed was a way for me to get a weekend, or part of a weekend, away from home. Of course, this was not at all difficult for me to do. I came and went on my own schedule, particularly now that I was driving. No one ever called my whereabouts into question. Still, I needed to say I was somewhere. Maybe I said I was going away with Sophie and her family for the weekend. I probably told Sophie I was not going to be around that weekend, to avoid a call from her. Even if Sophie had called my house asking for me, I doubt anyone would have made the connection that I was theoretically already with her. Or if they did ask about it, a breezy "our plans changed, and I went with Bonnie's family instead" would have put it to rest. Simple. The door was open. All I needed to do was walk through it. Mark was elated at the prospect.

"This is what we've been waiting for, Sweetie. Finally! I'll make you a nice dinner. We can play tennis, walk on the beach, lounge at home . . . whatever we want. We won't be trapped in the car. Just think of it!" He paused for a breath. "And we can make love, like we've been wanting. Like two people who love each other the way we do."

*Is this what I've been wanting? Am I ready?* Despite my uncertainty, I found myself unable to say no. It was all too difficult to resist. Maybe it was the sign from God I had been praying for, some indication of which way to go. Okay, I would go. Mark had enough excitement for both of us.

We took off on a Friday afternoon to make the hour-long drive to the town where he lived. In the style of the day, I wore tight, cut-off jean shorts and a brown, ribbed, stretchy bodysuit that snapped together at the bottom. Mark said I looked like someone poured me into my clothes. He meant it as a compliment, I guess, but I felt self-conscious and fat, despite my petite and athletic build. Maybe he read something into my mute response because he followed with, "Trust me. I like it!"

We stopped first at a park to play tennis. I was happy to be engaged in a familiar, safe activity. Mark and I could just be friends, batting tennis balls back and forth like I did with Sophie, who lived near a park and introduced me to this lighthearted activity. We weren't intense or competitive; we didn't even keep score. I had a momentary reprieve from wondering and worrying about what would come next.

His Cape-style house was roomy and comfortable, with a living room paneled in rustic gray wood, which Mark had rescued from a nearby demolished barn. On one wall hung a huge brass letter "J" for Johnson. Next to the "J" was a built-in raised fireplace with a slate bench stretched across the front, creating a cozy hearth. On another wall, rows of shelves displayed a TV, stereo, and lots of hefty books—classics, recent novels, and history books.

Mark prepared a simple dinner—grilled steaks, salad, and baked potatoes. Naturally, Mark had started a vegetable garden in his backyard. Everything about Mark's house seemed uncluttered and earthy. A lot like him.

Opening a bottle of pink champagne, Mark poured out two glasses and made a toast. "To us! And to finally being able to be together like two people who love each other."

That phrase. *Yes, he's right,* I thought. *We do love each other. It will be all right.*

"To us," I replied, smiling, clinking my glass to his.

Mark bustled around with dinner, and I tried to help, chitchatting about school. Without warning, and rather matter-of-factly, as if he were asking me about snorkeling, he said, "What do you think about masturbating? Do you ever do it?"

Embarrassment flooded my chest like hot lava spilling down a mountainside. No one had ever asked me such a personal question before.

"No, not really," I squeaked, mortified at the prospect of having to answer such an intimate and scandalous question.

"No?" he said, surprised. "You should try it. Emily masturbates all the time. It relieves stress. For example, when we are having a dinner party, and she's uptight about it, she just goes into that bathroom right over there," he pointed near the stairs, "and masturbates. She feels much better afterward."

I pondered that for a moment, intrigued and somewhat in awe of this woman. Who *was* she? She had the privilege of being married to Mark, living with him, going places with him, and having dinner parties with him. And she masturbated to prepare for the arrival of guests.

"What's Emily like?" I asked Mark, feeling a little bold to be exploring this woman in her absence, while sitting in her own kitchen. Also, I was eager to move the conversation away from masturbation.

"Emily? She is sweet. And kind. A good mother. She's becoming someone else lately though, now that she's started working part-time. She can also be cranky and demanding. I think she's discovered women's lib. Which is great for her, but she seems angrier than before. She certainly is angrier toward me."

"What is she angry about?" I asked, captivated.

"I don't know. Emily says she feels trapped. She thinks we got married too young. Hey, let's not talk about her anymore. Let's talk about us."

Emily was a much safer subject for me, and he brought her up, so I had to work hard to let go of dwelling on this pretty, sweet, angry-at-Mark, mysterious, masturbating person whose husband I was about to sleep with, under her very roof.

"Do you know how much I love you?" he asked with his natural, friendly smile, glancing over at me while he turned the steaks. "Do you know how glad I am to be with you right now, right here? You, and my children, are the happiest things in my life."

I noticed the absence of his wife's name in that honorable list, but I also noticed I ranked equal to his children. I felt privileged and grateful, along with some responsibility to Mark and our relationship. He was taking risks to be with me; that certainly proved the truth of his feelings for me. I owed it to him to hold up my end of the relationship.

I gulped my champagne and went over to Mark at the grill and hugged him. I reached up to kiss him, but he said, "Just a minute."

He walked us through the patio door back into his kitchen. "No need to put on a show for the neighbors."

In his kitchen, we stood and kissed for a few minutes. Mark ran those warm hands of his over my body, pulling me close to him, and I yielded to his embrace.

Pulling back enough to gaze right into my eyes, he said softly, "I'm going to show you how much I love you later. I'm going to be gentle and loving, and we're going to be happy together. Are you nervous about it? You don't need to be. You're in good hands. I know what I'm doing. I'm no sixteen-year-old boy!" Releasing me, he said, "I better grab these steaks, and let's eat!"

For a moment, my body hung in space like a limp dishrag.

With more swallows of champagne, I was comforted and excited by the knowledge that, indeed, he did know what he was doing. I saw how smart I was to pick an older, experienced man for my first sexual experience. I'd start off right. I'd learn everything about it, and I'd develop confidence and self-awareness. I was sixteen and it was about time; Mark and I had been close since I was fourteen.

But I did not develop self-awareness that night, nor did I learn about sex in a loving relationship. What I did not see—could not see—was the impact my relationship with Mark had on my young psyche. That impact lodged itself deep in the recesses of my being and simmered in unawareness for a very long time.

After dinner, we stacked the dishes in the sink and took our refilled glasses into his living room. We sat down on the slate bench in front of the fireplace and drank and talked. Then Mark put my glass down and pulled me onto his lap and kissed me. My heart raced.

"Do you know how long I've waited for this?" He breathed close to my ear.

We kissed some more, and his crotch hardened beneath me.

"Please touch me," he begged, and I made room for my hand to press against him. I had touched him this way many times before in the car. I suddenly realized we had far more space around us now, no longer hemmed in by car doors and gear shifts. I considered asking God to help me with this, but quickly decided I didn't want God around right now. He probably disapproved of this sort of thing. It was better to leave Him to deal with His other responsibilities for now.

"Here, sit this way," Mark suggested, moving me into a position facing him and straddling him with my legs on either side. We kissed more, Mark's hands on my body and my one hand around his neck and the other in the space between us pressing harder.

"You don't know how good you feel," he said and leaned back to rest against the stone wall of the hearth. This gave me more room to touch him. Mark unbuckled his belt and started to undo his zipper, but then said, "You do it."

Hands trembling, I fumbled with the zipper until it made its way all the way down. Mark's bulge was much more prominent now, held in only by his briefs. My hand covered him. Mark moaned, and I knew I was doing something right. This was as far as we had ever gone in our car encounters—a lot of rubbing. But I had never seen or touched this part of him without the protective layer of chinos. The room spun around me a little and had a hazy orange cast to it. My heart pounded, and my breath came in quick bursts as I reached the edge of my experience and wondered what was next.

Mark had a plan, though. "Stand up for a minute, sweetheart." No one had ever called me sweetheart before, not even my parents. *Is sweetheart—me?*

Lifting a leg over him, I stepped awkwardly to one side while he leaned back, raised up a bit and pushed his pants and underwear over his hips and legs, and tossed them aside. There was Mark, in his full glory, and I was paralyzed.

"Kneel down," Mark said, pointing to the floor in front of him. As he sat on the hearth, and as I kneeled, he gently guided my head.

I knew what this was; I had heard it described, seen pictures, and had even talked about it with my friends. But I had never done it. Mark gave me quiet instructions, and I did my best to follow them. I closed my eyes, braving only quick peeks, and tried to keep breathing. I felt awkward and far more terrified and embarrassed than excited.

Mark continued to be encouraging, moaning, "Oh my God, you are so good!"

I followed his instructions with more awkwardness, blood pounding in my ears, eyes now closed tight, trying to figure out how to breathe. After what seemed like an eternity, I heard Mark moan louder and louder. His body began to move, pressing himself farther toward me. The whole while, his hands were on my head, holding me in place, focusing me on my task. I had no idea whether I was doing things the right way, and I had no idea how long I did it, but Mark clearly enjoyed it.

Finally, he released his gentle press on my head. "Okay, you better stop now. This is getting too exciting. With more practice, you are going to be great at that. Thank you for doing that for me. It's something I have thought about and wanted for such a long time."

*More practice? I wasn't great yet? But he said I was.*

My heart sank, and my brain froze.

Mark pulled me close to him and held me in his arms for a while. I kept my eyes closed and, at some point, remembered to breathe again. Numbness spread through my veins, and my body was still. Then he stood up, took me by the hand, and led me to the stairs. Blood again pounded in my ears, legs rubbery, I followed him past Emily's bathroom of masturbation stress-relief and up to the quiet, dark upstairs.

"We'll use Little Mark's room if you don't mind," he said, leading me into his son's bedroom with blue curtains covered with football players and a twin bed covered with a matching bedspread.

Mark laid me down on the bed and began to take my clothes off. "What is this contraption?" he asked with amusement as he saw that my brown bodysuit stretched all the way down across my bottom and snapped there, the front connecting the back. "This isn't a message to me, is it?" He laughed.

*Is it?* I wondered. *Why did I wear this shirt? What a stupid thing to do.*

Mark unsnapped the bodysuit and peeled my clothes off. The pounding in my ears deafened me.

"You're so beautiful," Mark said, taking his shirt off, too. "I'm going to show you how beautiful I think you are."

He laid down next to me, but kind of half on me, in that narrow child's bed. He held me, kissed me, and touched me all over. Still, the pounding in my ears raged on. I kept my eyes closed as much as possible. If I couldn't see what we were doing, maybe it wasn't really happening. Of course, I was happy it was happening, I reminded myself. I was just scared, naturally.

After a bit of rhythmic movement against my side, Mark got up. "I'll be right back."

I heard him walk into the family bathroom across the hall and open drawers, muttering something to himself. I couldn't begin to imagine what he was doing or searching for. I didn't want to imagine. But he soon returned, holding a large jar of Vaseline. Now I was truly baffled. *What is that for?*

Looking through the crack of my eyes, I saw Mark spread the Vaseline all over himself.

"This is so it won't hurt as much," he explained. "This will make you slippery."

I was not a complete dummy; I knew sex could hurt the first time, so I was grateful for anything that would make it easier. I braced myself, feeling brave and now determined to see the thing through. I was never one to change my mind in midcourse. Once on a path, there was no turning back for me. To stop would create too much of a fuss. I bravely closed my eyes again, held my breath, and felt the pushing, pushing where it didn't seem anything should go.

At some point, it was over. I don't know when or how we got there, but in one moment, Mark decided the time had come for him to "pull out," as he described the method of birth control we were using. I wasn't sure what he did next because I had my eyes closed tight, but later I noticed that a towel was involved.

Mark lay down next to me for a short while, telling me again that he loved me. He stroked my hair. "Next time, it will be easier," he assured me. "The first time is always a little harder for the woman."

*Woman. Am I a woman?* I felt more like a Raggedy Ann doll that some child had mistakenly lost track of at the beach and was now bobbing in the water, far out from shore.

Mark suggested we go into his bedroom to sleep because

the bed was too small for him, let alone the two of us. I tossed and turned, waking from a dream state, disoriented by the room and the bed in which I found myself. In the dark gray hours of the early morning, my eyes slightly opened and I wondered, *Who am I?* I was a stranger to myself, inhabiting or visiting a foreign land. I longed for sleep to arrive and carry me away. I wanted to shut out the unfamiliar landscape and the two strangers in the bed, and find some part of myself I recognized.

Eventually, the light of real morning came. Quiet sounds of the bedside radio came on, music and voices calling all sleepers into the new day. I felt like I was in a movie, looking down at us from the ceiling, lovers tangled in their rumpled sheets, groggy from the events of the previous evening, allowing themselves to lounge before fully registering each other's presence. I lay there for a few minutes while Mark slept, hearing the murmuring of the radio, thinking of myself as the interloping woman, left over from the night before, and wondering how it had happened that I was there.

Oddly, I did not mentally review the activities of the previous evening, although I certainly knew what had happened. Emotionally, all I noticed was a peculiar sense of comfort I derived from the sounds of the radio. Perhaps I was grateful for the presence of some other people in the room with us, speaking in cheerful tones as though all was right with the world.

Eventually, Mark woke up. He watched me, stroking my long hair, and smiling.

"How's my girl this morning?"

"I'm okay," I replied. "A little sleepy, I guess."

Mark gazed at me and waited a few moments. As though coming to some decision, he said in an upbeat tone, "What do you want to do today? We have all day. How about some breakfast and then the beach? It's gonna be pretty warm today. I'll make us some eggs and coffee, and then we can pack snacks and drinks and take off."

"That sounds good," I replied, eager to get out of bed.

I started to get up, and Mark pulled me back, saying, "Hey, wait a minute! No need to be in such a hurry. It's only 7:30. Let's stay here and talk a little while." He was fully awake now, and I could sense his attention and gaze on me.

Mark reached for my hand. He said, "We had a very, very special thing happen between us—a sacred thing. We shared our love as two adults share love. I am so happy that I could show you, as a man to a woman, how much I love you and cherish you. It's okay if it was a little awkward—the first time usually is like that for two new people. They need to get to know each other, and over time they learn what each other likes. We will learn that about each other."

At those words, I sank back down into my spot on the bed, now acutely aware it was Mark and Emily's bed, and again feeling like I was somewhere I did not belong. Being in their personal space, perhaps more than what had happened in Little Mark's room last night, made me feel small and uncomfortable. I wanted to get out of there. A part of me started to worry Emily would burst into the house at any moment, catching me in her place. The thought was mortifying, and the more it crept into my mind, the more guilty and dirty I felt.

"Can I use the bathroom?" I needed to flee from that spot and from the conversation. "I really need to go."

He hesitated. "Yeah, you can use this one here. I'll use the kids' bathroom. Take your time. If you want to shower, go ahead. I'll get breakfast started. You want coffee, don't you?"

Heading for the bathroom, I said, "Yeah, definitely. Thanks."

Once alone in the bathroom with the door firmly shut, I sat down on the closed toilet seat and gathered myself into a ball. I stared down at the floor for a while. The warring factions inside me left me disoriented. I just had sex with Mark, my thirty-two-year-old friend, former teacher, and now lover, who was married with two kids. I was awash in conflicting emotions—sad and proud, grown-up and young, excited and lost, and pretty small. I couldn't keep any single feeling straight. I sat and stared into space, paralyzed. It was only my self consciousness about being in the bathroom for too long that spurred me to get up and, with a sigh, turn on the shower and step in.

The sound of the water, its warmth, the beautiful clean bathroom, the soap, and the solitude began to soothe me a little, and I wanted to stay there indefinitely. I stayed as long as I dared, not washing my hair because I was too nervous to take the liberty of using Emily's shampoo. What if she noticed some was gone? I dried off with a towel, wrapped it around me, and went into Little Mark's room in search of my clothes. I found them, inched my way back into them, and headed downstairs. Now I was ready to consider God again and offered a quick prayer for forgiveness, just in case what I had done was wrong.

I was pretty sure it was.

## seven

## MY DOUBLE LIFE

I FIRST NOTICED PHILIP WHILE SITTING IN SPANISH CLASS AT the beginning of my junior year of high school. Philip exuded down-to-earth reliability. I saw this quality in him despite his shyness. Philip also projected a sense of kindness and gentleness, and seemed an all-around nice guy who never had overly much to say. Maybe what drew my attention to him was his surprising command of Spanish. He seemed to know almost as much as the teacher, despite being a white kid with green eyes and sandy, cropped hair.

"How come you speak Spanish so well?" I approached him shyly one day as we walked together out of Spanish class.

"Well, my father comes from Ecuador, and my mother teaches French, so I guess languages are just in our family. My older sister speaks French, Spanish, and German."

"That's pretty impressive. I'd be happy just to learn to speak Spanish better."

"We could practice sometime if you'd like."

I could see he was a little nervous suggesting this, but I was intrigued.

"Okay, let's do that sometime. Thanks! It's so much easier for me to learn by having a conversation in Spanish."

We started taking walks together a couple times a week after school on my non-Mark days, and we did Spanish homework together. When Philip brought me to his house, I met his older sister Debbie, who was beautiful, smart, and just as down-to-earth and responsible as Philip. His mother was an understated, youthful, friendly woman. His father, short and compact, worked at the United Nations in New York. His parents seemed to like me, although we didn't establish a close relationship. They were Baptists and seemed to value honesty, simplicity, and good morals, and churchgoing was a big part of Philip's life. For all his goodness, Philip didn't seem to carry any baggage of guilt that I associated with his religion. Not that my own religion was free of guilt . . . far from it. My family just didn't talk about religious guilt—or anything—openly.

I soon learned Philip was working on his Eagle badge in Boy Scouts, the highest level a Boy Scout could attain. Philip was quiet, reliable, smart, cute, and kind. He was not part of the in-crowd; his friends seemed to be other serious, shy guys, mostly teammates from the soccer team, which I also came to learn was a great passion of Philip's. He played soccer on the varsity team, and I went to all his games. He took me once to a professional hockey game, and I tried but failed to follow the game. His favorite sports teams became my favorite teams.

I would say Philip and I struck up a fast friendship, but it was clear to both of us, right from the beginning, that we had the potential for more than friendship. In Philip's case, he was introverted and inexperienced with romance. In my case, I was reluctantly playacting Mrs. Robinson in *The Graduate*: my relationship with Mark made me the "experienced" woman courting an innocent boy.

Philip and I spent many late nights in his basement den or

in my living room with the doors shut, "watching TV." We kissed and petted like the teenagers we were. Although we loved it, we never once went over any lines beyond this. I don't remember even struggling with that decision with him; we both seemed to know where we wanted the limit to be, at least while we were in our parents' houses.

My social world consisted primarily of Mark, Philip, and my girlfriends: three separate worlds. I liked spending time with Philip, although I could never forget that I led a double life; it placed a wedge between me and my feelings for him. I wouldn't say I was in love with Philip, although I fully accepted him as my boyfriend, at least as much as I could, given my relationship with Mark. Philip and I were what I thought a girlfriend and boyfriend were supposed to be. But my duplicitous double-agent life dominated my world, as I met up with Mark most days after school.

Although Philip knew Mark, he didn't know *about* Mark. Although Mark knew Philip, he didn't know much *about* Philip. My girlfriends—Judy, Bonnie, Sophie, and Joan—knew Philip and knew *about* Philip, and they certainly knew Mark but did not know *about* Mark. My family knew even less. Occasionally there would be some overlap; they all knew each other periph-erally, but I was the only thing they had in common.

As the fall yielded to winter, and my relationship with Philip grew, another opportunity to spend an overnight with Mark emerged. Once again, Emily took their two children out of town from Saturday to Sunday, and Mark and I could have a repeat performance of our summer tryst at his house. This time Mark drove out on Saturday afternoon to get me, and on the way back to his house, we stopped for an early dinner at one of the fancier restaurants in the area. My parents had gone there a couple of times as guests of parishioners, and they had described the large fireplace, stone walls, beautiful table settings, and fabulous food. I had always dreamed of going there someday.

I was so excited as I walked into the darkened foyer and saw the white tablecloths and sparkling water glasses waiting to welcome us. Several tables were already filled with people, but Mark had called ahead to reserve us a table in front of the large fireplace, which had a cozy and crackling fire, offering extra warmth on a chilly day.

"We have a reservation for two," Mark told the man behind the podium. The man led us to a table against the wall, far from the fireplace, and I was dismayed.

But Mark corrected him. "We have reserved *that* table." He pointed to the empty table in front of the fireplace. "That's the table we would like." The man immediately apologized and steered us to the place reserved for us. I was grateful for Mark's protection; I would never have been able to speak up and challenge the waiter's behavior.

We settled ourselves in our seats and studied the menus. I already had decided on one thing I knew I wanted. My parents had raved about the lobster bisque there, and indeed it was one of their specialties. I couldn't wait to try it; the choice was an exotic one for me. The rest of the menu was less exciting, but I decided on the sole with breadcrumbs.

"I'd get you a glass of wine, but I don't think they'll bring it to you. But I'll get some and share it with you." He winked at me.

I was considering Coke or Ginger Ale when a new waiter approached us.

"The lady would like a ginger ale, and I would like a glass of Chablis." Mark took charge of the ordering.

"I'm afraid there is a problem." This new fellow seemed a bit serious, even stern.

"Oh, what's that?" Mark asked with lightness in his voice, suggesting he wasn't planning to take what the waiter said too seriously.

"You cannot sit here. You see, we don't allow children by the fire." The waiter sounded officious and disapproving.

My face reddened with the shame of doing something wrong, of being caught breaking the rules, and of being considered a child in this situation. Just when I was reveling in having such an adult and long-awaited dining experience, the waiter had called me a child.

Mark once again came to the rescue, saying in a calm but emphatic voice, "Oh, that's okay. We don't have any children." And he continued, undaunted. "Now, about those drinks. We would like a glass of Chablis and a ginger ale. Thank you."

I was amazed. What a great comeback! How did he think of it so quickly? Although I didn't meet the waiter's eyes, I smiled and sat a little straighter. When he stiffly receded from the table, Mark and I exchanged a glance and laughed conspiratorially.

"Imagine thinking we had children!" he said.

Although deep inside the sting of shame remained, I wanted to enjoy this dinner. It was a rare event for me to even be in a restaurant, much less this famed establishment, and with a man like Mark. He was my hero, my protector, my advocate, and my adult friend. I loved being with him, and I wanted the dinner to last forever. I tried not to think much about what would happen after dinner.

When we got to Mark's house, he put on music, made a fire, poured us some wine, and laid out blankets on the floor. We threw down some large and fluffy cushions and settled in there, talking and drinking our wine. It would have been a magical time, were it not for the rising anxiety I could not force down. I was finding it harder and harder to converse, and I became quieter. I excused myself to go to the bathroom, and when I returned to the nest by the fire, Mark—to my shock—was stretched out in front of the fire completely naked, his long body relaxed. His excitement, however, was obvious.

"Come over here, honey, I want to show you something. See this?" he asked, pointing. "This fellow here is showing you how happy I am to be with you, and how much I love you."

I glanced down, my eyes not wanting to linger there, and not knowing what to say. Or do. But Mark took charge once again in his gentle, confident way. He slowly got my clothes off, stoked up the fire, adjusted the music, and laid me down gently, talking lovingly the whole time. He invited me to explore his body. He guided my hand, kissed me, and caressed me by the fire.

The evening blended into night, in what seemed like hours and also just seconds. I found myself less shocked and embarrassed this time. It was easier for me to go through the motions required and keep emotion out of it. When sleep came, I was grateful, and I slept through to morning. When we woke up, the house was chilly, and I wrapped myself in a blanket. This time Mark made it clear he wanted a morning repeat of the evening's activities. From some unfamiliar place inside, the words emerged without my thinking.

"I'm actually a little . . . well . . . tired." I was apologetic, and I watched closely to see what reaction Mark would have to this, secretly thankful to whoever inside me found those words. If he seemed too disappointed or even slightly mad, I would readily go along with what he wanted. But Mark didn't press the issue. Except just a little, I guess.

"How about if you just watch?" Mark showed me what he meant to do with his hand. "Would you like that?"

*Oh my God*, I thought. *I can't possibly.* Not only did I have no interest or curiosity, I was repulsed and frightened at the idea of it. *Please, God, no!*

Again, some friend from deep within tried to come to my rescue. "Uh, I don't think so. Not now, I mean." I wanted to erase the word "now." "I mean, I don't think I'm ready for that yet." I wanted to erase the word "yet." My smile was apologetic.

Mark backed off. "No problem. Maybe sometime in the future. Some women think it's really sexy, but, hey, let's get some breakfast. Eggs? Coffee?"

I worked hard to push aside my guilt for declining his offer, and I continued to watch for signs of disappointment, disapproval, or emotional withdrawal, but Mark showed none of it. We got dressed, he made breakfast, and I tidied up the blankets and pillows, then we ate and chatted. Mark offered to make another fire and suggested we read for a while until he needed to drive me back home. Emily would be back by mid-afternoon, and it was close to a two-hour, round-trip drive for him to take me home.

The rest of our time together was amiable and relaxed; he inquired about my stated desire to study neuroscience in college, and we talked about the books we were reading. At the time, I was reading *Atlas Shrugged* by Ayn Rand, the epic work extolling the virtues of fierce individualism and capitalism. I found her writing to be captivating, the strength of her characters inspiring, and her economic and political views convincing. (I was impressionable.)

Mark encouraged me to explain what I liked about it. He listened carefully, and we went back and forth in the discussion. I loved his acceptance of me and his genuine interest in what I thought. If he challenged my views, he did it intellectually and not emotionally. This was why I loved Mark; he was so mature. He didn't get mad at things. He was supportive, smart, gentle, and understanding. And he genuinely seemed interested in who I was. I could tell he loved me; he treated me so well.

*eight*

———

## A CLOSE CALL

BONNIE RUSHED OVER TO FIND ME IN THE LUNCHROOM.

"Hey, guess what? I was just talking to Mr. Johnson, and he told me he has eight tickets to this coffeehouse in Queens Saturday night. This Saturday. And he said we can use them and invite anyone we want to go. He's going, of course, so that's seven tickets! What do you think? Should we go? I definitely want to go!"

"Wow! That sounds terrific. Yeah, I'll go for sure." Mark had already told me about the tickets, but we agreed Bonnie should spread the news, just to take attention away from him and me. I wanted to ease any jealousy there may be among the girls. They knew I was his favorite, and I already noticed Joan was a little testy with me when the subject of Mr. Johnson—they didn't call him Mark—came up with us girls.

We gathered up a group that included Bonnie, Sophie, Joan, me, and Judy. I wanted to ask Philip to go; even though he didn't often hang out with us, he still knew them all. Philip agreed and asked a soccer buddy to join us, but his friend backed out at the last minute. Our group was us girls, Philip, and Mark. I drove out to Queens with Philip, and the girls went in Sophie's car (the only one of us besides me who had regular use of her parents' car). Mark met us there.

We filled up a round table, and I managed to sit between Philip and Mark. *Perfect*, I thought! The music hadn't started yet.

When the waitress came over, Mark said, "The first round of drinks is on me, friends. Order up!"

We ordered sodas and iced teas, since none of us were eighteen yet. Mark ordered a beer. The drinks arrived with bowls of popcorn for the table. The lights dimmed, we settled in, and the place got quiet.

The singer wasn't anyone I knew, but he was good—folksy and funny. Some songs were lively, and everyone in the place nodded their heads and tapped their feet with the tempo. Some were serious and created a somber feel. During intermission, people got up to use the restroom or just stretch. Once everyone returned to the table, Bonnie took charge.

"Hey guys, let's order some food. How about a large cheese pizza? We can split the cost. I'm getting another Coke."

"And I'll have another Bud," Mark chimed in when the waitress arrived, and we all ordered more drinks. I noticed Philip ordered iced teas; his family didn't drink soda.

"What do you guys think?" asked Mark. "Do you like him?"

"I love him!" gushed Judy. "I wonder if he sells records. I'm going to ask him after the show."

"Yeah, he's cool," Bonnie and Sophie agreed.

Joan was a little quiet, and Philip had said almost nothing the whole night. I leaned over to him. "Are you okay? You're so quiet. Do you like the music?"

"Yeah, I guess. It's fine. This isn't really my kind of scene. I'm a little out of place. I wish Ben could have made it."

"You don't like being with all these girls?" I teased. Philip just looked so uncomfortable. "It's okay." He shrugged and focused on his glass of iced tea.

---

"Hey, Mr. Johnson," called Bonnie across the table. "Thanks for arranging this. It's so cool to be here."

"My pleasure, girls. And guy." He smiled at Philip, who nodded slightly.

Mark handed me a slice of pizza while he asked, "What concerts have you lovely ladies been to this year?"

No mention of the guy this time.

Joan piped up. "My sister and I saw Dylan at the Music Fair last month. It was so excellent!"

"Hey Joanie, that's a real treat. I'm jealous." Mark winked at her, and she beamed back.

"I can't top that," said Judy. "But my friends at the Ethical Humanist Society and our parents went to see Brotherhood of Man the other week. They're not widely known yet. But they will be!" She bubbled, always optimistic.

The lights dimmed again, and the mood shifted as we watched the stage. I placed my hand on Mark's thigh under the tablecloth, squinting out of the corner of my eye for a reaction. He smiled into the darkness. His foot moved closer to touch my foot, and my heart beat faster. I pressed a little harder on his leg, feeling those muscles I loved. Philip was right on my other side, but the tablecloth generously covered what went on below. I cast a glance toward Philip anyway, just in case he reacted to what he couldn't see. I recognized a twang of guilt, but mostly I felt powerful, expressing my intimacy with Mark in such a public yet private manner, engaging in my enormous secret relationship right there in the midst of my high school peers. What they didn't know!

"Just what is your relationship with Mr. Johnson?" Philip asked the next day when he came over in the afternoon.

"What do you mean?" I tried to sound innocent and hide my immediate terror.

"I mean, first of all, I think it's pretty weird for a grown man, a teacher even, to go out on a Saturday night with a bunch of kids. Why wasn't he home with his family? And I have to say, it seems like something is going on between the two of you. You seem pretty friendly." Philip sounded hurt, angry, and uncomfortable.

"Mr. Johnson has been friends with us bunch of kids for a while. We all work on the Organic Farm together. He's friends with all of us."

"Well, I feel like a chump. I didn't belong with that group last night; I only went because of you. He didn't belong there even more than me, but you seemed pretty happy he was there. You seem to think it was all normal. Now I'm not so sure about things. I don't like that guy." Philip kicked at the asphalt with his shoe.

"What's not to be sure about?" I tried to keep my voice calm. I suddenly realized I not only had to protect my secret, but I might lose Philip over this, and I did not want that. I really liked Philip, and I hated lying to him. He was a tie to normalcy in a romantic relationship, which was a comfort to me when we were together. But telling Philip the truth about Mark was not an option. Mark had convinced me no one would understand our relationship; it was essential to protect our secret. If I were going to lose anyone over this, it would be Philip. This deception was getting complicated and painful. Philip's innocence made my guilt come alive.

"He's a friend of my family. Maybe that's why he seems

friendly to me. There's nothing weird going on. You may not like him, but he's okay." I thought it would help if he knew my parents knew Mark. They had seen him on one or two occasions; he used to be my teacher. A "friend of the family" stretched the truth like a taut rubber band, but Philip didn't know that.

Philip countered my arguments with, "Well, I don't want to be around him. Next time count me out on any groupie plans." Philip seemed to sulk a little. "I don't even want you to be around him. No matter what you say, I think he's weird, and I think he's after you."

*Sheesh, this is too close for comfort. I have to be more careful from now on,* I thought in a bit of a panic.

Hiding my shaking hands behind my back, with a contrite voice, I said, "Well, it will be hard for me to not see him; he's there every day with the Farming Club, and I don't want to give that up."

"Okay, do what you want," he conceded with a gentler voice. "But I still don't like it."

I paused a little. "All right. There's honestly nothing to worry about. I'm really sorry you were uncomfortable last night." I was eager to bring this conversation to a close.

Philip shrugged and then smiled grudgingly at me. "I just really like you."

This was such a sweet thing to my ears; he was not one for words of love, even though I knew he liked me. There was goodness in Philip, and his liking me made me think there might be goodness in me, too. I loved just being with him to see a movie and hold hands—simple things. Philip was a boy my age that I could act my age with. I didn't need to keep my relationship with him a secret, and there was nothing about him to feel guilty about . . . well, except my lying to him about Mark.

But I didn't want to give up Mark; he was the only person who seemed to really know and love me, and he told me that all the time. Philip's sweetness in this moment broke the tension and endeared him to me even more. I smiled back at him and said, "I really like you, too!" We hugged each other . . . a sweet moment of reconciliation.

We moved on to our plans for the day. I continued to shake inwardly at the near exposure of my secret and at the idea my true relationship with Mark could be visible to anyone else. I would have to watch Philip closely and work to keep Mark far away from him. Trying to bring my two worlds together like that was a mistake. Too risky. The idea of giving up either one of them was not okay. I needed them both.

My double life with Mark and Philip continued without any further run-ins throughout the winter of my junior year when I turned seventeen. I saw Mark after school in our secret parking spot, and I saw Philip on the weekends, at his house or mine. Even though the Organic Farming Club didn't often meet during the winter, once early spring arrived, we began meeting to plant seeds in small mulch pots and nurture them along as the seedlings sprouted. Mark surprised us all one day with an invitation to his cabin in Rhode Island. We had heard him talk about this rustic cabin on a lake, and it sounded like a pretty cool place.

"Mr. Johnson is inviting the members of the Organic Farm to his family's place in Rhode Island this weekend," I announced to my mother, knowing it sounded like his family would be there, too. "I'd really like to go. Is that okay? I can take my car and drive some people, which would be helpful."

"Well, as long as he's there to supervise you kids, it's okay with me."

That was easy.

"Have a good time," she added distractedly.

We left on Friday after school, a caravan of cars loaded up with pasta, sandwich makings, cereal, sleeping bags, and games. About eight of us drove out in the afternoon, and some more joined us that evening. Philip was not among us, although there were a couple of guys from the Farming Club. Philip knew about the trip but had an away soccer game that weekend. I knew he didn't want to go, anyway. If it bothered him that I went, he didn't mention it. Some people had to leave earlier than others on Sunday, so it worked well to have a few cars among us.

We settled into the cabin, and after a satisfying pasta dinner, Mark announced, "Let's go over the sleeping arrangements. The girls have the two bedrooms off the porch, and the guys can crash here in front of the fireplace. I will be in there." He gestured toward a third bedroom off the kitchen. "That being said, everyone is on their own, but don't get your parents mad at me." He winked. Everyone laughed.

"Let's get some games going!" someone called out, and we grappled over forming charade teams and gin rummy players.

"I'll make us some hot chocolate," I offered. "How many takers?"

I went into the kitchen, and Mark followed me, saying, "I'll show you where the pots are kept. You'll need more than one." Alone in the kitchen, Mark leaned in close to me and said, "Do you know how happy I am when I see you across the room, here, in my cabin? It's as though you belong here with me."

I smiled up at him. It warmed my heart to be so wanted.

"On Sunday, try to be the last one to leave so we can have some time here alone," Mark said, as I stirred the warming chocolate milk.

"Yeah, I think I can do that," I spoke softly. "I don't have to drive anyone back." I was feeling good and stifled a chuckle as I smiled up at him. He and I carried trays of hot chocolate into the living room, ready to join in the games.

"Hey, Liz," called out a boy from the Club named Stuart. "We need another player. Come join our charades team!"

"No way!" I exclaimed. "I'm definitely not a charades girl. I'm sticking with gin rummy over here."

"Okay then, Mr. Johnson, you can be on our team!" Joan called out excitedly.

"Honored, my dear. But watch out, other team. I am an ace at charades!"

We all laughed hysterically at the charade antics, gin rummy long forgotten. Watching people act foolish, all in the name of fun, was way more entertaining. I loved every minute of it. I noticed how Joan beamed as she and Mark conspired to pick the movies or books to stump the other team, and when Mark gave her high-fives and pats on the knee, she glowed. I knew she loved his attention, but it didn't threaten me. I trusted Mark.

After the games ended, Mark went to his room, and the rest of us stayed up gossiping about teachers and classes. Mark and I could have no plan to sleep together with the whole group there, so I went to bed with the girls.

The next day, we split up into comfortable groups and went

on walks or made meals or sat by the fireplace. Mark joined different groups throughout the day. It was all very companionable, and I loved being around him with other people . . . friends, in the normal way kids do. Although we couldn't show our love in any way, Mark and I stole brief moments when it was safe, touched an arm, walked together, or whispered a quiet "I love you" to each other. Saturday night, we all played more games by the fire and sang songs late into the night, Stuart playing his guitar.

Over breakfast the next morning, I offered to the group, "I don't have any homework this weekend, so I don't mind staying later to help Mr. Johnson clean up."

"Sounds good to me," everyone agreed. Some had sports practice to get to, and others had homework or just told their parents they'd be back by late afternoon. Since there were enough cars for everyone to get a ride back without needing my car, it worked out smoothly.

Waving the last carful goodbye, Mark and I headed back into the cabin. Alone at last! About this, I had my now-familiar mix of feelings and non-feelings. It was exciting and daring to be so chosen by Mark, getting away with such a bold opportunity to be alone with him in this remote place. However, I was vaguely aware of that small nagging knot, like a pit planted in my gut, which radiated out a heaviness across my body, down my arms and legs, leaving me a little queasy.

Mark closed and locked the door to the cabin, and lifted me off my feet, twirling me around in the small kitchen.

"I thought this moment would never get here!" he exclaimed. "Let's quickly get things put away and make the most of these hours we have left."

As we tidied up and washed and dried every dish, my emotions slowly relocated themselves into a tiny, locked box buried deep somewhere I couldn't reach, until I couldn't feel anything. Not happiness, not fear, not excitement, not anything. Instead, my body was numb, and my mind was cottony; I was only vaguely aware of feeling nothing. This was my state of being now whenever Mark approached me as his sexual partner.

We went into his room, where the bed loomed. He slowly undressed me, telling me he loved me and that I was beautiful while caressing my body, then he lifted me onto the bed and joined me there. After some time, he said, "You know, there are ways a woman can experience so much pleasure. Ecstatic pleasure. I'd love to show you that. I know you will love it. It's what a woman's body is meant to know, to have, to experience. I want you to have an orgasm, and I can do that for you. What do you say?"

Mark had brought this up before, but not for a while. I was uncomfortable with the idea of losing control into something I didn't know. I didn't want more expression. I wanted less. I mostly wanted to endure the sex and be done. What I said was, "You know, that sounds great, and I'd like to do it sometime. But I don't think I'm ready for it right now. Give me a little more time, okay?"

"Sure, baby, whatever you want. Whenever you're ready, I'm here."

I was relieved he didn't push it, and we stuck with our usual routine, which was basically missionary position, with Mark pulling out just in time. Mark seemed happy with our encounters, and that made me happy . . . and relieved.

*nine*

——

# THE PRESSURE MOUNTS

SPRING TURNED SLOWLY INTO SUMMER, THE MONTHS AHEAD promising days of warmth and freedom. I loved the summer sun, the long days, the games of tennis, and the sleepovers with Sophie, Bonnie, and Joan. I read books, drove to the beach and the mall in my own car, took modern dance classes, and worked for a local dentist as a chair-side assistant.

One glorious day, heading into my senior year, I was sitting under the trees in front of the high school. I laid back in the soft grass and gazed up at the impossibly blue sky as it poked out among the vivid greens of the young leaves of summer. A blue so vibrant and deep I could disappear into it, and I would be in heaven. A green so alive, natural, and shockingly beautiful next to all that bright sapphire. Summer was my home season, when I could step outside and the warmth would embrace me. No shivering, no shouldering the burden of cold, no bracing, no shrinking from the dark. In summer, I emerged. In summer, I had the right to live, and the world welcomed me.

Mark and I continued to watch for chances to get away together. Another couple of trips to Mark's house for an overnight was part of that summer. We went directly to Mark and Emily's bedroom, skipping the room with the football curtains and blue bedspread. Those summer mornings, I again awoke to the assuring company of the voices on the radio. It was hard to stay connected with my body, and I watched myself from a vantage point on the bedroom ceiling. Looking down, I observed the tangled sheets, the jewelry box on the dresser, the family photos of children on the wall, and the form of Mark sleeping next to me. From up above, I saw Mark awaken, pull me close, rub my back, and move against me. I saw myself offering no resistance to this, as I knew it was coming. I lost my need to seek solace in his bathroom.

As summer ended, my excitement about senior year rose.

"Did you get in? Did you get in?" Joan, Bonnie, Sophie, and Judy hovered around me as I opened the envelope. We were gathered at Bonnie's house, each with our envelopes in hand, waiting to open them together.

"I did!" I shouted, relieved and ecstatic. We jumped up and down, hugging each other.

All five of us were accepted into a new experimental program for seniors called The New School. The program ran like a small college, where the students chose or created subjects to study. Some courses were The Poetry of Bob Dylan; News and the Media; Campaign '74; and any independent study we wanted. My two favorite classes I designed myself: one was a research paper, *The Pain Threshold in Dental Procedures*, combining my experience at the dental office and my interest in the brain, and the other was a course in writing book reviews. Using the *New York Times Book Review* section as my guide, I read countless books and wrote reviews for them. I was proud when our English teacher told me I had a future in writing.

Conveniently, the Organic Farm sat next to our New School building, and one of our spring class creations was Organic Farming with Mark Johnson, so we saw him often.

As my academic life blossomed, so did my relationship with Philip. In the fall of my senior year, he invited me on a backpacking trip.

"But I don't know anything about camping," I fretted when Philip said we'd hike for miles and camp overnight.

"Leave the planning to me," he assured me. "I'll pack all the equipment and food we need. I can do this. I'm a Boy Scout, you know. You just need to get a pair of hiking boots and break them in before we go, and you'll do great. I can loan you a pack."

We'd be together for a night, a first for us. Even though we didn't talk about it, there was no doubt in my mind about having sex with Philip; I was going to do it. I thought about being able to kiss him, hug him, and do the usual touching that we did, and then go all the way. I was going to be the experienced one, and although this gave me a small degree of confidence, it mostly terrified me. I did not, for all my times with Mark, feel experienced about sex. I was still shy, embarrassed, and confused. But we were seventeen, and this was an opportunity to explore normal teenage sex.

I did worry about birth control. With Mark, I left it up to him and his withdrawal method. But with Philip, I was too self-conscious to discuss the subject with him. That night, lying by the fire in our sleeping bag, happily kissing and talking, neither of us raised the issue.

*Well*, I thought, *if he doesn't have a condom, I'll have to rely on the stand-up-and-jump method I read about in a magazine.* It said that after intercourse if the woman immediately stood up and jumped, all the sperm would run out and down her legs and not allow pregnancy. It was my backup plan.

We made love, and I allowed the sensations flowing through my body to pull me forward freely. I relaxed into each kiss, each gentle touch, our growing excitement building together. We didn't speak but followed our instincts, laughing at our occasional fumbling. There was something beautiful about trusting, discovering, and just letting go. Even my worry about no condom melted away. This sweetness during sex was very new; I was not tensing, waiting for it to be over, as I did with Mark. Any guilt I had about being a teenager having sex with Philip was dwarfed by the constant shame and confusion that permeated my encounters with Mark.

True to my Plan B, I got up afterward, walked a few steps away near some trees, and jumped up and down a few times, praying silently. *Please, God, don't let me get pregnant. Amen.*

Philip asked, perplexed, "Are you okay? What are you doing?"

"I'm okay. I'll be right there. I just need to stand up for a minute," I said, too embarrassed to explain further. I couldn't talk about sex; I had no words. I was desperately hoping Philip had read the same article, but no luck there.

"Are you sure you're okay?" He sounded concerned.

"I read that this is good to do now—after . . . what we were doing," I said.

"As long as you're sure you're okay," Philip replied, puzzled, but not pressing the subject further. I didn't know what he was thinking.

I soon lay down with him again, under the sleeping bag, and we fell asleep in each other's arms, myself relieved that I had taken care of the birth control issue.

The next morning, Philip fired up the camp stove and made eggs for us while I made tea. We offered these to each other with a warmth and closeness that was palpable and so pleasant. Making love with Philip left me feeling tender and sweet, like a smile spreading through my heart. We made no direct reference to the night before, but we shared a peacefulness—an unspoken new beginning. Walking through the woods, I had a lightness in my heart, like all was well with *this* world.

Meanwhile, something about the freedom and stimulation of the New School, moving to a closer relationship with Philip, and perhaps the weight of time made me want, more than ever before, to tell Bonnie, Sophie, and Joan about my real relationship with Mark. The secrecy was a burden pressing on me, and I longed for the relief of sharing the truth with them. Part of me knew I was betraying our friendship by withholding this huge part of my life. I walked around with a chronic feeling of mild nausea, born of guilt and uncertainty. In those moments when I allowed emotion to come too close, I wanted to vomit it all out. Vomit out deception, Mark, sex, my shyness, my aloneness, my existence—all of it. But I kept quiet.

I noticed Joan's interest in Mark by how animated she was around him. She seemed to create a subtle air of competition between us for his attention and was often sullen or sarcastic when his name came up in my presence. I feared if I told her the extent of my relationship with Mark, it would hurt her and damage our friendship. I didn't want to flaunt anything; I just wanted to stop lying and deceiving, especially with them. I worried Sophie might have some judgment about it, although she would never desert me. I was too ashamed to consider telling Judy Weil, knowing her code of ethics would not condone what I was doing with Mark. I thought Bonnie would be the most open-minded and accepting of it, but Bonnie was distracted by some of her own romantic adventures. If I was going to share my secret with someone, I wanted their full attention. I ruminated on whether and how to tell Sophie.

By late winter of the school year, we all found out where we would be going to college the next fall. Judy was going to William and Mary, Sophie to U Penn, and Bonnie to Wesleyan College. Having been the recipient of a National Honor Society award and another merit scholarship that required me to attend a New York State system school, SUNY was my only option. My choice revolved around which SUNY city to pick. I chose Binghamton, and independently, so did Joan. I was glad I would have a friend at college. But at the same time, it did present a dilemma for me since I assumed Mark would visit me at college, which would be difficult to hide from Joan.

When I told Mark my decision about college, he shared my excitement.

"That is really wonderful, sweetie! I am proud of you. SUNY Binghamton is a good school, and it's not that far away. You love learning, so you will enjoy college. And remember, I will be waiting for you. Waiting for the time we can start our real life together. I want to marry you, you know!"

This wasn't the first time Mark had said this, but this time I pushed on the idea a little. "Mark, I know you say this, but how can you marry me when you are already married, with children?"

"I haven't wanted to share much about my home life with you." He lowered his voice. "But things have gotten pretty bad there. Emily wants a divorce."

"Oh, my God!" I exclaimed. "I am so sorry. What happened? Was it because of me? Does she know about me?"

"No, no, don't worry. She doesn't know about you. She says she's not happy with me; she wants to start over . . . find herself, she says. Whatever that means."

"Well, what do you think about that? Do you want a divorce, too?"

"I am mostly worried about the kids. I will be fine. I want to live my own life, too, with you. This is actually good news for you and me. It means we can be together like we want to."

I knew there were problems in his marriage because Mark had alluded to issues from time to time, but I wasn't prepared to hear it had come to this. I was sad about this breakup of a family, but I knew in my heart I was equally worried about what it meant for me. What dawned on me at that moment was that I didn't want Mark to get divorced. I didn't want Mark to wait for me, to marry me after college. What I wanted was freedom. I wanted to live *my* life, not a life with him.

As these new thoughts coursed through my mind like sludge, Mark said, "In fact, this summer I will be getting my own apartment. Think about what that means for us. We can be together much, much more. Almost whenever we want. And I can visit you at college on weekends when I don't have my kids."

"Wow, that does change things, doesn't it?" I feigned excitement. Mark didn't notice.

As the year advanced further into spring, the pressure inside me increased and wore me out. I juggled Mark and his pending freedom, Philip, my girlfriends, my family, my supposed church life as the pastor's daughter, and a longing to escape from my home life. I had headaches every day and yearned to disappear into reading books and my newest passion, running. With Joan and me attending the same college and Mark wanting to visit me there, the pressure simmered just under the surface. Every day, day after day, I agonized over how to handle this situation with Joan and college. Finally, I talked over my concerns with Mark. He recommended I keep our affair a secret until Joan and I got to college. Before the first time he visited, I should tell her but swear her to secrecy. He seemed to sense how to handle Joan best, so I agreed to this. It seemed the most reasonable thing to do.

Yet, as often happens with pressure cookers, the underlying volatility of the situation one day took on a life of its own.

*ten*

---

# BREAKING THE CODE OF SECRECY

"SOPHIE, I NEED TO TELL YOU ABOUT SOMETHING," I SAID ONE morning that spring when I was sleeping over at her house. "It's really important, and it might surprise you." I peeked over at her.

"I've wanted to talk to you about this for a long time but didn't know how. I really hope you'll understand and will still want to be my friend after I tell you." My voice shook.

Sophie sat up in her bed, folding her arms around her bended knees. "Oh my God. Of course, I will always be your friend. Don't even think it. What is it? Are you okay?"

I believed her.

My heart pounded, and my palms sweated. I took a couple of deep breaths to fight back the tears. "It's about Mark Johnson." I faltered over these few words.

Her face was open and soft. "I think I know what you're going to say. It's okay, you can tell me."

"Really?" I asked with some relief.

"Yes, but I think you should just go ahead and talk."

"Well, he and I are more than just friends. I mean, we are friends, but we're also more than that. I've been seeing him for a while." I let out my breath, which I didn't know I was holding.

"Oh my God. I knew you were going to say that. I actually

wondered about it." She was animated as she regarded me. "How long has this . . . have you . . . ?" She seemed a little at a loss for how to ask.

Eager now to tell the whole story, my words rushed out. "Well, it began kind of slowly. Really, ever since junior high, we started writing letters. And those times he and I went to the beach and none of you could go . . . that started things. And then he left our school, and then he came back. I don't know. It kind of slowly grew into something else. I wasn't sure about it at first. I felt kind of weird about it. Sometimes I still do. But I think he really does love me."

"Yeah, I'm sure he does," she reassured me.

"The first time we had a chance to be alone overnight was two summers ago, between tenth and eleventh grade."

"Wow!" she said. "I wondered if something was going on for a while, but not that far back."

"Why did you suspect something?" I asked, anxious to find out how serious this chink in the armor of our secrecy was.

"Well, just in the way you two would sometimes talk. He clearly likes you. That's obvious to anyone. You've always been his favorite. He likes us, too, but there just seems to be something different about the way he treats you. I can't pinpoint it exactly."

"Do you think other people see this, too?" I worried.

"Yeah, I do."

These words punched me in the gut.

"Some people, anyway," she added. "I've heard Joan wonder about it. Bonnie mentioned to me she thinks something is going on. I don't think Judy notices anything since she doesn't spend as much time with him as we do. I don't know about people who aren't one of us. Probably no one else sees anything. It's not like you guys do anything crazy that people can see. But we are your friends, and it's easier for us to tell."

If my closest friends already suspected something, it would make it easier to tell them. My heart had been heavy for so long with the guilt of hiding it from them. Now I worried about who else had suspicions, but mostly I was relieved to spill my long-kept secret to a person who was safe and trustworthy.

"I am curious. How do you manage to get time together?"

Sophie seemed baffled, so I told her about meeting him in the afternoons and parking in his car. I told her about the weekends at Mark's house, and I told her about the time at his cabin.

"Wow. That's pretty good. I know I could never get away with that," Sophie said.

I sighed. "Yeah, that part's not too hard."

"Who else knows about all this? Have you told anyone? Has he?"

"No one."

"Are you going to tell the others?"

"I don't know. I think I have to. But I don't know. Should I? How do you think they'll take it?"

"Bonnie will be fine with it; she suspects it anyway. And you know what she's been up to with her father's friend. I think Joan will not be happy. She'll be mad that you didn't tell her about it. And I also think she'll be jealous. You know how she is. She's always wanted more of his attention."

"Yeah, I think you're right. I don't know what to do about her. I can't tell you and Bonnie and not her. That would make it worse. Maybe I shouldn't tell anyone else. What do you think of that?"

"Honestly?" Sophie said, "I think you have to tell them. I

also don't want to have to keep this secret. I wouldn't tell anyone if you didn't want me to, but I would feel kind of funny being the only one of us friends who knew."

She was right, of course. Sophie was always practical and seemed to see the best way to do things. A deep wave of gratitude for her friendship moved through me. I wanted to ask Sophie what she thought of me, but I was too afraid to hear her answer. Even though she showed no judgment of me, perhaps it was my judgment of myself that fueled my fear.

We stood up, and I hugged her. I felt close to Sophie but, strangely, also distant from her. We had just shared something many would call intimate between friends, but I was worn out and stressed. Along with my thankfulness for Sophie's presence and friendship, at the same time, I wanted to flee.

Somewhere. Anywhere. Just go.

Telling Sophie about Mark started a sequence of events that pulled me along like a strong current in the shallow waters of the seashore. Over the next few days, I gathered my courage and talked to Bonnie.

"Well, it took you long enough to come out and tell me! So, tell me more."

Her enthusiasm for the details told me she wasn't mad and maybe even approved. "When did this start? What do you guys do? Have you slept together? Who else knows about it?"

Bonnie liked Mark a lot, and she was no stranger to the allure of older men, having recently had an affair with a friend of her father's. Of course, she shared that story with me immediately after it happened. Her family went on vacation to Indonesia with another family, and the other family's father seduced her. Bonnie had found it exciting and daring. Bonnie seized life; self-confidence was not a problem for her.

"Let me tell you, Joan is not going to take this well. I am sure of that. She's going to be jealous, for one thing. And she's not going to like hearing that you told Sophie and me first. I think you should just do it. You have to do it. But be prepared!"

Warned, I made plans to take a walk with Joan after school. Joan didn't often invite friends to her house, either; going for a walk suited us both.

"What is this thing you wanted to talk about?" she asked, after chatting a while about school. We sat down on a park bench. I took a breath.

"You know how we're all friends with Mark Johnson. Of course. Well, over time, it turns out that he and I have become kind of more than friends." I snuck a sideways glance to see her reaction.

"What do you mean?" Joan faced me, her voice sharp and accusing. She wasn't going to let me off any hook.

"Well, we spend some time together, just the two of us, and I know he loves all of us, but I think he loves me . . . in a different way." God, I was talking to her like she was a child.

"Oh, for heaven's sake! Just tell me. Are you sleeping with him?"

"Yes. Sometimes." I glanced at her, then quickly averted my eyes.

"How long has this been going on? Who else knows about it?" Her voice was demanding.

"A couple of years," I whispered, trying to minimize the time.

"A couple of years?!" Joan burst out, now glaring at me.

"Are you kidding me? You've been doing this behind my back—all our backs—all this time? What kind of a friend are you? What friend lies to her friends? Oh, did Bonnie and Sophie know about this all along? Am I the only one who didn't know?" her voice escalated.

"No. No one knew. I just told Sophie and Bonnie this week." My body clenched into a tight knot.

"Well, it figures you told them before you told me. I don't believe this! I can't believe you lied to us all this time."

"It was—is—important that no one knows," I almost whined. This was not going well, and I desperately wanted to get up and leave. "You know, he could get in trouble if people found out."

"Yeah, I bet he could! Shit!" At this, Joan stood up and paced a couple times back and forth.

In the silence I had a moment of panic. *Would Joan possibly tell people?* My breath became shallow.

"Well, don't worry, I won't spill your little secret. And I really don't want to talk about it anymore. I don't want to talk to you. And right now, I don't want to even be your friend. I'm turning around now and going home. And don't walk with me. Just stay away." She strode away and I took a deep breath.

We didn't talk about Mark again. Not for a long, long time.

I told Mark I had shared our long-held secret with my three girlfriends. He said he understood my need to tell them, although it worried him a lot. He planned to talk with each of them himself—I think to support or repair his relationships with them and maybe reinforce the need for secrecy.

As spring moved into summer, all of these conversations of

the heart took place, and my world with Mark took on a new color. The stricture of the secret loosened a bit. Even this confused me: my relief at finally sharing the secret was now tinged by feeling exposed and vulnerable.

Having secrets was oddly comforting to me, so unmasking this secret was like ripping off a scab with the tender skin now exposed to danger. What if more people found out? I would be so judged! What if Philip found out? My heart groaned under the weight of that thought. He would not like that deception, especially when he had already asked me about it, and I had lied to his face. It would be the end of our relationship, I was sure. My stomach was queasy, and my headaches pounded.

School ended, and the excitement of high-school graduation passed. I continued working at the dental office and signed up to take more dance classes. I anticipated spending time with Philip, Mark, and my friends before leaving for college. Mark was very aware of my impending move to college and wanted to spend as much time as possible together.

Right after graduation, Mark announced he finally found an apartment.

"I can't wait to show you. It's close by, and we can spend lots of time together. I want you to help me fix it up. It'll be mine in a week!"

"Wow! So soon. That's great! Maybe we can drive by sometime so I can see it," I replied with enthusiasm, even as my heart tightened.

"Absolutely! We're going to have some great times once I move in. Let's work on spending a night together in the next couple of weeks."

I was unprepared for the immediacy of the opportunity to be together so easily, even though I knew it was coming. I found myself dreading the idea of another night together. The more excited Mark got about being together, the heavier my heart became, and my head hurt every day.

Whatever night Mark would suggest, I considered telling him I couldn't go. But what would be my reason? I could say my parents wouldn't let me get away. I could say they were suspicious. I could make other plans every weekend, so I was too busy to go. But coming up with all these excuses made me weary. What would I tell Philip about being MIA for that night? Joan continued to shun me, and in fact, took any chance she could to be around Mark. I didn't know what to do with my dread. In the meantime, an unexpected invitation shortened my summer; my sister Judy offered to take Sophie and me on an RV trip across the country with her, her new husband Art, and Art's grandmother and his younger brother. I was so excited to travel, but it did put pressure on my plans with Mark and made him more eager than ever to get time with me.

One afternoon, with all the plans swirling inside of me, excess pent-up energy, and a bad headache, I ventured out along the same road I walked along on those days Mark picked me up after school. I walked all the way to our parking spot and spent some time staring at the large tree we sometimes sat beneath. I continued walking along the wooded streets with no clear destination in mind but an urgent need to keep moving. My chest tightened up, and I started to cry. Before I knew it, I was sobbing, and my head was throbbing so much I had to stop and lean against a tree for support. I thought I might throw up. I didn't know what was happening.

I separated from myself and looked down at me, as I did those first few times in Mark and Emily's bed. I saw an eighteen-year-old girl out in the woods alone, bent over sobbing and holding her stomach, then falling to the ground, face in her hands and shaking all over.

I don't know how long I stayed there, but eventually, my crying subsided, and I felt lighter, empty, and wrung out. I didn't know what had overtaken me, but the clearing in my body allowed a thought I'd never had before: I had to end my relationship with Mark.

I let that thought hang there; I didn't push it out or encourage it to stay. I waited for the thought to be replaced by the next thought. But it stayed, like a wisp of a cloud, hanging there in my mind. Suspended there, it took on more clarity and substance. *End the relationship with Mark. Just end it. Do it now.*

I was too empty to be shocked at the thought. It simply hung there in my mind like a kind friend who was not going to leave me. Soon, I was ready to walk again. I moved with intention, feeling each step on the ground, feeling my muscles move each leg. The thought stayed with me all the way home, and I found myself feeling a great sense of calm and peace and strength—even a little urgency. My headache was gone.

*eleven*

---

## BETRAYAL

I DIDN'T KNOW HOW I WAS GOING TO TELL MARK, BUT TO MY surprise, I wasn't worried about it. There was no doubt about my intention. I was like a horse with blinders; my focus was on only one thing. I did not want the blinders removed. I did not want to analyze or think. I did not want to waffle or crumble. The thought of being out from under this relationship bathed me with relief and lightness.

It wasn't until we had planned our next visit that I began to think about what to say. Even still, I didn't agonize. I thought I would just say I had been thinking, and I needed to stop seeing him. I was leaving soon on the trip, and then college, and it was a good time to break things off. He might understand. The explanation was reasonable. Still, I dreaded his reaction; I expected it was going to be big. How could it not, after all this time? I didn't try to picture it. I just held tight to my little life raft of planned sentences.

We took a blanket and walked to a private field we occasionally visited when the weather was warm. We walked through the woods. With each step, my legs got wobblier, and my hands began to sweat. My pulse raced, but I kept focused on my simple sentences. We reached the clearing and set the blanket down. In a last-ditch effort with God, I desperately prayed I could go through with this. Mark leaned back casually on his elbows, and I sat on my legs, with my back straight. It helped me remember my sentences.

"What's up?" he asked lightly. "You're so quiet. Come on down here."

"I'm okay," I replied, my voice quieter than expected. I cleared my throat. "You know, I've been thinking." I held my hands to keep them from shaking.

Mark waited, gazing at me from his place there on the blanket.

"I've been thinking that maybe this is a good time for us to change things. Like to stop seeing each other." There it was! I had said it. I couldn't take it back. There was no returning, only going forward now. *Right? Please, God, help me!*

Mark sat up immediately. "What? What did you say?" He waited and made me repeat it.

I took a quick breath. "I said I think it would be good to stop seeing each other . . . like we have been."

"Why?" He nearly shouted. "What are you talking about? What do you mean, 'Stop seeing each other'? What does that mean?"

"I've been thinking that I feel a lot of pressure. It's hard in some ways to be seeing you like we have been. Even though it's so good, there are ways that it's hard." I wasn't sure where these words came from; I hadn't planned to say them.

"In what ways is it hard?" he demanded. "What do you mean by that?"

"I hate lying all the time."

"Well, you just told your girlfriends, so you don't have to lie anymore. Who else do you want to tell?" Mark's voice got louder and a tiny bit accusatory.

"Well, I don't want to tell anyone else, but I still have to lie a lot. Like to my parents. I think they suspect something."

I was desperate, grasping at straws now. Lying was second nature to me. I didn't know how else to explain myself to him. There were parts of me even he didn't see or understand.

"Oh, I see. I bet you don't like lying to your little boyfriend, is that it?"

His sarcastic tone sounded mean, and I felt sick. He was putting a lot of pressure on me. He had never gotten mad at me before. I had a moment of panic, thinking he wouldn't like me anymore and that I was losing a friend. I had thought—hoped— he'd still want to be friends with me. But this was not going well. I wanted him to understand and see things from my perspective. Just a little, maybe.

"No, it's not about him. I am just tired of being deceptive in general." I seemed only capable of short sentences.

Mark gaped at me, saying nothing for a minute.

"How can you do this to me, now, of all times?" He stared. "I am going through this divorce, and I need you more than ever. This is the worst time in the world to do this to me. I just got my freedom, my own apartment. What are you thinking?"

"I know. I feel bad about that," I said. "I didn't mean for the timing to be so bad."

"Well, then why don't we just take a little break for a few days. You need some time to think things over. We can talk more about it in a while. You know, you're leaving very soon. Going on the RV trip and then off to college. These next few weeks are our last time together for quite a while. We should be making the most of them." His voice was calmer now. He put his hand on my leg for a moment, then took it back.

"My leaving soon is why I thought this was a good time to change the way we see each other. I still want to do things with you. I just want it to be more like friends."

"Friends?" His voice rose again. "What are you talking about? I need more from you than friendship. We love each other. We have a unique, extraordinary relationship, different from anyone else. We need to guard it and take care of it. I thought you knew that. I thought you wanted that too." He was quiet for a long time.

I stared at my hands, dreading what might come next.

Then he sighed and said, "I don't know. Maybe I was wrong about you. I don't understand what you are doing. You are ruining something so special."

"I don't want to ruin it, believe me," I said. "I just need to change it." My voice was shaking, and I wished I would cry, so he would know how hard this was for me. But I could not cry. I was tense and paralyzed.

"Well, this kind of change is ruining it." Mark sounded angry again.

"I'm sorry," I whispered. I took a shallow breath and cleared my throat. "I just really need to do this. I'm sorry."

"You sound like you've made up your mind. You don't even want to discuss it. You don't want to take time to think about it more. You are just declaring this is over." His tone was biting, almost cruel.

"I just have to," I breathed. I was praying he would end this. Would let it go. Would let me go.

We sat in silence for a while. Then Mark said, "Let's go. I'm going to take you home."

My relief blended with terror. *Was it over? What had I done?* I desperately wanted to be home, in my room. I needed to put the blanket over my head and close my eyes for a long, long time. Just shut it all out.

We rode in silence and Mark dropped me at the end of my

driveway. I glanced at him as I got out of the car. His hands gripped the steering wheel, his eyes straight ahead, his jaw set.

"I've got to go," I said, at a loss for words as I slid out of the car.

He drove off as the car door closed.

I rushed to my room, grateful no one was around to see me or stop me. I closed the door and dove onto my bed. I pulled the covers up around my head, pulled my legs up into a fetal position, and started to cry. I wanted to cry forever. I stayed there as the sun set lower in the sky, and I eventually heard people downstairs. Mom was making dinner. I stayed in my room until I heard her voice call up, announcing dinnertime. I dragged myself out of bed, washed my face in the bathroom, and tried to make myself appear normal by pinching my cheeks to draw out some color. I went downstairs, sat on my stack of newspapers, and had a quiet dinner.

The next morning, I drove over to Sophie's house, feeling tired and weak. I wanted to tell her about this. Telling someone would help make it real.

"What's going to happen next, do you think?" she asked. "What do you think he's going to do?"

"I wish I knew. Mark left in such a state. He was so mad. I wonder if he'll ever speak to me again." I was honestly sad at that prospect. I didn't want to lose him altogether. I wanted him to love me. I just wanted him to love me as a friend. I wanted to still be special to him. Maybe not in the same way, but still more important than anyone else.

A few days after my bombshell with Mark—I still hadn't

heard anything from him—I got word from Bonnie that Mark wanted to get in touch with me. I guess she had run into him, and he told her his version of our breakup. He made me sound like an insensitive jerk, but Bonnie was a good friend and remained faithful to me and the way I presented the situation to her. Bonnie suggested I take him up on his suggestion to meet at the high school. I walked the familiar mile trek along the turnpike to the high school, a route I had walked so many times over the past few summers, going to meet Mark after his summer school classes ended.

As I walked, I wondered what Mark had to say. I wondered if he was going to try to talk me into resuming our relationship. I wondered if he would still be angry with me. I wondered if he was ready to be just friends. I was nervous; I hated conflict and tension. Leaning again on whatever God was, I prayed it would go well. I mostly prayed Mark wouldn't somehow make me change my mind.

When I got to Mark's classroom, he suggested we take a drive over to the pond and sit on the grassy banks. This spot was very public; we had only gone there once or twice over all the years. I was happy, though; it meant he didn't plan on any intimate contact between us. My spirits perked up, and I cautiously relaxed just a little. We settled on the blanket by the pond.

"Let's talk about this. Let's talk about us," he began. "Let me hear again why you are doing this. Because I don't understand."

I sighed. "I am so tired of lying. I feel guilty all the time. I have headaches all the time."

"There is so little of the summer left for us." Mark's voice was gentle. "Let's not throw that away. Then if you still want to end this between us, at least you will have given it another chance. I think you're doing this too soon. Let's spend some good quality time together and talk it through."

I sighed again. I was tempted to say yes, tough it out a few more weeks, and then be done with it. What harm would a few more weeks be? I hesitated before answering. In that hesitation, I imagined a weekend in his new apartment "talking it through," and something in me froze into a solid block of wood.

I shook my head and whispered, "I just can't do it. I am so sorry." As I spoke, my voice got stronger. "I know it makes sense to wait, but I just need to change things now, not later." I don't know where my resolve came from. I don't know where these words came from; I hadn't planned any of them. I hadn't planned any of this.

I braced, ready to absorb his reaction. To my surprise, he didn't keep pushing.

"I am just so sorry." I bowed my head.

"Yeah," he said. "I'm sorry, too. I am so sad about this, you have no idea. I am beside myself." But something in his voice didn't sound sad; it sounded mad. It made me want to end this talk and get away from him.

"Well, don't worry about me. I can find consolation in other ways," Mark said. I assumed he meant he'd do some heavy drinking. But I didn't ask.

In early August, we left on our RV trip. It promised to be fun, and I was eager to get out of town. The trip would be a good buffer between my disaster with Mark and the start of a new life at college. In addition to Sophie and me, the final roster of people was my sister Judy and her husband Art, Art's nine-year-old brother Paul, and his sixty-nine-year-old grandmother we all called Nanny. The six of us each had our own sleeping space in the RV. Sophie and I shared a double-bed loft over the cab. We could just barely prop our heads up on our elbows while lying in bed without hitting our heads on the ceiling. Nanny slept on the kitchen table, which converted into a modest single bed, Paul slept on the little couch across the aisle from the kitchen table, and Judy and Art slept in the large bed in the back.

Art did all the driving, and he was tense and snappy the whole trip. Judy was energetic and upbeat, providing the glue between us all. Paul was a great easygoing kid, and Nanny was amazing. She did most of the cooking and was full of stories about culture and food from the "old country" . . . Italy.

We had a great time and saw many beautiful places: the Grand Canyon, Yellowstone, Yosemite, the Badlands, and a variety of state parks. It wasn't until Art careened down Route 1 along the western coast, ignoring Judy's pleas to slow down, particularly when a large logging truck loomed toward us on the narrow windy coastal road, that I realized they were not getting along particularly well. Sophie and I sat in the back of the RV, enduring the tense silence with our eyes bugged out and our white-knuckle grip on the handrails. I too wanted Art to slow down but didn't want to encourage his anger by suggesting his driving was not safe.

After this near-death experience, we settled into our campsite. Judy and Art took a walk. Sophie and I decided to take a hike in the opposite direction to get our blood flowing again. We recounted the drive and laughed the tension out, then found some rocks to sit on. We sat in silence, gazing at the woods in the fading daylight. Sophie began talking.

"This is kind of awkward, but I think you should know about it," she said. I was intrigued.

"Before we left on this trip, Mark spent a lot of time with Bonnie and Joan and me, too."

"Yeah?" I asked, snapping to attention. Why was she saying this? "What do you mean? What is 'a lot of time'? What kind of things did you do?"

"Well, it's hard to say this, and I really hope it isn't hurtful to you, but it turns out that at different times this summer, Mark slept with each of us." Sophie sounded embarrassed and watched my reaction.

"What?" I said, jumping up, dumbfounded. "Are you kidding me? How? When? Why?" I didn't know what to think or feel as I let her words sink in, but my heart was racing.

"It was after you broke up with him," she rushed to assure me. "In my case, there was just one night a bunch of us were at my house, and my parents happened to be away. We were in my basement listening to music and stuff, and Mark just asked me to go upstairs with him. At first, I didn't know what he meant, but we went into my parents' bedroom, and he began telling me how sad and confused he was and asked for a hug. One thing led to another, and well . . . it happened. I'm sorry it happened, and this whole trip I've been thinking about how to tell you. I really don't want you to be mad at me. I *really* don't want to hurt you. I want to apologize for what I did. I told Bonnie and Joan, and they told me he had slept with them, too. Joan more than Bonnie, I think. I don't know exactly when or where." She sounded distraught and worried.

I paced in front of Sophie. I couldn't take in more words. My limbs buzzed and shook. My heart pounded. I heard sound rushing in my ears. I stared at her. How could this be? Questions flooded my brain, but I couldn't speak. I pictured Mark with each of them, one after the other. I heard his voice seducing them like he had with me. I saw their breasts in his hands, him moving on top of them. Then I shut those images out like a steel door clanging shut. For a second, before that door closed, I felt rage—at Mark. It flew out as fast as it flew in. Gone.

I sat down and hung my head between my legs, forearms on my thighs.

"Are you okay?" Sophie leaned toward me, worried.

"I feel sick, actually," I mumbled. I wanted to cry. What did it all mean? I thought he was mine. I thought I was the special one. What about "no one will ever love you like I do?" My heart hurt. I wasn't mad at my friends; I was sad and stupefied about what love meant. I started to ask questions in an attempt to clear away the confusion, as though the answers could remove the sadness.

"How many times? How did it happen? Where did this happen? What did they think about it? What does it mean to them? What can it possibly mean to him? What was it like for them? What does it mean to *you*? Would you do it again? Would they? Were Bonnie and Joan doing it while we nearly died barreling down Route 1 today?" I didn't give her a chance to answer. I just needed to purge.

I knew I wanted answers. And maybe Sophie tried to answer. I don't remember anything more from this conversation. What did it mean to love someone? I had absolutely no idea.

Did I feel betrayed? I was having trouble identifying my emotions. I thanked Sophie for telling me, and we spent the rest of the trip as though the conversation had never happened. This technique I learned well from my family; uncomfortable subjects must be avoided at all costs, never mentioned again, and all feelings associated with them erased. I intended to enjoy the rest of the trip. Perhaps I felt so hugely betrayed—by him and my friends—that I shut out whatever emotions I had about it, walling them off, and enabling me to move on in my life.

Over time, the details about Mark faded away, along with my feelings for him. In the years to come, I didn't give my relationship with Mark much regard and didn't speak of it to any of my boyfriends unless I was getting very serious with them. When I did mention it, it was just a matter-of-fact accounting of my first sexual relationship. Other than it being unusual, I didn't think anything was fundamentally wrong about it. Maybe hearing about Mark being with the others normalized it for me. Maybe, maybe, maybe. I parked it all in a recess of my mind and rarely took it out.

What I didn't understand for a very long time was that, even though I shut my experience with Mark out of my mind and heart, its impact remained in my body and nervous system, where it unconsciously governed my life. In the next decades of my life, I thought I had normal relationships with people (especially men), made appropriate life decisions, and had healthy access to my emotions. But I was wrong.

# twelve

## MEN

I BEGAN COLLEGE WITH THE EXPECTED JUMBLE OF NERVOUSNESS and excitement. I adored being on my own in a place where I was supposed to be on my own. I embraced college fully, even as an introvert. I found a small circle of friends, guys and girls, and soon discovered I was the object of attention from men.

Where Mark left off with me, he took up with Joan, visiting her throughout freshman year. I was more curious about their relationship than jealous or angry. I wondered if Mark said all the same things to Joan he used to say to me, and I wondered if he made her happy. But I didn't dwell on it; I shut that door. Joan and I found our way back as amiable friends, primarily by not talking about Mark.

The first weekend Mark came to Binghamton to visit Joan, I stayed vigilant to avoid running into them. As the visits continued, Joan would mention them to someone in my presence, never directly to me, thereby sending me the clear message that questions about these visits or how their relationship was going were not welcome. One time I saw him from a distance, walking with Joan across campus. A tinge of a feeling started to arise, but it stuffed itself back down in a nanosecond. Mark and Joan were a couple; I accepted that. I lost touch with Bonnie, Sophie, and Judy, which made me sad, but I guessed it was just what happened with friends. Emotional attachment to other people was not a strength of mine.

The next time I saw Mark was the summer between my freshman and sophomore years when I came home and worked in Howard Johnson's, a local restaurant with a famous ice-cream counter. One night, just before closing, I saw Mark come in and take a seat at the far end of the counter. My stomach churned. It never occurred to me he'd come to where I worked. How did he even know I was there? Had he been watching me come and go?

I had to serve him, so I went over. He smiled at me and said, "Hi there! I would like a cup of coffee with cream and sugar, please." It was the way he drank coffee in those takeout cups from our parking-lot days.

"Hi, Mark." I tried to smile, but my mouth was tense. "One minute and I'll get that for you." I hurried away. When I placed the cup down in front of him and turned to go, he stopped me.

"Hey, Liz. Wait a minute. Can we talk?" I slowly faced him but did not return his direct gaze. "I'd like to catch up. I want to know how you are. Let's go somewhere when your shift is over."

"Hey, Mark. It's nice to see you. Thanks for stopping by. I hope all is well with you. But no, I can't talk. Sorry. Take care." I busied myself bussing dirty dishes and moved away. He paid up and never came back. I sighed in relief as I watched him go, a little surprised at my firmness. I had a fleeting curiosity about what he had in mind by talking with me after work, but I quickly pushed it aside. That part of my life was over.

I returned to school in the fall, promising myself never to go back home for a summer. I was independent from my parents; I paid my way through college with scholarships and jobs. My parents drove me the five hours to college my freshman year and did not come back until the day of my graduation, four years later.

My life at school was happy. I loved learning, and I loved being on my own. I quickly fell into a relationship with my biology TA. Dave was the graduate student who was assigned to help teach my undergraduate class. He lived off-campus and was several years older than me.

On Friday afternoons, I would meet him at his lab in the basement of the bio building, and he'd drive me to his place for the weekend, a couple of towns away. He was a serious student, friendly, very cute, and I was fond of him. Mainly we'd study all day in his sunny, plant-filled apartment and have sex at night. The sex part would be expected, right? Seeing an older guy was cool, and there were no complications. Dave didn't know or socialize with my friends, and he didn't ask much of me other than the weekend studying and sex, neatly compartmentalized. The guys my age at school didn't interest me; they seemed like boys to me.

Throughout my freshman year, I continued to see Philip on occasional weekends. But by sophomore year, our relationship remained friendly but tapered off, and I was with Dave every weekend. The striking resemblance of my situation with Mark —being with an older man, a teacher, in a sexual relationship isolated from the rest of my life and friends, didn't occur to me at the time. I was just living my life.

In my sophomore year I discovered martial arts and my life changed. Wanting to learn to defend myself, I stumbled into a karate school led by a Japanese master and didn't leave for six years. Sensei taught us how to meditate and I learned the basics of Buddhism, a thread that would run through the rest of my life. Karate also brought Ethan into my life.

Ethan was a steadfast, devoted guy with a dry wit and many cynical opinions and judgments about people's behavior. "That's ridiculous!" was one of his common expressions, said both fondly and disdainfully. And he gave me sight. When he learned I stopped wearing my glasses back in high school, preferring to walk around in blurriness than appear uncool, Ethan changed all that.

"How can you possibly walk around and not see clearly? That's ludicrous!" He laughed with scorn. "Do something about it! Go get contact lenses. Or just wear your glasses. But this is not acceptable!" This is how Ethan showed care and love, and I loved him for it.

I got contact lenses, and the world took on a crispness I forgot was possible. Once I got used to sharp vision, I developed a real fear of losing it. I worried about world war breaking out and separating me from my contact lenses and glasses. I feared I would not be able to survive, floundering like a near-blind person in the haze. This worry about pending disaster of some kind stayed with me for most of my adult life. My feeling unsafe in the world lived in my nervous system, and its origins predated Ethan and contact lenses. For a long time, I didn't know that feeling unsafe originated in my non-attached family, which led to my misplaced attachment to Mark and the damage done by that relationship.

Ethan's clear sense of ethics quickly ended my time with Dave. "You have to stop seeing him. You can't be with him and me; you have to choose one of us. Do it now, go talk to him. Or else we can't be together."

"But it's so abrupt just to say, 'I can't see you anymore starting right now—goodbye!'" I complained. "Maybe I should give him some time."

"Don't be silly. He's a guy, he'll understand. Trust me. Besides, you know it's the right thing to do," he said more gently.

My fear that Dave would be angry about breaking up proved to be unfounded. He wrote me a sweet, funny poem and wished me well. I was relieved and just a bit sad.

Ethan and I bonded through our love of karate and being an integral part of our dojo—karate school—community. Our lives centered around the dojo and following the Zen path of discipline and devotion to meditation. My martial-arts training made me strong, and I was a leader, which gave me self-confidence. I earned my black belt, taught new students at the dojo, and offered self-defense classes to women in downtown Binghamton.

Ethan finished his graduate program in computer science the same year I finished college, and he immediately got a job in Boston.

"You should take this program too," he encouraged, even though it meant we'd be apart for the next three years. "Computer science is fun and not that hard, and you'll get a good job when you're done. You can ask me for help if you need it."

I wasn't sure computer science was right for me, but I was drawn to financial self-sufficiency, and by staying longer in Binghamton, I could continue studying with Sensei. Ethan and I continued our relationship across the distance for the next three years and planned to live together in Boston when I finished graduate school.

❦

To support myself in grad school, I worked at a dental office once again and also as a technician in a neuropsychology lab. I took karate classes at the dojo and meditated daily. I discovered the mystical spirituality of the Carlos Castañeda books and was intrigued by the expanded consciousness they depicted. I found my dear friend, Rose, during these years, someone who has been a pillar of my life ever since. My life was full, and I was happy.

The dentist I worked for liked me a lot. He was a young guy, but big and imposing. I was naturally somewhat intimidated by him, being both a doctor and my boss. He was a periodontist, performing oral surgery to repair patients' gums. Our appointments were long; the patient was fully reclined, covered with dental napkins, various tubing, instruments collecting on their chests, and a tray table hovering over them. Sometimes it seemed the patient was not actually in the room; they became so separated from us, although they were fully awake. Over their reclined bodies, we discussed books, politics, and dentistry. He sometimes snuck in some double entendre that seemed sexual. These made me uncomfortable, but mainly, I ignored them, not knowing what to say.

One night after our last patient left, he lingered, watching me clean up.

"What do you think about oral sex? Is it something you like to do?" he asked.

"What?" I pretended I didn't hear, stalling for time as my heart pounded. What was I supposed to say to that?

"Oral sex. Giving head. What do you think of it. Do you enjoy it?"

Legs now trembling, I replied, "Actually no. I don't. I mean, I don't like it much." I was hoping to dissuade him, so he'd go away. I realized we were alone in this office, and my tension mounted.

"You don't like it much? Maybe you need some practice. I can give you that opportunity right now," he said smoothly, moving closer. "What do you think? No one is here to interrupt us. I'm sure I can get you to like it. I'll return the favor. I bet you'd like that."

I started to think about what self-defense moves I could do.

"Listen, I don't really want to do any of it. Nothing against you. Sorry. I need to finish up here. I have a lot of homework to do." I tried to sound firm, but to me my words sounded unsteady.

"Okay. Never mind. Let's forget I mentioned it. I'll see you tomorrow. You can lock up here."

He left the room, and in a few minutes, I heard the front door close. I quickly went to the door and locked it. Not that he couldn't let himself back in, but it gave me a sense of safety anyway. *Sheesh,* I thought. *That was a close call.* I dreaded returning to work the next day.

After that, he was cold toward me. His usual affability was now replaced by stiffness, condescension, and criticism of my work. Soon, he let me know he no longer needed a part-time chairside assistant and would need to hire someone who could work more hours. When we parted, he was formal and stiff, and I was anxious and resentful. I didn't say anything to him about what happened that night. Even though I needed the work, I was relieved to be out of there. I didn't know it was okay to be angry or that I could have said something to him or anyone else. Still, I was proud that I rebuffed his offer.

❧

I loved my graduate school life. My little apartment in a modest house on a shaded side street was furnished like a hotel room, but it was all mine. I could come home from class, the lab, or the dojo, and the silence wrapped itself around me like a trusted friend. I could breathe it in. I was alone but not at all lonely. Outside of school, karate and meditation were my focus. Drawn to Eastern spirituality, I moved further away from the Christianity of my upbringing. I still believed in God, but that was evolving in ways I couldn't yet articulate. I fantasized about moving to a Zen monastery in Japan, where I could retreat into a lifestyle of monasticism and meditation. But in my non-cloistered life, karate gave me a sense of physical strength and safety. When a friend asked for help moving a refrigerator up two flights of stairs, I happily obliged. This was an era when I walked down dark streets at night without concern because I knew how to preemptively plan my defense as I walked.

Ethan and I agreed we could see other people during these three years apart. I dated several men, although Ethan was too loyal to see anyone else. I didn't intend to date, but the opportunity was always present, and there was rarely a point in time when I wasn't seeing some man—sometimes more than one at a time, this being familiar to me. The influx of men and the attention they gave brought a constant sense of validation. They were all more like friends to me. I didn't much want the sex part, although it cemented their interest in me. Female friendships and even the love of my friend Rose didn't reach the deep need for validation that came along with a man's sexual interest . . . another legacy from Mark. After a childhood of being invisible, the attention of men fed the part of me that longed to be seen. The more men, the more validation. At the same time, I liked the freedom of being unaccountable to anyone, and when the time came to move to Boston in 1980 and live with Ethan, my projected husband-to-be, the prospect felt stifling.

As the months drew closer to my move to Boston, some sense of preparation caused me to stop seeing men entirely. I harbored a growing discomfort with sex and sexuality. Whenever I saw two people kissing, whether in a movie or real life, I'd turn my eyes away. It went beyond kissing; I developed an aversion to anything sexual or even romantic. I concluded asexuality was my sexual orientation.

Ethan held it lightly. "Don't worry too much. This is just a phase, and it will change when we can finally be together. It won't be much longer now."

"I hope you're right. I don't know what's wrong with me."

"Nothing is wrong with you," he comforted. "Keep the faith!"

Maybe I was unconsciously preparing myself to be with Ethan for the rest of my life, a visceral rebellion against what I took as an obligation to include sex in this long-term, committed relationship. It was all unconscious to me. I was a sleepwalker through my life.

Once we were together in Boston, with both of us having solid jobs in high-tech companies, we settled into life, and my asexuality subsided. We lived in a cute little cottage on a small windy road, with a creek running in the backyard. Despite the oil embargo that nearly paralyzed the country, we took a road trip across America and into Canada. Our lives centered around opening and teaching in our own karate club. Although we had fun, and Ethan was sweet much of the time, I often felt judged as doing something wrong (leaving old food in the refrigerator) or not being good enough at something (remembering the last names of new students). It wasn't easy to live up to his standards. I responded by withdrawing and shutting down, a reflex I would lean on many times to come.

Into this withdrawal from Ethan came Michael, who worked in my office. We had a secret office affair, the deception being a familiar and comfortable old friend. Lying to protect an illicit relationship was how I first learned to be with a man. But our secret was revealed when a friend of Ethan's inadvertently caught me. I signed up for a dance class as a front enabling me to spend time alone with Michael at his house. Unbeknownst to me, this friend was in that class, and it came out I was never there.

"How can you do this to me? To us? How can you be so dishonest? You lied to my face about taking a dance class, and I believed you! Instead, you were off with some guy. I thought I knew you!" Ethan cried. "Your behavior is appalling. I can't trust you. I thought we loved each other. I don't even want to be with you anymore!" Ethan pounded the wall with his fist.

I cringed. "I am really sorry. It was wrong to lie. I don't want to hurt you, but I know I have." I averted my eyes, ashamed and sad. Ethan paced.

"You'll need to find someplace to live. I'm not leaving this house. You can stay here until you find something. Use the other room in the meantime. We'll go our separate ways. I need to get away from you right now."

He left the house, and I set myself up in the spare room. We lived with distant coolness until I found another place to live. I also dropped out of the karate club.

I was sad to leave Ethan after being together for six years, and along with my guilt about sneaking and lying, I was also relieved. His perpetual dissatisfaction with me was oppressive, and now I had Michael. Except for his rule of secrecy, he was very accepting and easy to be with.

An affair was how I ended the relationship with a man I thought I would marry. Secrets and lies were what I knew best.

I moved into a weary little attic apartment in a different town, delighted to live alone again. Music was my companion. The sounds and words penetrated my soul and became one with me. Bob Dylan was my hero, even when he was born again and sang religious songs. I found them to be magical and not insipid. I listened to Beethoven's *Clarinet Concerto* until the rich tones made me cry. In my freedom without a committed partner, there was room for me to explore and expand my inner world. God's presence was around and inside me. This was not the God of my childhood. This God was an expansive, loving presence with whom I had moments of clear union, filling me with peace and joy.

I lived there for the duration of my two-year relationship with Michael. For most of those years, we maintained secrecy. None of our work colleagues knew we spent most nights together. Michael wanted to keep it quiet, and I was okay with that. The relationship with Michael was comfortable for me. We were very fond of each other, but neither of us wanted any real commitment. After time, it languished, and in my little living room, it came to a head.

"Liz, what are we doing? Are we going anywhere? I can't tell what you want from me."

"What do you mean? I like things as they are, don't you?" Dismay crept over me.

"I do . . . sort of. You just don't give much; I guess I'm ready for more. You also don't ask for much. Things are just . . . stale.

I'm sorry, I know I said I didn't want more commitment, but for me, something is missing. I can't find you."

I sank back into the couch, not knowing what to say for a while.

"See?" His voice was soft. "This is what I mean. What are you feeling right now? Do you feel anything?"

I sighed. "I'm not sure what I feel. Sad? Disappointed? Confused? I don't know how to be any other way than how I am. I'm sorry that it isn't enough. I don't know what it would mean to give more. Maybe this is as far as we can go."

He wrapped his arms around me, and we sat quietly for a long time. It was easy to be quiet with Michael. When he hugged me goodbye, the image of sand sifting through my fingers came to mind.

After we parted ways, I spent some time dating. I didn't seek them out, but I was never without a guy. Even though I was shy, I was friendly, and I enjoyed these relationships; they kept me engaged and busy, but I can't say I was "in love" with any of them. I'm not sure I knew what that even meant. I floated around like a wispy cloud, not knowing what I wanted or what I was capable of in a relationship.

Then I met Adam.

*thirteen*

———

## MARRIAGE?

ADAM WAS THE FIRST MAN I HAD TO CONVINCE TO DATE ME, and his reticence made me want to gain his attention even more. He was handsome, friendly, kind, and attracting him to me seemed aspirational. He shared my interest in Eastern spirituality and was doing professionally what I sought to do. I had entered a graduate program in counseling psychology, where Adam was—perhaps it's no surprise—an adjunct professor. He was six years my senior and an established social worker.

Adam was elusive at first, but eventually, we became a couple. He was used to living alone and a bit set in his ways, so making room for me was challenging. He had a lovely, neat, and clean house, a benefit of his meticulous nature, which I appreciated. I loved his laugh, calmness, and gentleness. Adam came from a good Jewish family, and despite my being a shiksa, his parents grew to love me. We attended all the high holy services at his parents' temple, which I enjoyed, and it pleased his parents very much. I enjoyed this foray into Jewish ritual; its more casual, chaotic flavor was a refreshing difference from the strictness of my father's church.

After some time, Adam's parents were not subtle about their desire that we get married. Adam was thirty-five, had never been married, and they believed it was time for him to do so. My past years of mostly aimless dating and Adam's comfort-able, established life made me want to settle down, though I was ignorant of what it meant to be married. I wanted to belong to someone, to be seen, loved, and accepted. I wanted to matter deeply to someone. I wanted to be emotionally safe and not alone, and I wanted a family. Marriage represented all of that, and I naively thought marriage would ultimately provide it all, despite Adam's reluctance. I was flattered by his parents' ac-ceptance of me and their hints about marriage. I was unaware of the wounds embedded in my psyche that drove my decisions and actions; I was unaware I had no idea what love was. But I wanted it.

Adam and I became involved in a spiritual group studying esotericism, and we did long daily meditations, often together. We attended regular meetings of the Wisdom Studies group, and learned about theosophy, a blend of Eastern religions, fo-cusing on mysticism and spiritual evolution. Adam was all-in with this group; I was more cautious. Spirituality was close to my heart, but I wasn't quite sure what I thought about this group and its self-proclaimed leader-master. The group's focus on sensing subtle energies and the evolution of the soul set up an atmosphere where people compared themselves with each other according to various scales and ratings.

One day, Adam was noting how "less evolved" my soul was than his, concerned it made me a less suitable partner.

"Don't worry about Liz's soul," the leader told Adam. "She's a very old soul. Focus on your own evolution, keep on the path, and all will become clear."

I appreciated his support, but I still was not all-in about this leader; I was wary of anyone who claimed to be the return of the Messiah. But Wisdom Studies was a shared interest for us, and being a spiritual seeker, I wanted to be open-minded.

Adam had a strong sense of family, and how family members took care of each other. One evening, I went to dinner with work colleagues, and afterward, we went to another place to get a nightcap. I didn't pay attention to time, and when I headed for home, it was quite late. Adam met me at the door.

"I'm so glad to see you! Where were you? I was so worried. When you didn't come home after dinner, I called the restaurant, and when the recording said it was closed, I was beside myself. Where were you? Why didn't you call? I pictured you in a ditch somewhere and was about to call the police."

"Oh! I didn't think you'd worry because you knew I was out with work friends. I'm sorry. It just never occurred to me to tell you I'd be late. I'm okay, though."

"Geez, Liz, I'm glad you're okay, but next time let me know if you're going to be this late so I don't worry."

I was stunned. I wasn't used to someone tracking my coming and going or worrying about me. I found this to be thoughtful; was that what it meant to love someone? But I was also chagrined that I needed to "check in" with my whereabouts. I had a lot to learn.

Our relationship was full of fits and starts and a fair amount of ambivalence—on his part this time. I was certain I wanted to marry him. Sure, he wasn't very crazy about me, but perhaps my proven ability to attract men gave me confidence that I could ultimately attract him, too. Maybe like others approaching thirty, I thought marriage "should" be the next step in life. Perhaps I thought marrying Adam would bring me the comfort of home and family. Maybe marriage to an emotionally unavailable man unconsciously felt safe because I was emotionally unavailable myself. However, I believed we could address our issues. We didn't discuss or analyze our relationship and its problems very much. We didn't have a very close relationship, although we seemed to be unaware of this. We were more like pals; the thing we did most was spend time with his parents. Occasionally we'd go out with friends—mostly his friends. We didn't do much alone as a couple. If we looked harder under the hood of our relationship, we would have found only a little go-cart engine, sputtering gray smoke and stalling out.

One day, he and I were having a tiff, probably about his ambivalence toward me. Finally, in a small fit of exasperation (a small fit was all I ever had), I took the bold step to suggest maybe I should take my toothbrush out of his house, and we should take a break from each other. He sadly agreed, and while I collected my few things, he wandered slowly around the kitchen.

When I returned to the kitchen, toothbrush and jacket in hand, he closed his eyes, held up his hand, and said, "Hang on just a second. Something strange is going on. I'm not sure what. But I'm a little light-headed or something."

Curious, I stopped and waited. Adam was not prone to strange behavior. He was a feet-solidly-on-the-floor kind of guy. He shook his head back and forth, like he was wrestling with thoughts. Then he started to pace.

"Adam, are you okay? Does something hurt? Should we call a doctor?" I was worried he might be having a mild heart attack.

"Just hold on. I don't know what's happening, but I just need a minute. I'm not sick or anything. I don't need a doctor. But don't leave yet."

My heart beat faster as I watched Adam slowly pace, turning his head, like he was trying to hear something. A small but insistent internal dialogue tugged on the sleeve of my mind.

*"I know what's going to happen!"*

*"No, you don't. How can you? You don't know anything."*

*"You're right. I'm getting ready to go now. But still . . . I think something strange is about to happen. It's crazy; I'm going to shake it off. But it's getting harder to breathe. I'm beginning to feel light-headed, too. It's because I know what he's going to do."*

*"You do not. Just get going. He's being some kind of drama queen. Nothing exciting is going to happen here. This is Adam. He isn't going to pleasantly surprise you with anything."*

*"Oh, yes he is! He's going to shock you. He is going to ask you to marry him."*

*"Stop it! He is not."*

*"I know you doubt it. But I know this. He is about to ask you to marry him."*

*"Don't believe that for a second! That is ridiculous. He doesn't want that. He doesn't love me that way. We have no business even thinking about marriage. Our relationship stinks."*

*"Watch and see."*

Adam gazed at me with wonder in his eyes, and he said, "I am being directed to ask you to marry me!"

*"Ha! I told you!"*

I was dizzy. Adam babbled and shook his head, then said, "Wait. Wait just a minute. I better sit down. I want to be sure I got this right."

I waited to see what he would say next, although I knew. I seemed to know everything in that moment.

He sat down, and then he stood up. He paced some more. He stopped, he paced. "It is definite. My guide is telling me in a message being pressed into my mind: 'Ask her to marry you.'"

"Liz." Now, finally looking straight at me, he said, "I am supposed to ask you to marry me!" His face held surprise and amazement. He laughed lightly. "Do you believe it? I checked again and again, and this is the message: Liz, will you marry me?"

Through the pounding in my ears and head and chest, the words came. "I know. And yes, I will."

Who were we to argue with the spirits whispering in our ears? It didn't make any sense, but we both had faith in spirit and intuition. Whether that was indeed the force behind these messages, I don't know. I believed God had a sense of humor. Or at least a far bigger plan than I had. I was simultaneously calm and excited like a schoolgirl. I was going to get married!

"I don't believe I am going to be married!" said he.

"I'm so excited we are going to be married!" said she.

We went—in twenty minutes—from breaking up to getting engaged. Some may say this was all a psychological reaction to the prospect of losing the relationship. Some may say God was guiding us. Some may say we were foolish or at least irresponsible. Today, I believe it was all of these. I put my toothbrush back in his bathroom, and we proceeded to call our friends and family and announce the good news. His parents were thrilled.

After that initial visitation from the spirit guides, we were left on our own to cope with the situation in which we found ourselves. Our five-month engagement period was fraught with difficulty. Adam seemed to wake up one day and comprehend how his lot had been cast.

One evening while sitting in our favorite Chinese restaurant, Adam shook his head in wonder. "I can't believe you are the one I am going to spend the rest of my life with."

This may sound lovely, as though Adam was gazing tenderly into my eyes, saying he was the luckiest man on earth. But that's not what he meant. He said those words from a place of deep dismay. Adam didn't actually want to marry me; he just took it on faith that it was the right thing to do . . . what he was "supposed to do." Somehow this marriage would evolve his soul. Someone wiser than he was knew something he did not, and Adam was determined to see it through. We knew we had issues. Adam often didn't want to have sex with me and admitted to being confused about that. The sex itself wasn't the issue for me (I was fine with less sex). It was how it represented his insufficient enthusiasm about me. He said he would work on this problem in therapy, and I trusted him.

We went ahead with wedding plans. Adam's mother was delighted, and I was happy, too. She gave me a lovely bridal shower and invited every Jewish mother in Brookline. She fussed over me and bought me a fancy, expensive dress for the bridal shower. All this was like a dream, and I accepted being fussed over with gratitude for the attention.

We were meticulous about creating a wedding ceremony that could make both his Jewish parents and my Lutheran parents happy, as well as reflect our own spiritual leanings. This was no easy feat, and there was great parental tension about whether anyone could say the name of Jesus at the wedding and what house of worship could possibly hold this event. In the end, we booked a beautiful, large, wood-paneled room in a private college, hired a female justice of the peace, left Jesus out of it, but invited God in, and wrote the entire ceremony ourselves.

For my part, I was comfortable leaving Jesus out, as I was still mystified about who and what he was and what to believe about him, but I did want God there. And I wanted my parents to be comfortable, at least a little. They accepted Adam and his Jewishness, although I am sure it was with reluctance. They were certain Adam's soul could not go to heaven, and they were, by extension, worried about mine.

The closer the date approached, the greater the tension grew between Adam and me. About a month before our wedding date, we attended our friends' wedding. These were crunchy-granola psychologists who also wrote their own vows. We were a cozy gathering clustered together in their living room. Adam and I stood side by side, listening intently, acutely aware we would be standing in their ceremonial spot very soon. They contemplated each other with love and ease. Their smiles were gentle, and their gaze upon each other long and luscious as they shared their vows.

"You are my best friend, my partner, my soul mate, my lover. I accept you into my heart with joy and gratitude, and will love you, care for you, walk by your side, teach you, and learn from you every day for the rest of my life."

*How beautiful and intimate these vows are*, I thought. And I noticed how much hearing them distressed me. The pit in my stomach spoke the truth: Adam and I did not feel this way about each other. I knew in my soul the truth of the words Adam had the honesty—or heartlessness—to say to me on our drive home.

"You know, I can't say one single thing to you that they said to each other."

"I know." We rode the rest of the way home in silence. Although I knew the truth of his words, they crushed me.

Once home, we traded our fancy clothes for shorts and Tshirts, sat on the couch, and talked. With dread in our hearts and voices, we faced each other and uttered the words out loud: "Maybe we should call this off."

This was an emergency. We were four weeks away from our wedding date. All the friends and family were invited, the travel plans established. The vegetarian caterer was paid, the wood-paneled room booked, purple bridesmaid dresses bought, my Mexican wedding dress altered to fit me like a glove, and the table linens selected.

We called Adam's therapist and presented our sad and desperate case to her the next day. Adam admitted his ambivalence; I brought my despair. Her altogether unhelpful advice was that we had to make this decision on our own. She would not offer an opinion other than we needed to examine what was in our hearts and tell ourselves the truth we found there. But we were simply not up to the task of telling the truth. Maybe Adam still felt obligated to fulfill the wishes of his spirit guide, even though he didn't understand them. I was ill-equipped to tell the truth, even to myself. I preferred the fantasy of love over the reality of being unloved. We could not carry the unbearable weight of the cancellation option. His parents would be devastated, we would be failures, and gifts would have to be returned.

We couldn't do it. Adam gamely redoubled his promise to work on his issues of doubt and lack of attraction to me. *Maybe*, I thought, *I can make it all work by sheer force of will*. I asked myself, *Doesn't every married couple have some problems? Isn't that part of marriage? Wouldn't we be working on them together?*

When the wedding day came, I resolved to enjoy it.

I succumbed to the primping of the female in-laws and their desire that I wear the requisite amount of makeup and get my hair right. Then Adam and I sat in silent meditation together—a ritual we both loved—thinking it would open our hearts and prepare us for our wedding day. Why, then, did I feel so alone?

After our meditation, Adam took my hands, breathed deeply, and smiled. "Well, shall we do this?"

"Yes, let's do this," I replied, trying to smile back.

We performed well during the ceremony, exchanging our personally written vows that were lackluster but had the right spiritual buzzwords. During the reception, Adam danced to Sister Sledge's "We Are Family" with everyone but me. He and I didn't dance together, sit together, or spend any time together throughout the wedding celebration, and I let it happen.

*fourteen*

─────

# BLACK ENERGY

FOR MANY MONTHS, I STRUGGLED WITH A LOW-GRADE SICKNESS that I believed was heartache, the kind of loneliness that can exist while in a relationship with another person. I had no energy, no enthusiasm, no interests, and I took no joy in the things I once loved to do. My blood-sugar level plummeted, and I passed out a few times in crowded places. I wondered if I had mono. After some tests, my doctor announced what I had was not mono but clinical depression. Even though I was trained as a psychotherapist and was in a struggling marriage, I never considered I could be depressed. *Silly me.* I thought depression was only for other people. This diagnosis of depression made me depressed. The only thing I found helpful was the doctor's suggestion that my husband and I seek counseling.

It took a while before we followed that advice. I struggled with my marital problems alone, choosing not to confide in friends or family. Maybe it was fueled by shame, but struggling alone was familiar to me. I carried a core belief that no one would care about me and my problems didn't matter. I didn't matter. My marriage seemed to confirm that. The more I understood I was not welcome in our marriage, the more quiet, angry, and withdrawn I became. Adam didn't mind the withdrawn part, but he definitely did not like any anger from me. Then one event occurred, which finally pushed us into couple's therapy.

One day I came home from work, placing my purse and briefcase in their designated spot on the bookshelf. I noticed Adam was frowning.

"Hi. How are you? Is everything all right?"

He faced me squarely with a scowl on his face. "Tell me the truth. Were you thinking about me today?"

I paused, not sure what he was really asking.

"I don't know. I guess? I was working, mostly thinking about work stuff. Why? Should I have been thinking about something specific? Did I forget about something?" I was puzzled.

His voice was stern. "There was black, angry energy coming from you toward me all day long. It interfered with my work, my aura, and my meditation. I want you to stop it! Right now. Stop sending me your angry, black energy!"

"What? Are you kidding me?" I finally blurted. "I was working. Sorry to say, I don't think about you all day long, and I don't send you black energy."

"You need to cop to this. I know we aren't exactly happy together, but I am very sensitive, and your resentment hurts me. It reaches me from three towns away. Don't pretend you don't have anger and resentment."

"Yeah, actually, I do have resentment." My voice started to rise. "I resent—I am *hurt*—that you don't act like you want to be married to me. For example, you took off your wedding ring one week after we got married. That tells me you don't want to be married to me. You don't really want anything to do with me. You treat me and our marriage like shit." My voice was now shaking. "I have resentment about that. Yeah."

"That ring exuded black energy! It hurt my hand to wear it."

I was accustomed to containing my emotions, stuffing them down as far as possible; I hated confrontation. But in that moment, some foreign force took over my body. I stepped over to the coffee table, and in one swift and beautiful act of violence, I swept my arm across all the books, ornaments, and magazines and sent them flying across the room. I stormed out and strode down the hall into the bathroom. I slammed and locked the door behind me, collapsing onto the floor in a ball, and wept. Desperation, futility, and self-contempt overwhelmed me. I thought I could not stand to stay in this life one second longer. Our marriage was intolerable, life was unbearable, and most importantly, I was unbearable. I entertained all sorts of ideas of dying right there on the bathroom floor—dying of a broken heart, a fucked-up, infuriating marriage, and an inability to know what to do or how to become someone else. Some part of me sensed I was only half alive, half present, a shell of a person in my marriage and in life. The pain crushed my heart.

I stayed there, huddled on the floor in a frozen ball, hardly breathing and wondering how or if I could ever face another human being again. It seemed unthinkable. I stayed there, almost catatonic, until time covered me with a soft blanket, melted the stress hormones coursing through my bloodstream, and I fell asleep.

When I awoke, it was as though a storm had passed through me. The air was still, and I could walk among the rubble of myself as though it were a graveyard with its silent sleepers. I was breathing again, and I wanted to get up. An urgency forced me to open the bathroom door and walk out into the space of my house. Adam was nowhere. I grabbed my jacket and walked out into the cold evening air, walking aimlessly for miles and miles. I contemplated what to do about my shambles of a marriage. I tried to invoke God in some way, to provide comfort, if not guidance. Nothing seemed to help except the physicality of walking. It eventually burned through all the anguish I was carrying, and I felt greater peace and resolve by the end of my walk. I decided the time had come: We needed to go to couples counseling. The distressing doctor with the unwelcome diagnosis of depression was right after all. We needed help. I needed help.

Over the following months, Adam and I labored on in couple's therapy. We had few, if any, breakthroughs or points of light that could move us into a real, loving marriage. I had chosen for my partner an intelligent, kind, capable man, trained in interpersonal skills, but when it came to relationship and intimacy with me, it simply did not work. We were two emotionally unavailable people. Neither one of us wanted to be the one to call it quits first, so we plodded along in therapy with little change.

One day, in Cynthia's office, she asked Adam to describe his feelings for me. After some thought, Adam said, "Liz is a truly good-hearted person. I care for her, and I want good things for her. She deserves them. If she ever needed to be picked up at the airport, I would be happy to help her out."

Adam stopped. We waited.

Silence.

"Is there more?" Cynthia prompted, and we waited some more. But Adam was done.

I could endure no more, and with a tight voice, I said, "Okay. I get it. That is not enough. We do not have the basic ingredients to make a marriage work, so let's stop. Let's agree it isn't working, and it won't and cannot work. Let's end this now."

The pivotal pause hung in the air.

Adam's face had an open-eyed, listening, taking-a-deep-breath expression. "If that is what you want, then I agree."

"That's what I want," I said with conviction and just a little bit of anger.

After an excruciating silence in which those words settled upon us like a shroud, the three of us talked about how to dismantle our marriage.

Adam's parents were the hardest to tell. The four of us sat at their kitchen table, where we had shared so many meals, and I watched their faces crumble. Disappointing and hurting them, plus the prospect of losing them as parents, filled my heart with sadness. We drove to New Hampshire and sat around my parents' dining room table. Their reaction focused on the failure associated with divorce, but they had never fully approved of this marriage, anyway. My father sat us down on lawn chairs under the pine trees and talked with us as though we were members of his church, and this was a pastoral conference, talking about not doing this lightly and praying for guidance. My mother waited until she had me alone in the kitchen.

"Have you tried to have sex? That often makes everything better," she said casually, keeping her eyes on the carrots she was chopping.

Shocking! In my family, mentioning the word "sex" was entirely forbidden by unspoken decree. I was astonished that my reserved mother would suggest this solution to me, implying sex was something with which she had any familiarity. However, she must have had a lot of familiarity with it, as evidenced by her ten pregnancies.

"Ah, well. I'm afraid it's a little too late for that," I managed to reply, which ended the conversation.

She had tried to help, and that was sweet. How could she know I had moved into the spare bedroom long ago?

The four of us chatted about the weather for a while, then we left, all of us knowing Adam and my parents would never see each other again.

I was both relieved and sad to be getting divorced. But I saw this as a second chance at life. Stretching before me, I had an opportunity to pick myself up from the ashes of judgments, rejection, and self-contempt, restore my broken heart and shattered self-esteem, and find out who I was as a woman, friend, mate, and a person. It was 1986, and I was thirty-one years old, an excellent time to start over.

I moved into a sweet little garden apartment in a nearby town, where I began to reconstruct myself. My attempt to establish a private psychotherapy practice proved to be too difficult now as a single person, so I leaned back on my past career and found a new job at a small software company in Boston. The people who worked there were colorful and intriguing. I was single and free and began forming friendships that suggested maybe I was not worthless. The trampled-down part of me rose from the ruins of my marriage during the two years I lived in that sunny apartment. I wanted to start over. I thought I knew how.

## *fifteen*

---

## LOST OPPORTUNITY

DURING MY POST-DIVORCE CONVALESCENCE IN THE GARDEN apartment, I went back to Long Island to attend a family event and took that opportunity to contact Mark. I was doing some soul-searching about myself and men, so I thought I might learn something from seeing him again. I had a mild curiosity to see what had become of him after his divorce from Emily. Some years before, I heard he had remarried and was still teaching. My agenda was vague; I just wanted to revisit my past and see him again.

He sounded genuinely pleased to hear from me, and we agreed on a day and time to visit. We met at the pond near the high school.

As we settled onto a blanket on that summer afternoon, he said, "I'm really so happy you contacted me. I love hearing from my former students. Tell me about your life. Are you married? Kids? Are you working? What do you do?"

I talked about my software job, and he said, "Oh, I am so glad to hear that. It's a great field these days. Isn't a college education great?"

I described my recent master's degree in counseling psychology and my unsuccessful try at opening a private practice.

"I always knew you were a thoughtful one. Good for you. I know it's hard to set up your own business. Maybe you'll go back to it someday. What about marriage? I don't see a wedding ring."

"Well, I was married for a couple of years, but it didn't work out. I've been divorced now for about a year."

"Oh, I'm so sorry to hear that. I hope our relationship from back then wasn't the cause of that in any way."

This oblique reference to our past caught me off-guard. I replied, "Oh, no. Not at all. Adam just didn't really want to be married to me. It's okay. We're on friendly terms."

"Well, I'm glad of that. You were always special to me; I only want what's good to come to you in life."

"Thanks," was all I said in response. Why didn't I ask Mark more about this and find out what he thought about our relationship from back then? This was a question that would haunt me far into the future.

Mark talked about his family, and after a while, we parted ways.

I spoke the truth as I understood it at the time. It was true I didn't think anything harmful had come from our relationship. I still believed Mark loved me back then, and what we had was unique and good. I didn't learn anything about myself and men. Not that day.

It would be many more years before I understood just how wrong I was. When I think now of this lost opportunity to confront Mark, to tell him how damaging it was to take a young girl's trust and abuse it, I get angry. I am enraged by his audacity that day by the pond to allow me to believe I was unharmed. Clearly, he had some notion that what happened between us was wrong; he hoped it wasn't the cause of my failed marriage. By the time I understood exactly what that harm was, Mark had passed away. My rage and sadness over what he took from me, and his colossal betrayal of my trust, took years in my therapist's office to unearth.

Before I found my way to Patricia's office, though, I had several substantial detours.

The software company I worked for had a very social culture; our office was small enough to encourage interaction with people and big enough for many varied types of relationships to form. In those years, I held an offbeat social theory about people and monogamy. I wondered whether monogamy had passed its original purpose of helping to raise children more effectively. If human beings followed their truest instincts and resisted societal conditioning, I argued, we might find ourselves free to love each other with fewer social restrictions, such as monogamy and heterosexuality. One of the social restrictions I resisted was adultery, and I found myself in more than one relationship with married men from this company. At the time, I didn't pause to think about why I did this or the harm inherent in it.

The next chapter of my life started with a dream I had of a tornado chasing me and a co-worker across a field. The next day, I found myself walking into the office with that same co-worker, Joe. I didn't know Joe, other than seeing him in the office, so this was an auspicious coincidence.

When he casually asked, "What's new?" I replied, "Well, this may sound a bit odd, but believe it or not, I had a dream last night that had you in it."

"You poor thing," he said with a short, quiet laugh and a

sardonic smile. "I hope I wasn't embarrassing myself. Or you."

"No, neither of us had time for embarrassment. We were busy being chased by a tornado."

"A tornado! That sounds serious. Did it get us?" He smiled.

"I don't know. All I remember is how busy we were trying to keep ahead of it."

As we parted company at the reception area, he suggested, "If you remember more, let me know. Have a great day."

"Sure thing." I suddenly felt foolish to have mentioned the dream at all.

I greeted coworkers and friends as I crossed the room to my cubicle. I sat down and prepared for a staff meeting scheduled for the afternoon. We had a code review planned, and I needed to read over everyone's comments and write my own. I was focused on this well into the mid-morning when I saw an email from Joe cross my screen.

Sorry to interrupt. I was wondering if you wanted to discuss your dream further. We could get lunch, and I could psychoanalyze you. Dr. Freud at your service.

A slight jolt. *What have I done? Do I want to get lunch with this guy?* My fingers typed the answer.

Oh boy, I'm in trouble now. All my inner secrets to be revealed. It might not be pretty, but I'm game if you are.

———

Don't be silly. It will be a delight. How is 12:00? Out front?

———

Ok. See you then.

After we ordered our food, Joe said, "We don't have to talk about your dream if you don't want to. I didn't mean to be over-bearing."

"I don't mind," I said. "I think dreams are fascinating. I usually can't make much sense of them, though, especially my own. Maybe the insights of Dr. Freud would be helpful."

"Okay. Tell me everything," Joe said with a bad Viennese accent that made me laugh out loud.

I reviewed the dream again, and I told him about my dread of some impending doom, originating in my college years. "Usually, I think of war or a natural disaster—like a tornado—that's going to strip me of everything I have and leave me penniless, homeless, and without hope. In these doom scenarios, I particularly worry about losing my glasses and contact lenses because then I will truly be lost, deprived of my ability to see clearly and be able to take care of myself. I guess I don't like losing control. That feels dangerous to me."

I laughed a little at myself, then added, "You know, I studied karate for ten years and have a black belt, so you'd think I'd feel a little safer in the world. But I guess karate won't help against war or tornados." I winked.

"I'm in trouble now, having lunch with a woman with a black belt," Joe quipped, his dark eyes smiling. "Seriously, that is very impressive. Good for you."

"Yeah, I didn't know it then, but now I wonder if it was the lack of feeling safe that drew me to the martial arts in the first place. It did make me strong, although I don't practice anymore."

We talked for nearly two hours. The mention of the word "chaos" somewhere in the conversation led me to talk about my recent divorce from Adam. Joe was sweet and gentlemanly in his chastising comments about my ex-husband.

"Marriage isn't easy." He shook his head. "We've been married for almost ten years, with two kids, and there have been many times I wondered if we could get through some hard times. But we do."

I enjoyed our lunch. It was easy and fun. And strangely natural. I found Joe to be an appealing mix of humility and intelligence. His humor was full of gentle irreverence. Getting to know someone new was a common practice of mine during the year after my divorce. I was open and interested in giving voice to the person inside me that was shut down for the years of my marriage. I liked people. Given my shyness, I was pleased to discover people liked me. This gave me an apparent strength and confidence which belied the depth of the wound I didn't yet know I had.

Had I understood the extent of the emptiness and loneliness that stemmed from those years of being a lost child growing up in a world of fog and isolation, would I have chosen a different path? Had I understood the self-worth Mark stole from me, would I have chosen a different path? Of course I would have. But I was unaware of all of it, and I chose instead a path that brought me great love and great pain.

Joe and I made a date to go running together after work one day. Spring was in full bloom, the weather was warm, and the days stayed light until 8:00 p.m. We met at my apartment to change into running clothes, and I took him along my favorite four-mile loop. Joe was lean and athletic and could easily outpace me, but he slowed to my speed. I wanted running together to be something Joe and I could occasionally do, an activity that could be an excuse to bring us together from time to time.

I liked Joe. I liked his easygoing way. He seemed established in his life, although not pretentious. He was easy to talk to, comfortable to be with, and he seemed genuinely interested in me. I knew he was attracted to me maybe a little bit because as I locked my apartment door behind us, he said, "You have beautiful hands." He added, "World-class beautiful!"

I thought my hands were okay, one of the few attributes I could believe someone might find attractive. Still, I wasn't fooled; a man doesn't say that to someone unless he was testing to see how it would be received. I was pleased by the comment and flattered. It wasn't the usual kind of come-on, but it showed some originality.

"Wow, no one has ever said that to me before." I held my hands out in front of me. "Thanks!" Not a particularly witty response, but I guess it conveyed an open door.

"People should say that to you constantly. What's the matter with them?" he said, smiling and seeming to chastise them all.

We chatted throughout the run, then walked the last few yards, caught our breath, and went back to my near-empty living room (with a post-divorce shrunken bank account, I had only a couch, loveseat, and TV). Before I could identify my feeling of sudden awkwardness, he said, "Would it offend you terribly if I told you I wanted to kiss you? I know I shouldn't, and I'm sure you must think poorly of me, but I can't help just telling you."

I stood face-to-face with him and sensed that gap in time when all sounds shut off, and it feels like the heart is taking a small gasp, like when something mildly scandalous is about to happen. I was happy he wanted to kiss me. Wasn't it what I wanted, too? And so we kissed, standing in my spacious, sunny room with running shorts and salty skin. Once we started, we—neither of us—could stop.

I didn't regret what happened. Maybe I should have felt

more guilt. Of course, I should have, but my overwhelming sensation was peace, and happiness. That was odd because guilt and shame just came along with breathing and being me. But here, I knew something big had happened, and I suspected the same might be true for Joe.

Over the months that followed, Joe and I met at my apartment almost once a week. To fill the gap between our visits, we had our company's electronic communication to hold us together. (This was before the days of smartphones and texting.) Our visits began with sitting on my couch, always touching each other's leg, arm, or knee. Through this bare touch, we transitioned from the outside world to the universe that filled my little apartment when we were there together. We experienced a completion with the other that I—and he said he—had never known before. More than once, he said if he were a female, he would be me.

Yet Joe brought a dominant theme to our relationship: his deep-seated commitment never to leave his wife, Suzanne. He described her as lovable, funny, kind, smart, and strong-willed, yet very dependent on him. She struggled with PTSD and anxiety, along with other neurological issues. She was, understandably, emotionally fragile, and Joe vowed she could never learn of our relationship. Plus, he loved his kids and did not want to disrupt his family. His guilt over all this pained him, and he convinced me Suzanne would literally die if she knew of our relationship.

Over the summer months, we lived in this secret limbo existence of joy and guilt. I knew I should be appalled at myself for being involved with someone married. But it had a familiarity and normalcy to it. A relationship constrained by not only its secrecy but also its built-in time limitations brought a sense of safety. There was something about living a compartmentalized life that offered freedom and security inside each compartment. I contended my relationship with Joe was my own business, and no one besides the two of us could understand or appreciate it. To us, it had enormous proportion; to anyone else, it would appear seedy and small. The parallels between this relationship and my relationship with Mark so many years prior were simply not in my awareness. I rarely thought about Mark. Compartmentalizing my life into separate secret boxes was a psychological concept I didn't apply to myself until years later.

When Joe and I spent time together, I was one hundred percent with him and in a state of quiet joy. Despite the despair and angst about what to do with our relationship, when we were together, there was peace. We couldn't go anywhere public, so we spent all our time together in my house. Driving in a car together was risky, and we didn't want to spend a second of our limited time searching for places with anonymity. Even at work, we didn't have lunch together anymore for fear of starting rumors. This caution was all for the protection of Suzanne.

## *sixteen*

---

## IN LOVE?

I SLOWLY BEGAN TO HARBOR A DEEP-SEATED YEARNING TO have a child. Our child. I was in my thirties, and my biological clock was ticking. My longing for this became as physical as hunger; it came from someplace inside that I could not silence. My desire was not rational, was not well-considered, yet it consumed me.

One day, lying in bed as the late afternoon light gently faded, I broached the subject with Joe.

"Do you ever think about . . . like imagine . . . us having a child? I know we can't, but just to imagine it?"

He was quiet, and for a moment, I thought I had pushed things too far. He shifted onto his side to see me better. "I think about that all the time. I didn't want to bring it up because it's too sad." He sighed and was quiet for a moment. "What about you? Do you think about that? Would you want to, if we could?"

"I want to have a child with you more than anything else." My voice shook as I said these words.

He touched my face, and his face glowed. "I would be honored and ecstatic to have a child with you. But we never can."

"I know," I replied. But in speaking this secret, my obsession now had a hook to hang on, and I spun a cocoon of hope and love around it.

"Can we just spend a few minutes imagining it, though?" I asked, smiling. Because I knew he'd want to do that, too.

"Okay, but just this one time," he conceded.

We both sat up.

"Here's one scenario. I could be a single mother and you could still see me like you do now. I'd say the father was an anonymous donor. Or maybe I could become friends with you and Suzanne, and then you both could visit us as friends."

"As long as we're fantasizing," he said, "maybe I could tell Suzanne about our love, and she'd magically recognize its beauty and allow us to have this child, and the three of us could raise it together."

"Ha! That's a very long shot!"

"Yes, forget I said that. What was I thinking? It would never happen; she is way too possessive. In fact, we should probably stop talking about it. It's just too hard."

We stopped talking, but I couldn't stop thinking about it.

A few weeks later, I brought it up again.

"What if . . ."

"Listen," he said gently. "You need to find a husband. Someone who you can really have a family with."

"Yeah. Maybe. But I want this with *you*."

"I know you do. So do I. But we need to let this idea go."

We were silent and sad.

After a while, Joe said, "How about this? Let's give you one-and-a-half years to find a real relationship, a real life partner. You have to honestly try. You know we can't do this forever. Eventually, something is going to have to change, and it needs to be you finding a man. A husband. Someone, not me. You need to live your life, and you need to have a child. If you haven't found that person in a year and a half, then I'll agree to father a child with you . . . anonymously. I'll support you both as much as humanly possible."

He gripped both my hands. "Look at me. You must promise me you will try hard to find that person to fall in love with."

"But I love *you*," I reminded him.

"Look at me. You must promise me."

After a moment, I said, "Okay, it's a deal," happy to have that much.

We named it the one-and-a-half-year plan. This "plan" kept the possibility of our child alive, yet gave us the freedom to move the idea from obsessional center stage, where the weight of its unlikeliness could break our hearts. We tucked it away into a corner and occasionally referred to our one-and-a-half-year plan with fondness.

One fateful day, a work-related event conspired to place the three of us—Joe, Suzanne, and me—in the same place together at a dinner table in a restaurant. I was nervous and intensely interested to see up close who she was. My stomach roiled the whole time, torn between wanting to scrutinize this woman and an urge to pretend she didn't exist.

Suzanne was open, quirky, and had an intensity that surprised me. I noticed how her raven hair matched the color of Joe's. Most notably, she was obviously attached to Joe. She leaned into him often, smiling and laughing easily. A part of me understood why Joe married her and why he was driven to protect her. A big part of me carried guilt over what I was doing to her, another woman. Another part longed for a life with Joe, longed to be in her position of belonging in his outward life. I felt ill.

I returned home with my heart and mind thrown into a tumult of emotions. Suzanne was real to me now, and the fact that I willfully acted in ways damaging and disrespectful to her filled me with misery. My feelings for Joe were so powerful, but it didn't take much to find the brutal shame lurking beneath them.

I talked to Joe in my mind. I told him everything was different now. Suzanne had become a real person to me, strengths and weakness together, just like all of us. The slim grip I had on navigating our situation had slipped away, and I was drowning in a sea of turmoil. I didn't know how to simultaneously hold my love for Joe, this new authenticity of Suzanne, and my guilt. I wondered if this was a glimpse into what he carried on his shoulders all the time. I knew the right thing to do was end our relationship and go on with our separate lives. However, I seemed incapable of doing so. I wondered if this was what drug addiction was like.

When he was finally able to come to my house again, we sat on my couch as we had a hundred times before, and I said with weightiness, "You know, there is a way I can see that you and Suzanne belong together. Although I know things are not perfect between you, it does seem that you can be happy with her. I can see how anyone could love her and want to take care of her."

"Yes. She's very lovable," Joe agreed with pride and humility. "That's why this is killing me. It's killing her, too, in ways she doesn't even know. I'm a shitty husband for her." Joe buried his face in his hands and shook his head. "I'm hurting her, and I'm hurting you. What a shit I am!"

"No, not a shit," I said, putting my arms around him. "Just a human being—a complicated, messy human being. I don't make it easy for you, either. I am at fault, too. None of this is easy."

We sat in silence for a long while. Moments like this were unusual for us; we rarely dwelled on our sorrow and guilt when we were together. I should have ended our relationship then; I should have been strong. But I wasn't. After several more moments, Joe pulled away and got up. "I'm so sorry. I've got to go. This is not about you. It's my struggle. I just feel too shitty right now to be good company."

"I understand," I said. "This is so hard for you. I'm sorry. So, so sorry."

Standing on my balcony, I watched him drive off. Then I went inside and cried.

I hired a therapist to help me cope with my love for Joe, his intractable commitment to Suzanne, and my guilt and confusion. Sitting across from her, I outlined my struggle—our struggle.

"I am not your typical therapist," she said. "I will listen to you, and I'll tell you the direct truth about what I see. I like to keep things to the point, and I usually don't see people for more than three sessions. Will that work for you?"

I was a little taken aback but thought maybe a no-nonsense slap across the face was exactly what I needed. I laid my tale of love and angst before her and then asked, "Okay, tell me what you think." I took a breath and leaned forward.

"You're having an affair with a married man who claims he will never leave his wife for you. You are considering having a child together, even under these conditions, which you would raise with or without him. He says he loves you very much, yet his actions are disrespectful to both you and his wife. Is that love? Is that healthy love? You say you love him deeply. Do you love yourself deeply? What you are doing is disrespecting yourself. It seems to me Joe is conflicted about his marriage. I suggest he see a therapist to help him get clear about that. Then he can see what he wants to do. What you two are doing now is unhealthy for everyone and bound to end in a lot of heartbreak. For you, my advice is to end this relationship with this man. Step back and find out what you want in a relationship. If it's love and commitment, you must start with a healthy and strong sense of self. Otherwise, you will have trouble."

I leaned back to absorb her directness; I had a lot to think about. "Strong sense of self" was the key phrase that tumbled around in my head. Didn't I have that? Yet everything she said rang true. I reached out to my friend, Rose, who knew about Joe and was a psychologist herself. Rose was, by nature, open, honest, and kind. She wanted me to be happy and saw my situation with clearer eyes than mine. She affirmed what my therapist told me.

With that wake-up call, I encouraged Joe to see a therapist, too. He agreed, but instead, they went to couples therapy with Suzanne's therapist for a short while. Joe tried to reveal to Suzanne that some part of him had ambivalence about their marriage and suggested there may be some delusion between them. She denied any delusion and was tenacious and protective of her view that things were okay between them. I didn't hear much else about their work in therapy, but I sensed it took the internal battle raging inside him to new levels and likely contributed to what was to come.

## *seventeen*

---

## THE ONE-AND-A-HALF-YEAR PLAN

IN THE MEANTIME, HONORING THE ONE-AND-A-HALF-YEAR plan, or maybe as a way out of the tangle I was in with Joe, I sought a relationship with a man with whom I could have a "real" life. And I tried to find that "strong sense of self." Meeting men and forming friendships had come easily for me through this period of my life, although I question whether I brought much honesty and real attachment to any of them.

One of these friends was Jason. Tall, lean, with a friendly face and a boisterous laugh, he worked in a different department in our office but was often with the crew who went to a local fern bar for after-work drinks on Fridays. We often chatted together. I noticed he seemed reluctant to leave, even after most of our coworkers headed home. Rumors in the office grapevine suggested he had problems at home.

"Isn't your wife expecting you for dinner about now?" I nudged him one Friday when we were the only ones left.

"Yeah. I guess. Whatever time I get there, there will be hell to pay." He finished his beer. "But that's standard for us. I can't do anything right, so there's little incentive to try." He sounded dejected.

"But you're right," he continued, sitting up straighter. "I

should head out. Thanks for staying to talk. I really enjoy it. I hope I'm not too much of a Debbie Downer."

I laughed. "Not at all. It's okay. Anytime you need to talk, I'm here."

"Don't you have a date waiting for you? It's a Friday night. I bet a dozen guys from the office would trip over themselves to go out with you."

"Nope. Not tonight." I smiled, wanting to steer the conversation away from me and my love life. "I lead a pretty quiet life. Going home to listen to some Mozart and read a good book."

Over time, Jason opened up more about his marriage in crisis. I listened and offered him friendship and companionship. In turn, he offered friendship and companionship to me while I privately navigated the turbulent waters of my life with Joe. So good at keeping Joe compartmentalized from the rest of my life, I never spoke to Jason about him. Occasionally I wondered whether he could be the healthy real-life partner I could take into a future without Joe. But since we were both underwater navigating our respective lives, I didn't dwell on it. Joe sensed Jason was becoming close to me, but he didn't ask much about him. As I think back on it, delusion held a steady presence among all of us.

One day, Jason and I sat over lunch at Legal Seafood, where we sometimes went when seeking variety from the corner deli. Jason didn't eat much in those days. He had little appetite, was quite gaunt, and his hands often shook. He was not in good shape emotionally, and I worried about him. Not only was his marriage shaky, but I also knew he had a baby on the way. He seemed so sad, so troubled. And yet, in some ways, so alive and bright and sincere.

"Tell me what books you're reading," I said.

"I love all things Arthurian; King Arthur is my hero." He leaned into a story about Guinevere and Lancelot, now wholly disinterested in his already neglected food. I ate like a glutton, finishing everything on my plate. I listened, glad to see Jason have a spark in his eye. He was an exceedingly sweet guy, and I wanted him to be happier than he was. He was in a tough situation. His pregnant wife was on strict bed rest, and she was living at her parents' house so they could take care of her while Jason was at work. The truth is their relationship was in a precarious state.

"I don't want to bore you with my troubles." Jason sighed when I asked him about it.

"You won't be boring me. I would like to know and understand more about your life. The good parts and the hard parts. It's okay, as long as you want to talk. No pressure."

He buried his face in his hands. I noticed his long, graceful fingers and how big his hands were. His shoulders started to shake, and I heard a single sob before he moved his hands away.

"I'm sorry. I'm just a mess. Are you sure you want to know me?"

I nodded slightly and waited.

"I had no business getting married. I thought—we both thought—it would be good. And parts of it were good. We had a lot of fun together and lots of the same interests. But even before we got married, I felt like a screw-up, that I couldn't do anything right."

This was something I understood from my years with Adam. And Ethan.

"I suggested we work on some things in the marriage, and just then, we became pregnant. We're both happy about that, don't get me wrong. But it put a lot of pressure to make every-thing work, and it just didn't. Right away, the pregnancy had complications. I tried to take care of her, but we ended up fighting a lot. She's staying at her parents' house until the baby is born. It's not clear if I'll even get to be at the birth, she's so mad at me. I want to be this child's father! I love him so much already."

He looked away.

"I'm so sorry it's so hard. I can't even imagine." I tried to console him. "I'm here if you want to talk about things or not talk about them. If you just want some company, let me know."

The Jason I came to know over that fall and winter was gen-tle, considerate, earnest, and troubled. A man alone. He hadn't told his family or any close friends about the issues in the mar-riage, that it was headed for divorce. This was a man in a dire, difficult bind. I liked Jason, despite my involvement with Joe. I confess to being apprehensive of Jason's home situation, which was a mess. But I had a mess of my own, full of guilt, despair, secrecy, and unrequitable longing. Why did I get involved with married men? They were like magnets. What was wrong with me? Despite the directive from my no-nonsense therapist to figure out what I wanted in a relationship, clarity about this eluded me. Rationally, if not emotionally, I knew continuing with Joe was not sustainable, and I had to disentangle from him. But what *did* I want? I knew I wanted a family. I knew I wanted to be loved and accepted. I wanted to be done with se-crecy, deception, and guilt. Getting more involved with Jason did not come free of secrecy.

Jason was erratic during those months. Sometimes he would be sad and shaky. Sometimes he would be more energetic and interested in doing things. He had that Southern knack for flirtatiousness, something I had no experience with and didn't know how to interpret. When Jason oscillated from sad and weary to friendly and flirty, I was suspicious. Which was his real feeling? If he was sad, how could he want to flirt? I was more comfortable with sad than flirtatious; I wasn't yet sure I was ready for anything romantic with him.

Sometimes I allowed his friendship, and sometimes I distanced myself. If we each were in different situations, I thought, I could imagine exploring a relationship with him. What I failed to recognize was that I was already in a relationship with him. It was a friendship. Wasn't it? Granted, I kept him at a certain distance. Granted, I was not honest with him by withholding the fact of my deep connection with Joe. But something was growing in my feelings for Jason. I really liked talking with him and being around him. His presence comforted me. Even while going through his own personal hell, he was kind and attentive, even nurturing to me. That was hard to resist. I wondered what life would be like after Jason's marriage ended, and he was free. I knew he came with a child, but as complicated as that might be, I welcomed it.

Still, Jason and I were in our separate battlefields. Arrows, smoke, ash, advance, retreat, pain, and guilt were all around and within us. It was no way and no time to begin a serious relationship. Perhaps we should have waited for the dust to settle, but we didn't. Each in our morass of confusion, each ultimately just seeking love and stability, we stumbled right into each other's hearts.

# eighteen

## AN ABRUPT ENDING

TO MY SHAME, I STILL STRUGGLED TO END THINGS WITH JOE throughout this deepening relationship with Jason. I navigated the ship of my life in choppy, muddy waters, lost at sea and rudderless. In the late winter of 1989, Max, Jason's new son, was two months old, and Jason lived in a small studio apartment by himself. Max's presence was a sheer joy, and yet these were not happy times. Divorce negotiations were raging like hormones out of control, and Jason's parents nearly disowned him for leaving his marriage. From their vantage point, he was shirking his duties as a father. Jason still knew nothing of my relationship with Joe.

The burden of keeping my love for Joe, this huge part of myself, secret from Jason grew heavier and heavier. Telling him about Joe seemed like the honorable and necessary thing to do. I didn't think Jason would like it, but I thought it would explain some of the mysteries of my inconsistent behavior, he would understand and be sympathetic for my dilemma, and it would bring us closer. To my mind, my honesty would be a gift to him because it spoke of my love and respect for him.

I worked up my courage and asked Jason to come over one Saturday night. We sat in my room, talking easily for a while. I knew I had to bring this up somehow, but now that the moment was here, my mind became blank.

"There's something I'd like to talk to you about," I started. My voice hesitated, and my breath was shallow.

"What's up? Is something wrong?" He appeared attentive but still relaxed.

I was quiet for a moment, examining my hands, which got his full attention. "What is it? You can tell me anything you want, you know."

"Well, I need to tell you about something going on with me. You might be a little surprised, but . . ." I glanced up at him, reading his face. *He's still with me, I thought. Shit.* Harder to back down now and abandon this idea.

He took my hands in his and said, "Hey, it's okay. Whatever it is."

I plunged ahead, taking him at his word "Well, you know Joe, who works on the AI project, right?" Of course, he knew him. We all worked at the same company. "Well, for a while now, he and I have had this relationship going on, and because of my feelings for you, I think it's time I told you about it. No one knows about it." I felt like shit. My heart raced, and my mouth was dry. I watched.

"What do you mean? What kind of relationship?"

Jason's face reflected attentiveness, fear, and anger. *Shit.*

"We have been in a relationship for a couple of years." I hoped that would explain it. The tension in his expression was making me very nervous.

"Are you saying that you two are sleeping together? Are you doing that . . . still? Now? Even since we have been together?"

My heart thumped heavily in my chest. I nodded slightly. This wasn't going how I envisioned. I thought Jason would appreciate my telling him and would understand this was a relationship preceding him.

"Well, we have been trying to end it for a while." I sounded so lame. I should have said, "Yes, but it's over now." But I didn't make that white lie.

"What do you mean, 'you've been trying to end it'? How exactly do you feel about him? About me? Where do I fit into this picture?" Now he was up, pacing.

"This is what I'm trying to tell you. I was in this relationship before I met you. Then I met you, and I've been—we've been—trying to end things. It just takes time." I could hear myself almost whining. Why was he not getting it? A tendril of defensiveness rose inside me. *Joe came before him.*

"Time? How much time do you need?" He sat down again, head in his hands.

I was feeling protective. "I don't know. Look, I wanted to tell you about this because I value you and our relationship." I already knew this wasn't going to help.

"Well, you took your sweet time telling me. I can't tell you how betrayed I feel. Stupid and betrayed."

Now I stood up. I so wanted this conversation to be over. I wanted him to leave. Now I was pacing. I had no more words; I was guilt-ridden, devastated, and full of regret. I didn't think it would go this badly. Where was the sweet, thoughtful guy? How could I have been so wrong? I hated men!

After some interminable silence between us, Jason spoke up, this time in a much gentler voice. "Okay. I get it. I think I get it. I don't like it, and I have a million questions. I am sick over this. But I hear you. I do think you should have told me a long time ago. This news makes me confused about you. I wonder what other secrets you have."

I quickly interjected, "There are no more. This is big enough, right?" I tried a lighter tone. I was grabbing onto any glimmer that he might be softening.

"Yeah, it's big enough. Listen, you need to decide what you want. Do you want to be with him or with me? Don't worry. This isn't an ultimatum or anything. But you need to get clear about what you want. I can tell you right now, I'm not leaving you or going anywhere, but I don't think I can stand you being with both of us for long. Please, figure this out." I could see his sadness and disappointment.

"Thank you for not running away. I didn't know how you would react."

"How did you expect me to react?" he demanded.

*Shit.* I ruined the direction we were going in.

"Sorry. I thought you might be more understanding that this was going on before I even met you."

"I get that. But it doesn't make a difference. What matters is that we've been together, and I didn't know about it. It's still going on. That's just wrong!"

I blew it. My frustration with this conversation was mounting again, and buzzing filled my ears. But Jason softened again and hugged me for a long time before he left. We agreed to talk the next day.

When he left, I sank onto my bed, pulled the blanket over my head, and sobbed. What a mess. Filled with shame, I desperately longed to go back to my cave of secrecy, where life was safer, where I could avoid conflict. Telling the truth was *so* hard. I wouldn't blame Jason if he gave up on me; it would prove my unworthiness. I didn't deserve his forgiveness, but I wanted it.

But now Pandora's box was opened. I had to "figure things

out," as Jason pointed out. I had no idea how to do that, but early the next day, I sent Joe a message.

> Last night, I told Jason about us. It didn't go so well. Sigh. We need to talk.

No reply came for ten minutes, and I went out of my mind. What was he thinking, feeling? Then I read:

> I'm glad you told him. It was good to do that. It is the right thing. I'm not surprised he didn't like hearing it.
>
> Everything is a mess!
>
> Let's talk about it next time I come over. It'll be okay. We'll figure it out.

Several days later, when we were together at my house, it was miserable. I was weak and disoriented. We sat at my kitchen table, not on the couch, as we usually did. Joe was gentle but withdrawn.

Taking my hand, he said valiantly, trying to be resilient, "You need to live your life, and I need to live mine, too. I need to figure out the mess of my life. I have to let you go. I don't want to. Every part of me is screaming that it doesn't want to. But we need to try harder."

*Try harder.* That sounded like this wasn't the very end. "Yeah, let's try harder," I agreed, my muddled heart hanging on by a thread of hope and desperation. We talked more, saying nothing definitive, other than agreeing we'd skip our weekly visits for a while.

On Saturday morning, just a few days later, the phone rang. It was Joe.

"Hi! I'm surprised to hear from you." I couldn't imagine what prompted this unexpected call. Joe never had the privacy to call on the weekends. "Is everything okay?"

"I'm good. Surprised you, huh? Sorry. Everything is okay. Well, not exactly. I'm so sorry to bother you on the weekend." His words were gentle, but he seemed nervous.

"Not a problem for me at all. I'm so happy to hear from you. But what's going on?"

"This is not actually a happy call, and I can only talk for a minute."

My mind raced with possibilities. Suzanne was hurt. He was hurt. Someone in his family died.

I immediately asked, "Where are you? Where are you calling from?" expecting to hear he was at the payphone down the road from his house.

His reply, "I'm calling from home," sealed my fear. "Can we get together? Now? Just for a minute?"

*Just for a minute? On a Saturday?*

"Um, sure. But what's going on? How can you do that?"

"I have done something very, very bad," he said. "And I am so very sorry. I can't tell you how sorry I am. Can you meet me? Now? Are you busy? I'm sorry to bother you."

"Of course, I can meet you. Do you want to come over here? But can you tell me what's going on?" I knew something very strange and terrible was happening, but I could not imagine what. What did he do that was very, very bad?

"I have told Suzanne about us," he said. "I had to. I couldn't do it anymore. I'm sorry. I just broke. I cracked in two."

I went silent for a few seconds.

"You did? Why? Why did you do that?" Of course, he had just told me why he did it, but that hadn't registered yet.

"I'm sorry. I have been—I *am* a complete idiot. I have deeply hurt the two people I love most in the world. Now we all have to live with my failure, and it's not going to be easy. Not for any of us."

After a slight pause, he said, "I need to ask you to do a hard, hard thing. I am asking you to meet with me and Suzanne. And to listen to me tell her I love you, I've had an affair with you, and I love her and want to stay with her, if she will have me. She wants us to talk in a public place, so can you meet us at the gazebo in the Boston Common? This is what she wants me to do."

I took half a shallow breath.

"Why does she want to see *me*? Doesn't she hate me?" I could not process this at a very sophisticated level.

"Sometimes, it's easier to face your demons. This is what she wants. I would understand if you say you won't do this. But I have to ask you."

"Of course, I will come." Ever the people-pleaser. "I can leave now."

"Liz?"

"Yeah?" I replied, waiting expectantly for whatever he would say next, hanging on every word, since I was overcome by confusion.

"Liz?" he implored. "No matter whatever happens, please know that I love you with my whole heart, and I always will. I am just so sorry."

"I love you, too," I whispered back. My mind had already started reeling in a chaotic blur, and I couldn't take in anything more.

We hung up, and I rushed to change my clothes and get

ready. Get ready? What does one wear on an occasion like this? Something frumpy or something nice? What should I do with my hair? I tried to force my mind to imagine the conversation, but I couldn't get far. Then the unwelcome thought arose. Would I be safe? What if Suzanne, consumed with rage, was waiting for me with a kitchen knife hidden in her purse, unbeknownst to both me and Joe? These things happened. Maybe she'd kill us both. She was highly emotional, almost hysterical at times, Joe had told me, and extremely possessive. Surely this news has put her over the edge, destroyed her life, as Joe had so often anticipated. It would kill her, he had said. Seeing me might trigger the kind of desperate rage that drives one to murder.

Then I was seized with another thought. If this was going to kill her, why did he tell her? Why did he do the very thing he feared most? Our whole relationship was founded on the principle we had to protect Suzanne, no matter what. Telling her made no sense at all.

I planned to say as little as possible. But what if she grilled me with questions? I would just go, listen, apologize to her, and leave. I would sort through it all with Joe later. I had so many questions.

All these thoughts flashed through my mind as I fumbled around with my clothes, hands trembling, throat parched, grabbing my car keys, dropping them, rushing. There was nothing I could do but rush. Adrenaline, confusion, and anticipation of the unknown were rocket fuel in my veins. The kitchen-knife scenario crept back into my mind. Maybe it would be a gun. Some people kept them in their houses. Then back to *why* did he do it? What possible reason could there be for hurting her like this? I began mentally preparing my apology.

It seemed like an excruciating amount of time to arrive and park in the underground garage. The closer I got, the more my heart pounded. I was grateful I didn't drive into a wall. My Jell-O legs almost buckled underneath me when I stepped out of the car. I took a deep breath and prayed this would go as well as possible, and we would all emerge alive. I walked over to the gazebo and saw them both. I wanted to turn right around and flee. Only adrenaline compelled me forward. I was relieved to see Joe step forward to greet me.

He murmured, "Thanks for doing this. I know it's a lot to ask."

I followed him into the gazebo. Fortunately, we were the only ones there. Suzanne stood, leaning over and brushing leaves from her shoe with her foot propped on a bench. Oddly, I noticed she wore black tights and a brown suede jacket—kind of put together, and not too distraught. I relaxed slightly about the likelihood of violence.

She straightened up when I came near her and said evenly, "I'm not going to give you a hug, although I ordinarily would, because I'm usually friendly. I hope you don't mind. I'm not feeling very friendly."

"Of course not," I quickly replied. *A hug?*

"Let's sit here," Joe pointed to an area along the curved stone bench that lined the perimeter of the gazebo.

The stone's coldness started to permeate my body. Suzanne sat between Joe and me. We were each a good three feet apart along the curved bench, but we could see each other. Joe leaned forward and turned toward us, forearms on his legs.

"Liz, thank you for meeting us. I know this is hard for you. This is hard for all of us. Last night I told Suzanne about you and me, about our affair, about our relationship. It nearly killed her. I am so very sorry about everything."

Then he got up and kneeled in front of me, taking my hand in his two hands. I almost grabbed it away. He looked straight into my eyes. This made me nervous. Why provoke Suzanne with this display of affection? I jerked my hand slightly.

"Liz, here is what I want to say. I love you. I am in love with you. I shouldn't be, but I am. That's the truth." I was dumbfounded and terrified.

"But I also love Suzanne. I love her very much, and I have promised to live my life with her. It is what I want to do. It's what I am going to do for as long as she accepts me. I'm sorry you are hurt. I'm sorry she is hurt. I have hurt two people who don't deserve that. I've put my family at risk and it's all my fault. You and I cannot see each other again. We cannot even talk to each other again. We cannot have any contact at all. This is what Suzanne is asking, and I agreed. I wanted to tell you that. I'm sorry."

I was still in a state of shock, so I barely heard what he said. I was worried about what Suzanne was going to do. I was watching her out of the corner of my eye. *Was she going to yell? Sob? What happens now? Am I supposed to say something?*

"Oh. Okay," was all I was capable of saying. *Oh? Okay?*

Joe stood up, and Suzanne and I quickly did the same. Before I could launch my prepared apology to her, Suzanne said, "Liz, I really feel sorry for you. I mean that. There must be something deeply wrong inside you, that makes you get involved with married men. You must be a lonely person, and I'm sorry for you."

"Suzanne, all I can say is I am sorry. I am *really* sorry. I didn't mean to hurt you." This is what I managed to say. My frantic practicing for this apology on the way over had not helped. My words sounded so wooden, so vastly inadequate.

"I accept your apology," she said. Then she added, "I have to go pick up the kids from swimming practice now. Joe, I'll meet you at home."

I watched her go and wondered how she could leave like that, so sudden and unexpected. And she left me there with Joe, alone?

Joe said, "I'm sorry." I was beginning to wish he'd stop saying that and say something more substantial, like explain what the heck had happened. "We can't stay and talk now," he said. "Let me walk you to your car. We'll talk soon, I promise."

"How can we do that? Didn't you say we can't have any contact?"

"That's right. We can't. But I owe you an explanation, and I will give it to you. We can't speak for a while; I don't know how long. But I will find a way for us to talk. Maybe only once."

"I definitely need to understand this. I am so shocked by it all." I didn't want to be there anymore. "I don't need you to walk me to my car. It's just down the steps over there, in the garage. But I do need you to explain this to me!"

"I will. I promise. Soon. Thank you again for coming here. I just needed to say those things in front of Suzanne, so she could know it was real. It's what she needs to be able to start healing."

"I understand. I guess. I've got to go. *Please* call me soon."

I left, feeling Joe watching me. I drove home in a stupor, heart racing and limbs weak. The car mostly drove itself, it seemed. I parked in my driveway and stumbled into my house. I sat on a chair and replayed the time in the gazebo. I played back the words I heard as best as I could remember them, while the scene became foggier and foggier. What still caught my breath was Joe taking my hand and telling me he was in love with me, referring to an affair. And my lame apology to Suzanne and her saying she felt sorry for me because I must be sick inside.

I got up and paced in my living room. I focused on Joe's assertion that we couldn't spend any time together anymore, or even talk. My stomach clenched. How can that be? How can we not talk about this? But strangely, I took the constraint of that rule literally and seriously; I was utterly beholden to it. This provided an odd sense of comfort to me, and I took it as my punishment. My just punishment. I hated it, and I accepted it. The world had shattered into a million shards of glass, and I needed to hold onto law and punishment to glue it together. It was the only guiding principle for how to live in the aftermath of this destruction.

But I was also enormously frustrated by this edict. A million unanswered questions ran through my mind and tore at my heart, but there I stayed, in confusion and guilt. I never got to outrage; I never got to see myself in that conversation, if you could call it a conversation, as anyone mistreated. As the other woman, I was too guilty to deserve any consideration for my place or my needs in this strange new world. I did not think, not for a long time, that anything unfair might have happened to me that morning—only to Suzanne. I was sure I didn't deserve to consider myself mistreated; my pain was not worthy of attention; my feelings did not matter. I didn't recognize that I too might have been betrayed that day. I knew only guilt, loss, and overwhelming disorientation that resulted in a kind of emotional shutdown lasting many, many years, echoing the shutdown I underwent at the end of my time with Mark.

Serendipitously, it was within the hour of my return from the gazebo when the phone rang again. My heart leaped with the possibility it was Joe, ready to talk and begin explaining what happened. There was so much to explain.

"Hello?" My voice was expectant.

But it was not Joe; it was Jason.

*nineteen*

———

## OPEN AND CLOSED

JASON IMMEDIATELY HEARD SOMETHING IN MY VOICE AND asked what was wrong.

"Something *is* wrong," I whispered into the phone. "I mean, I'm okay, but I'm also not okay."

"Are you hurt? Can you tell me about it? In what way are you not okay?"

I didn't have the stamina to lie or put him off. "I'm not hurt. But I got a call from Joe this morning. He told me he told Suzanne about our relationship. She made him promise to never see me or even talk to me again. He wanted me to meet them both in Boston so that he could tell me this in person and in front of her."

"Yikes! Did you go?"

"Yes, I did. It was so surreal." Now that I said this out loud, the events became more palpable to me, and I found myself crying. Shit. I was not supposed to cry on Jason's shoulder, of all people.

"Oh, sweetie, do you want me to come over and be with you?"

I hesitated to bring Jason further into this. Yet so few people in the world even knew about my life with Joe. Under the weight of all my guilt and shame, a small wave of comfort arose at the prospect of sharing this with someone. I also was protective of the events of the morning. My life had just been ripped apart, and I didn't want Jason to assert his own needs into the mix. Despite my inclination to retreat into isolation, I accepted his offer. I longed to lay down just a little of the burden of isolation I had been carrying since the day of the tornado dream.

In the time it took Jason to arrive at my house, the crack of vulnerability that opened on the phone moments ago was now closed. I was again in the grip of guilt and ambivalence about sharing this with him. When Jason arrived, he was kind, gentle, totally focused on me, and dedicated to whatever I needed. His needs were not present that afternoon, as complex as they must have been. And still, my instinctual urge toward isolation and secrecy fought to reemerge during our time together.

"Would you like to take a walk?" he asked gently, seeing me paralyzed there on the couch.

"Yeah, let's do that. It might be good to move. Thanks."

We walked through the quiet wooded path of a nearby park.

"I just don't get it." I sighed for the nineteenth time, shaking my head slowly.

"Maybe it's as simple as he said; he just broke. Maybe he carried so much guilt, and he just fell apart. Or maybe he was testing the water with Suzanne; maybe she said something that he took as a slight sign that she might not be as devastated as he thought she'd be. Maybe she is stronger than he thought." He stopped walking. "Obviously, she is stronger than he thought because this didn't kill her like Joe always said it would."

That was a good point, I thought.

"You know," Jason said, "It's okay if you want to cry. In fact, it would probably be good for you to cry."

"Yeah, probably. But I just can't right now. I have too much swirling around. Too much confusion."

"Yeah, I bet. Well, just sayin' that if you want to, don't hold back on my account. If you can't do it now, you might be able to later. Whenever, it just might help."

"Thanks," was all I could muster. We continued walking. It felt good to move.

"Sometimes grief takes a while to come out and be recognized," he said after a bit.

*How does he know this stuff?* I wondered.

"Yeah, I guess that's right." I had no idea about grief. "You know, you're being awfully sweet to me. I don't deserve it. I don't deserve you, of all people, to be so sweet to me about this."

"Well, maybe I like you a little." He smiled. "Besides, you definitely deserve for me to be sweet to you; you've just been hurt."

I appreciated his gentle, caring way. I can't say I completely opened to Jason during our walk, but I allowed him to come near me. And that was good enough for him.

Over the weeks ahead, I respected this directive to not see or even speak to Joe. I accepted the chastisement of this injunction. I was guilty; it was what I deserved. I almost believed some wrathful, punishing hand of Suzanne/God would strike me down if I ever transgressed from this directive. Our time was over.

Yet, it drove me mad. I wanted answers. Didn't it matter that I was left in limbo? Didn't I matter?

Eventually, I received a message on my computer. Joe reiterated how sorry he was, that he "just broke," and it almost killed Suzanne. He said he had acted out of a desperate hope he could somehow be with me and continue to take care of Suzanne. If he showed her how much he loved me, she might allow it. Of course, he was completely wrong.

He ended his message with:

We must let go of a way of being that we shared. We must let go of our dream of having a child. None of this is meant to be. I am so sorry. It is utterly clear to me now. I love you. I'll carry you in my heart forever. I wish that were enough for both of us.

I told him I understood and how grateful I was for what we had. I would love him forever. I "released" him into his life. As if it were as easy and simple as that.

Weeks passed, and part of me eventually felt a short-lived flash of anger. But mostly, I was just lost. I didn't cry much, which Jason thought was very odd. Jason again encouraged me to process my grief. I knew it was a healthy thing to do, but I had no idea how to do it myself. Knowing about grief and doing the grieving are two different things. Passive feelings like paralysis and detachment were familiar to me, not active ones like joy, anger, and grief.

"Yes, yes. I am processing my grief," I lied.

"It doesn't seem like it from the outside," he said.

"How can I process this in front of you, of all people? It feels very uncomfortable and strange to me."

"You don't have to process it in front of me, if you don't want to. But you should know that it's okay with me if you do. As long as you process it somewhere. It would be very good for you."

"Okay." I wanted to change the subject. I felt like a grief failure.

I found spending time with Jason to be helpful. But I did not want to discuss Joe with him. I could not get past feeling guilty about Joe, worried about Jason's feelings, and undeserving of any kind of help. How could Jason be so generous with me? Where were his feelings? I was impressed with his devotedness; his caring toward me seemed so sincere. Yet, I had a limit to how much I could be with Jason. There was a place in my heart that still only wanted to be filled by Joe, and it seemed sacrilegious to allow anyone else there. So I was with Jason . . . but not entirely *with* him.

Jason had more emotional clarity about love and relationships than I did. For all my psychological training and intended self-reflection, I exercised an astonishingly small degree of actual self-knowledge in this area. I was unpredictable. Poor guy. One day, I would be free and happy with him, and inexplicably, the next, I would retreat into solitude and the freedom it offered.

One September day, we planned to go out to dinner to celebrate his birthday, and he arrived at my house upbeat and eager to be with me.

"Have you decided where we're going?" he asked, after kissing me hello and sitting down on the couch.

"I still have to change. I'm not sure where we should go. I'm just not sure we should go out tonight," I said in a stressed voice.

Disappointment filled his face. "Why? Is there something wrong? Did something happen?"

"No, nothing happened. I just think I need to be alone tonight. I don't think I would be very good company. I just have confusion about us."

"Can you tell me more about it? What confuses you?" He spoke gently but had laser attention.

"I don't think I'm a very good partner. I don't know if I'm ready to be in a serious relationship. I'm afraid of hurting you." I was saying everything except, "I have to wash my hair." I hated myself, and I had to suppress an internal urge to run.

I needed air. I didn't know what I was doing, and my incompetence was oppressive and frightening to me. Feeling miserable, I wanted him to leave. The evidence of my relational ineptitude sat on my couch with a wounded and disappointed face. I couldn't bear it.

Jason didn't lose his temper. He was infuriatingly kind— kinder than I deserved.

He said, "Can I sit with you and hold you for a few minutes before I leave? Just for a couple of minutes."

"Yes, of course," I said apologetically. I was afraid to lose him, yet I didn't want him too close, too often.

That spring, Jason and I took a previously planned trip to Belize in Central America. I was still brokenhearted yet pretending I wasn't. Seeing more and more of Jason, I believed I was allowing this relationship to grow.

I gave him my full attention during this trip, to be open to a new life and allow the possibility of falling in love with him. I knew he was already in love with me. I was flattered and, most of the time, grateful for the companionship and attention.

We traveled around this beautiful, developing country by bus, sometimes sharing the space with chickens, on our way to snorkel, ride horses, or visit ancient ruins. It was fun, and I discovered Jason was a comfortable travel partner. Part of me began to wonder again if he could be a serious, long-term relationship. He was loving, attentive, smart, handsome, kind, and clearly interested in me. I found myself falling in love with him.

But I was still, like a defective appliance, not functioning quite properly. My heart was behind a wall, and I didn't know it. On the outside I was an open, loving soul, ready to embrace her life and Jason, but on the inside, I was a befuddled, defended person. My life was ruled by the tyranny of the wiring inside me that made me unable to fully participate in a relationship of openness, love, and honesty. I knew only how to live inside a secret or isolated world and engage in deceit and denial. To me, that's what being in a relationship meant; these elements had the comfort of familiarity. Without them, I was rudderless. I should have seen the trouble that could come from a beginning like this. But I did not. If Jason took note of this inauspicious beginning, he chose to move forward regardless.

Still, somewhere inside, I knew I had stumbled upon someone extraordinary who loved me in a way I had not ever known before. Could I really say yes to this beautiful gift?

## twenty

## MARRIAGE!

NURTURING WAS SECOND NATURE TO JASON. HE MADE ME FEEL like my comfort—both physical and emotional—was the only thing that mattered. Despite my caution, he was a lamb, and increasingly I let down my guard and accepted his sweet attention.

In Jason's world, things slowly began to improve. His family's judgments of him and their shunning eventually thawed, now that they saw Jason was not neglecting his responsibilities but was constructing his life in a way to meet them best. They saw the tenderness with which he held his son and the fierceness with which he fought to keep Max in his life. It appeared life might assume some regular pattern. I too, finally, released my lack of confidence in having a healthy relationship, and happily anticipated a future with Jason. It was like a dam on a river giving way to flowing water.

In the early months of Max's young life, his mother banned me from being in his presence. Jason hated this exiling of me. The only reason he initially tolerated it was out of fear his divorce settlement might strip him of the right to see Max. I hated it, too, but the role of the secret girlfriend ran in my blood, so I had to remind myself I no longer was the exiled interloper; I had a right to exist in the relationship.

In October 1990, when Max was almost two years old, Jason and I moved into a charming, sunny apartment together. Jason took Max to Texas to visit his parents for a family reunion and to celebrate his mother's fiftieth birthday. I was not invited. Although his parents liked me, Jason worried that introducing the new prospective wife along with the previous wife's very young child at a family gathering might not be welcome. Once again I was the other woman, and I understood and accepted it. I knew my place. Jason very much didn't like it, but he went ahead, not wanting to threaten the newly re-knitted relationship with his parents.

"I will never do that again," Jason said when he returned home. "I will never visit my family without you again! You belonged there with me, and I am so sorry I didn't bring you. Please forgive me."

For him, keeping me home was a betrayal of our relationship. It was unacceptable, and he wanted me to recognize it as unacceptable, too. This was so new to me, being valued, validated, and respected. No longer kept in secret, I had rights! The night of Jason's return, I loved him so much, and I knew my life was going to be with him. I wanted to release everything I had been holding back and embrace that life.

"Let's make a baby," he whispered into my ear. "Let's make a baby."

What a thrill those words had! All my suppressed maternal longing soared. I wept because I had a man who was ready to have a baby with me. I never felt more loved or understood than at that moment. I knew Jason and I were going to spend our lives together, so I had no hesitation about having a child with him. I suspected I was one of those women who would take a long time to conceive a child, so I thought, *Why not start trying now?* We were enchanted, and it was a moment beyond thought; it was perhaps the most spiritual moment I had ever experienced, and I said, "Yes!"

My desire to have a child was an overwhelming, physical, emotional, and spiritual drive. I could feel our child in the ether, so close that a force field enveloped us and drew us together to form this baby.

Indeed, within weeks, we received the ecstatic revelation that I was pregnant.

We planned our wedding for the week after Christmas, so Jason's family could stay on from their Christmas visit and be at the wedding. We were euphoric. Every day we came home from our respective workplaces and soared together like powerful, blissful electromagnets. My ambivalence was gone, along with any remaining concerns about my "sense of self" and knowledge of what I wanted in a relationship. Gone? Or buried?

Then, six weeks into the pregnancy, I developed debilitating morning sickness. Scarcely able to rise out of my bed, shrouded in the ghastly yellow-green sheen of nausea, I somehow managed to buy rings with Jason, plan a ceremony, invite friends, and arrange for food and flowers. Or rather, we got others to do it for us.

In the days before the wedding, I was helpless. "I can't stand how dusty this apartment is!" I groaned from my familiar spot on the couch, pushing myself up. After a week of emergency acupuncture treatments leading up to the wedding day, nausea remained constant.

"Don't you worry about that for one second." My soon-to-be mother-in-law, Sandy, jumped to the rescue. "I'll run a cloth over everything, and it will sparkle. You'll see. All you have to do is rest. I've got it covered. And tomorrow, I'll run out and get plates, napkins, candles—you just tell me what colors you want, and I'll get it all."

Sandy and her husband, Al, were excited about a new grandbaby and wanted to be part of our lives. They welcomed me as a new daughter-in-law, and I embraced their love and acceptance. I was delighted to have new parents who were engaged and involved with us.

Diane, a friend I had recently met at my new job, rivaled Sandy for organizational skills, and together they contacted guests, made a menu, and ordered cake as I watched woozily from the couch. My wedding dress was a loose-fitting, white sheath dress I borrowed from a friend.

We held the ceremony in our living room, next to the Christmas tree, in front of the fireplace. Twenty of our friends and family cozily pressed together while my father presided. My father, now without a larynx, could not give voice to the words of the service. Instead, my mother used her vocal cords to provide sound as my father silently mouthed the words. I was delighted to have them officiate. I would take whatever parenting might be available, even at the age of thirty-five.

In this wedding service, we used the name of Jesus liberally. Although I still had discomfort with Christianity, I lost my militant defense against it. I held a sense of the sacred, of a divine presence in the world close to my heart. Still, I only darkened the doors of a church when visiting my parents during Christmas. Not to be too Christian, our ceremony included a guided meditation framed by the tones of a Tibetan singing bowl.

Despite its short notice, the wedding was lovely, and I

think of it with much warmth and joy, if not some first-trimester fogginess. Jason stood next to me, holding my hand and providing a steady presence to lean on. Thankfully, I did not have to lurch away from the ceremony and into the bathroom for any upchucking. This had been a genuine possibility.

Max, who had just turned two, was with us, along with Jason's parents and his sister Jennifer, my parents, and two of my four siblings, Judy and Peter. I don't know why the other two, Pat and Andy, weren't there. Along with some friends, we somehow all magically fit in our apartment. The atmosphere was happy and gentle, and it all went smoothly. For me, the dominant feeling of that day, breaking through even all the queasiness, was a calm sense of intuitive certainty that I was doing the right thing in marrying Jason.

During my pregnancy, we lived in a little cocoon world. I struggled to go to work each morning during those first few months, barely got through the day, and collapsed with relief and the bone-aching tiredness that came with pregnancy. I wasn't eating much, but Jason prepared whatever I could manage—pasta, mac-and-cheese, scrambled eggs and toast. I struggled to get it all down but couldn't keep it down. The white bucket was my constant bedside companion. Many times, when I wasn't near the bucket, I'd make a desperate dash for the bathroom, often not making it.

"I am so sorry," I'd groan to Jason, who scurried right behind me and held my hair back in a ponytail.

"Don't worry about a thing. This is the least I can do. You're doing all the hard work here," Jason said, as he gently rubbed my back. I would hear him swabbing down the bathroom after I crawled away. After the vomiting and swabbing, we watched *Jeopardy* every night at 7:30, and then I immersed myself in reading *The Winds of War*, which kept me busy for a good part of the pregnancy. Jason worked in the next room while I slept. It was a sweet routine.

I had some physical discomforts to manage during the pregnancy, but I was ecstatically happy anyway. Having a child was what I wanted more than anything else in life. I loved the concept and the actuality of being pregnant, of nurturing a new life inside my body, so close we were in many ways one life. I felt full of grace, almost holy. I loved getting bigger and bigger. I loved the tight firmness of my bulging belly and the round movements of an elbow or foot, like an ocean ripple under my skin. I liked the weight of my belly, even when it became an ungraceful, grunting feat to get in and out of cars and chairs. I loved our child with a burning passion, and I loved that we spent every waking and sleeping minute together.

The sudden breaking of my water one midnight ushered in labor, and the midwife told us she would meet us at the hospital. When the contractions began with some earnestness, I was shocked into a new experience of "discomfort," as the midwives called it. I immediately demanded to know just how long it was going to take.

My demands were met with gentle smiles and a not-very-reassuring, "You're doing just great."

Time warped as I saw shifts of nurses come and go. I was clearly in an altered state, still drug-free but staggering through a haze of pain.

The hours passed midnight and turned into the next day. And still, I screamed on. Jason was always there. I could hear his reassuring voice right next to me. As active labor passed the thirty-hour mark and concern mounted, I heard the word "induce" float over the haze that used to be my mind.

Several excruciating hours later, the resident came with the Pitocin, and then the party really began. I now faced a refreshingly new and deeper understanding of pain. But then panic gripped my entire being as I realized there was absolutely no way my baby was going to fit through the passage out. It was a huge mistake. God had gotten it so shockingly, awfully wrong! My body was going to rip apart, or maybe the baby would just have to stay inside me for the rest of my life. That would be okay; I liked being pregnant.

The midwife said, "You are doing so great. You are having this baby. This baby is coming out now. Just keep pushing. You're doing great!"

David was a little peaked, the poor thing, after his thirty-six hours of laboring to enter the world, but he was healthy, and I soon had the unutterable thrill of holding him in my arms, the contractions, pain, and screaming already forgotten. David's presence was a light, a joy, and I fell immediately, unconditionally, and unabashedly in love with him.

## twenty-one

## MOTHERHOOD AND CONFLICT

ALMOST ANYONE WHO HAS HAD A CHILD KNOWS THE ALL-
consuming nature of that first year of life. To say I was a happy
new mother is the hugest understatement I can imagine.

That joy, I think, blinded me to Jason's experience during
this period. While he was also deeply in love with this child of
ours, and his first son, Max, he was also eager for his pre-
pregnancy partner to return. He longed for the continuation
of—or more accurately, the start of—the familiar honeymoon
period most couples have in their first year or two of marriage.
Since our marriage had begun with morning sickness, followed
by months of pregnancy, childbirth, and new infancy, the honeymoon phase never came. For me, I was joyful to finally have what
I most wanted—a family to love and to love me.

One evening, we bundled David into the infant seat and
went out to eat in an Italian restaurant nearby. I carried on
about David and how happy I was, and didn't notice Jason's face
getting glum and dark.

As we waited for our food to arrive, he asked, "When do
you think we can spend some quality time together?"

"Isn't that what we're doing right now?"

"That's not what I mean."

"What do you mean?" I asked.

"Haven't you noticed how far away we are from each other? You're preoccupied, and we barely talk, at least about us."

His voice had an edge to it, which got my attention. "I'm not sure what you mean." I was almost afraid to say it, since I sensed part of the problem was exactly that: I didn't know what he meant.

"How can you not know what I mean?" His voice rose. I shrunk down in my seat. "You carry on about how happy you are, but where am I in that?"

"I thought you were right here with me." My heart tightened.

"Well, I am not right there with you. You don't let me in. I'm surprised that you don't know that, or maybe I shouldn't be surprised. We don't talk enough for you to notice anything about me. Not to mention we haven't made love since David was born."

I surveyed the restaurant to see if people were looking at us. As usual, when I was emotionally uncomfortable, I wanted to flee.

"I'm sorry. Let's talk, then," was all I could muster. My concession was half-hearted and sullen. I didn't know how to begin talking, and even if I did, I had already moved into that familiar frozen trance state I escaped to when emotions got too strong. It felt like my existence was threatened.

"Well, how do *you* think we are doing?" he asked, pointedly.

"I think we have a new baby to take care of. I have been really, really happy, and I thought you were, too. Now I discover that you aren't. How could I have been so wrong?" I squeezed back tears.

"I am happy with David, as you well know. I miss you, however. This is the problem right here. You don't even know how

I'm doing. Do you care? Do you want to know?" His voice rose again.

I think I didn't want to know. I didn't want to face the truth that I was the happiest I had ever been, and he was not. My happiness crumbled like a dried-up leaf. I couldn't tolerate this conversation and the pain of it any longer. I said, "I think we should go."

The truth was I had always been brain-dead regarding real intimacy. Not in any of my strings of boyfriends, not in my first marriage, not even with Joe, did I honestly and fully participate in life with another adult person who loved me. If I wasn't compartmentalizing or living in secrecy and delusion, I couldn't be open. Jason took it as his right to have me fully present in our daily relationship. But my wounded self lived behind a protective wall, and I didn't know it.

I really didn't comprehend what Jason thought was missing. It was vague to me. Still, I resolved to please him and give him whatever it was he needed. I didn't understand all my efforts came from behind a curtain of self-imposed isolation, and therefore did not—could not—hit the mark. I tried to be kind and thoughtful, so it was hard to fault me for anything noticeable. Just like in my childhood, the problem was what *wasn't* there. I was replicating the emotional neglect of my childhood with Jason—and with myself.

Jason would go along with life for a while, and then when I least expected it, would bring up something I had overlooked about him, or us, or some request he had made about our relationship I had completely forgotten. I never knew when this would happen. One minute we'd be eating dinner or watching something on TV, and the next moment I would find myself on the witness stand trying desperately and unsuccessfully to account for my failings. Mostly I froze and couldn't find any words, at a loss. I was always trying to avoid saying or doing something that might trigger his upset—whatever that was, I rarely knew. I thought our sex life was okay, but whatever effort I put into it rarely seemed to register as enough to him.

When this happened, I became depressed. I began to believe I would never be good enough. Jason never explicitly said I was not good enough; this was a construction I put on myself. Yet he was unhappy and asking for more. What else was I to conclude?

During these talks, I slid into a state of self-loathing. Why couldn't I understand better what he wanted? Why did I always come up short? I, too, wanted us to be close. I hated myself for not getting it and for not getting it right. I believed I was truly emotionally deficient, as though some vital part of me was missing. What else could explain my complete incompetence about how to be in this kind of relationship? What had happened to us?

A year after David was born, when I was engaged in those numerous numbing attempts to give Jason the kind of relationship he wanted and always coming up short, I made a grave mistake. I am doubly ashamed of what happened next because I accepted attention, not from the one who longed for me to receive it—my husband—but from someone else who unintentionally took advantage of my lostness. I reverted to my old ways of living secretly, lying to myself and others, and trading myself for some positive attention.

Denise worked for my software company as a human resources manager in a satellite office and lived in another city.
She came to town occasionally for a week at a time and for
company-wide events. She was very popular; everyone loved it
when she was around. Denise was full of life, witty, energetic,
and she paid attention to me. When she was in town, she offered
friendship, a girlfriend to do things with, like get out of the
house and have dinner. She wouldn't get angry unexpectedly,
and she was someone with whom I could be carefree. She accepted me for who I was, which pulled me under. No helpful
warning bells went off—no recollection of how I felt chosen by
Mark. I unconsciously reenacted my relationship with him.
That lonely fourteen-year old girl buried inside me was still
running my life. She was the part of me that was relating to Jason
in a protected, transactional way—the only way I knew how.

It happened on a girls' weekend away, planned with several
friends from work. I was excited to be part of the group. Jason
knew them all, including Denise, and was fully supportive; he
would stay home with David. When everyone but Denise can-
celed, he was okay with just the two of us going, even though he
knew she was gay. Previously, he and I lightly joked about the
idea of my having a sexual encounter with a woman, thinking it
might add something to our faltering sex life. Maybe in the
back of our minds, Jason and I each thought this could be that
opportunity. Perhaps I took it as his unspoken permission and
leaned on it when the opportunity developed that weekend.

In the moment, what happened seemed organic and innocent to me. She was my friend. Maybe there was a thrill of
the unknown. Did I unconsciously wonder if I was gay, which
could be the root of my intimacy problems with Jason? No, I
was in a trance mode; the little girl inside me wanted atten-

tion, acceptance, and proof that she was worthy of existing. The real question was: why wasn't I allowing myself to receive this from Jason? Why seek this in secret relationships?

Sitting together on the bed watching a movie, Denise asked, "Have you ever had an experience with a woman?"

"You mean a physical experience?" I knew what she meant but needed a moment to think.

"I mean sex. Have you ever had sex with a woman? Made love with a woman?"

"No. Well, once in college, I held hands with a woman in the back seat of a car, but it never went anywhere."

"Did you want it to?"

"I wasn't sure. I was too scared, I guess. So, it was okay to let it go."

"Do you want to now?" There it was. "We can go slow. If you don't want to continue, we'll stop. I promise." She smiled. "Scout's honor."

I heard my heart beating. A room with blue curtains covered with football players and a twin bed with a matching bedspread flashed before my eyes. Then it was gone.

"You can think about it. No pressure. Although maybe it's better if you don't think about it *too* much."

"Okay," I whispered.

She kissed me with the brush of her lips, then asked, "Is that okay?"

"Yes," I whispered, nervous and excited. She snuggled up to me on the bed, the movie abandoned, and we kissed more. It was light, with no pressure. Then some switch went off inside me, my brain shut down, and I tumbled in slow motion off a cliff, trusting I'd have a soft landing.

I called upon my old skill of compartmentalizing, screening out thoughts of Jason and shutting the door. I didn't call him that night as we had planned, and in the morning, he called the B&B. The owner told him there was no answer from our room, and we hadn't come down for breakfast, but he'd leave us a note. I still didn't call him; I clung to the thought that this was *my* experience. On my drive home, I weighed my options. I could keep it to myself, and life would pick up right where it left off. Jason didn't have to ever know. But should I keep it secret? I was pretty sure he'd be mad, at the least, because I didn't call. What would I tell him? Now back in the "real world," I was terrified. The second I walked in the door, I knew something terrible had happened.

One look at Jason showed he was devastated. My heart plummeted, and my hands began to sweat and shake. I closed the front door behind me.

"Hi!" I tried to smile. He was pale, like he hadn't slept.

"Why didn't you call me? You didn't call last night. You didn't return my message this morning. Why didn't you? At first, I didn't know if I should be worried. But then I assumed you were too busy for me. Too busy with your girlfriend." He paused to see my reaction.

Did he know? Should I tell him? I was sick to my stomach. I didn't speak.

"So that tells me. That's it. You had sex with her, didn't you? You won't have sex with me, but you had sex with someone else. How do you think that makes me feel?" He hung his head in his hands, and his shoulders shook.

Seeing his pain filled me with agony. I wanted to die. Just die right there, of shame and disappointment in myself.

"How about telling me the truth? I thought we were past your lies and deception."

I crumpled onto the couch. "I am so, so sorry," I began. "I don't know what's wrong with me." Now my voice shook. "I so don't want to hurt you. Ever. Maybe I thought you'd think it was okay. I thought you said it was, but maybe you were only joking about how my being with a woman might help our sex life."

"Well, if I thought that, I was very wrong. I feel betrayed and more hurt than I've ever been before. I'm not sure I can get past this."

Those words filled me with terror. "I am so very sorry. Let me try to make it up somehow. I made a big mistake. Please don't say we can't get past this. We have to! I'll do anything I can." I couldn't bear the thought of losing Jason.

"Then talk to me! Tell me what happened. Tell me what I mean to you. If you even can." His voice was flat.

I took a deep breath and tried hard. "It just happened so easily. I mean, I wasn't thinking. I feel so bad now, so stupid, so guilty. I should have known it was wrong. I should never have gone." I was drowning in my guilt and remorse. "I love you. I want to be with you. I want us to live a happy life together. I am so sorry I always screw up."

"Please don't say that. It doesn't help. What you did was wrong and incredibly hurtful. But we'll work on it and get through it, somehow. I just need you to talk to me."

I promised I would.

Unfortunately, the way I expressed my guilt was not to talk but to withdraw, my natural and primary coping mechanism. I found it exceedingly difficult to say anything other than, 'I am sorry,' and retreat in shame and confusion. I wanted it to *go away*. Of course, it didn't. It festered like a cut that would not scab over. But it festered in the dark because I couldn't deal with it. It was overwhelming. Not only did I hurt Jason by having an affair, I doubly hurt him by my inability to talk about it adequately.

I felt profoundly and fundamentally broken. I did not want to be who I was. But I didn't know how to be any other way, and clearly, who I was did not work. There were echoes of feelings of desperation from my ill-conceived marriage to Adam. I was not good enough and never would be. I went to a very dark place, and I went there alone. I often believed that were it not for being a mother, I would not come back from that place. It was just too hard. I knew Jason had no idea how bad this period was for me. If he had, he would have acted with more concern about it. He had concern in general, of course, but he did not know—could not know because I didn't show him—how serious these dips were.

Jason and I lumbered on, trying to hold it all together, while feeling disconnected, confused, and sad.

# twenty-two

## PARENTING AND THERAPY

JASON AND I BEGAN TO SEE A COUPLE'S THERAPIST. TALKING about our relationship was easier during that hour in Chris's office than by ourselves at home in our broken-record conversations.

During one memorable meeting, Jason wanted to talk about Denise.

"I am so . . . So. Very. Sorry!" I wailed. "I wish I could undo it all. I don't know what else I can say. What can I do? I don't even know how to do the basic things you want in this relationship. I am so guilt-ridden and confused all the time. I feel so awful. Just so awful. All the time." Anger swelled up in my chest, and my body broke into a sweat and began to shake. I was afraid to look at either of them.

"What's happening, Liz?" Chris asked. All eyes were on me.

Through clenched teeth, I sputtered. "I can't tell you how hard it is for me to sit in this chair. All I want to do is to run out the door. You have no idea how hard it is to be me, how much I do not want to be me, and I do not want to be here." I pounded my fists on my thighs. I wanted to hurt myself. I was teetering on the brink of a dark night, and I did not want to go there, not in front of people.

After some long moments of silence, I took a breath and

gritted my teeth. "It's okay. I can stay. And I'll try to talk." I tried hard not to cry.

"My feelings of self-hatred and failure are so strong right now. I'll disappear into oblivion if I give in to them. I want to stuff them down and get rid of them."

"That's okay. Those are intense feelings, and you don't have to be with all of them right now. It's okay to back away from them a little bit, until you sense you are safe enough to feel something, just what you can tolerate." Chris coached me. "Does that sound okay to you? And keep breathing. It will help."

It did help. When Chris asked for one small positive thing I could say about my feelings for Jason, I was able to get past my shame and remorse enough to say, "I love you so much. You're strong and steady, and you're holding us together. I so appreciate that. Thank you."

"Okay," said Chris softly. "That's great. How do you feel now?"

"I want Jason to know these things, how I love him, and also how sorry I am. I'm a little calmer now because I said them."

"How about you, Jason?" Chris asked.

"I hate this. I don't want Liz to suffer like this. I just don't know what to do with my anger. But right now, I'm okay. It helps to talk here. It's harder at home."

"We can build from there. When you're at home, and those feelings overwhelm you, allow yourself to back off a little, just like we did here. That's not stuffing them down. It's just keeping them from overwhelming you, which will shut you down. We'll attend to all the feelings a little bit at a time. Let's talk about homework for this week. Set aside time each night to just focus on yourselves and say three things you are feeling. Just listen to each other, no judging. Just name three emotions you feel."

I was comforted by his permission to back away yet not stuff my difficult feelings. It was a start.

I believe Jason watched my misery with his own sense of sadness and frustration. With his anger about Denise, he learned to wait patiently for me, but his anger didn't disappear.

Over the years, we revisited the subject of my affair several times. I tried to offer more information about why I did it and listen to his hurt and anger. I think he sensed my remorse, but I don't think we inched the needle very far. We had deeper realms to excavate. We both remained baffled about why I couldn't just be open to him. I used to be, in the beginning. Wasn't I? What happened to that person? Where did she go? Was she ever really there? This was the question. *Who* was driving the bus of my life?

At the same time, we loved Max and David and loved being parents. We had fun making birthday parties, creating gingerbread houses, staging Easter-egg hunts, and decorating our Christmas trees. Back then, in the 1990s, we used giant hand-held video cameras to record the boys' antics during these holiday activities. From an early age, Max loved hamming it up in front of a camera.

"Here is our Christmas tree! Come with me." He pointed with a flourish, taking the future viewers on a tour of the ornaments. "Here we have a beautiful golden globe, and here is a paper chain I made in school. You'll see at the very top of the tree is the menorah I made. This makes the tree about Jesus *and* about Hanukkah!" Max was pleased with his knowledge of both traditions.

"Wait, it's my turn!" David tried to horn in on Max's monopoly of being the film star.

"Okay, David. You tell everyone about the ornaments you made. Here, I'll help you! Start with this one."

"I can do it!" David cried, and Max acquiesced, stepping out of view. And on it went, both boys vying for attention, which they readily got from their doting parents.

We visited Jason's parents in Texas during summer vacations, where we all lived in their swimming pool during the blistering heat. I basked in the joy of being part of Jason's family. His family showed me what family could be—involved, active, and present. I think Jason and I both tried to make things work well, and sometimes it seemed they were working. We had confidence that we loved each other with tenacity and tenderness. Then, sure enough, our issues would come to the forefront, and we would go around and around again. This usually happened when we had one of those precious opportunities to go out to dinner alone. Perfectly lovely restaurants lined up like dead soldiers lying in the dust, never returned to because they were a site of one of our excruciating relationship discussions. We would be sad, mad, and distant for a couple of days, and then life would again sweep us up, and we would carry on with it.

We were caught in this entrenched cycle but tried our best to enjoy the beautiful life of good health, great kids, and the privilege we were given. Never through any of these times did I ever consider ending our marriage. And never did either of us say anything overtly mean to the other. Some passive-aggressive comments, yes. Jason used sarcasm to vent his hurt. I believed things were going to get better. And, except for those horrible "discussions," our life together was pretty good. We had a role reversal: Jason, the man, wanted more contact, more relating, more emotional intimacy.

I, the woman, scratched my head and said, "Honey, don't we already have that stuff?" while emotionally backing out the door. We learned to live with it—most of the time. We had a family to raise and a deep-seated desire to find that elusive peace and happiness between us.

In the midst of "living with it," my mother called late one night, just a few days after our Christmas visit to New Hampshire. A call late at night was never a good thing, so I braced for the worst.

"Daddy is gone," she said. "He wasn't feeling well after dinner, so we called the ambulance. They did what they could, but he had a heart attack, and he died peacefully in the hospital."

"Oh, Mom, I am so, so sorry! How are you doing? Are you with someone? Should I come up tomorrow?"

"I don't think you have to. I'm here with Pastor David, the hospital chaplain. He is a great comfort. I'll need to make arrangements. I'll call you when I know when the service will be. Right now, I need to call the others."

"Okay, please let me know what you need. I love you."

The conversation was short and to the point, but it rattled me. I wasn't sure what to feel. *What does one feel upon learning that their father has died?* I wondered. I knew it was significant news, and it troubled me, yet I just had an empty space inside. Jason wrapped his arms around me.

"Should we drive up there tomorrow? Even though she said no, do you want to just go?"

"I'll call her in the morning and see what's happening," I said, just wanting to sleep in his arms.

A few days later, Jason, Max, David, and I drove to New Hampshire for the family gathering. My mother had taken care of everything. A modest service would take place at the funeral parlor, followed by a small reception at home.

The day before the service, we mingled at the house, along with my siblings, nieces, and nephews, eating cold cuts and fruit salad. David was three years old, unaware of the solemnity of the occasion, running around among our legs and helping us smile. Amid this activity, the need for quiet overtook me, and a desire to spend a few minutes alone with Dad. I drove over to the funeral parlor and pulled up a chair near his casket, where it rested in a dignified space in the darkened room. The room was otherwise empty and silent, almost like there was no air in it. I sat and waited. I wasn't sure what I was waiting for, but in that moment, it became clear to me he was just a man trying to do his best.

"I understand, Dad. I know you did the best you could. I know you loved me in your own way. Yes, you were mostly absent to me. Yes, you knew nothing about me, which hurt. I understand you were in pain, and that's why you drank. I'll never know what your demons were. I don't hold your lack of involvement in my life against you. It makes me sad, but it's okay. I just want you to know that. I hope you are at peace now."

I sat a while longer in the silence, in case he said anything back. I imagined hearing him say, "Yes, I loved you. All of you. And I'm sorry for my shortcomings. Thank you for understanding and for your forgiveness. I wish you only the best in life." My heart held peace, no anger or resentment. I had closure.

When I think of him today, it is with fondness for his kind heart and sadness I didn't know him better. I carry the loss of not really having had a father, but I've known that loss my whole life.

I was approaching forty. I knew our marriage was not optimal, but since time had shown I was unable to fix it, I half-accepted and half-ignored it and focused on creating a happy home. Jason loved me and was devoted to me. Despite my internal struggles, my love for him was strong. I loved our son David, and I loved Max and the family we were. Max and David were happy children, and being a mother came (surprisingly) naturally to me—the only thing I was confident about in my life. Undeniably, I have parental flaws, but I was unbridled and free in my love for these children. The force of life flowed through my motherhood, and it felt entirely right.

Given that my parental role models were a bit on the neglectful side, my devotion to parenting seemed remarkable. I showered Max and David with attention, wanting to be part of every aspect of their lives. Wanting another child was like one of those inner cords pulling me in a direction, gently, firmly. Despite all the relational inadequacies I brought to my marriage, they were not with my children, and I opened my heart to this pull.

The pull included the desire to have a girl. This idea took hold in me, and I gave it more and more space until I found myself researching how to coax the odds into yielding up a baby girl. I created charts and graphs and was excited to give it a try. After two months of following the suggested schedule and methods, we learned we were once again pregnant, and we were joyful at the news. The sixteen-week amniocentesis test confirmed we, indeed, had conceived a girl, and I savored the news deep into my heart. It was the beginning of solidarity, an unconditional bond that we shared, this daughter and me, in our family of males.

If I had thought my pregnancy with David was difficult, the first five months with Savannah truly brought me to my knees—and my bed. My nausea with this pregnancy rendered me unable to go to work on any consistent basis. I took days and sometimes weeks off at a time when I could no longer safely drive myself the half-hour commute to the office, nor make it through a one-hour meeting without needing to either lie down or vomit.

Morning sickness made it difficult to be very effective—or popular—at meetings. With some incredibly good fortune, I worked for one of the country's most progressive, family-friendly software companies. My manager reassigned my work and assured me my job was not in jeopardy.

Then, happily one day, near Thanksgiving, the nausea tapered away. In my relief and excitement, we planned a fortieth birthday party for me in January, to which we invited dozens of friends we knew from our workplaces. I spent almost two months enjoying the delights of my substantial belly—its taut skin and comforting heft—and feeling the baby move in there.

One day, on my drive into work, I noticed a mild, strange sensation in my belly that came and went. Several times I convinced myself it was nothing. What must have been some maternal instinct made me seek advice and call my midwife, Amy. I hoped she would say it was nothing.

Instead, she said, "I want you to come into the office now."

I drove myself there, curious about what she'd find, but not worried. She poked, prodded, and hooked me up to monitors. I wanted to update Jason, but before I could ask to use their phone, Amy said, "We're going to have you take a ride to the hospital. I'm calling you an ambulance."

*What?* "Is something wrong?" My voice rose as my heart pounded.

"You're having contractions that we need to stop. The hospital is better able to help with that." Amy placed her hand on my shoulder and smiled. "They'll take good care of you."

At the hospital, my contractions stopped with time and intravenous hydration. However, Amy ordered me to my home and bed for the rest of the pregnancy. This meant no walking, no stairs, no car rides other than weekly doctor's visits, and no bending to pick up dirty socks. I wondered how I was going to manage *that* for two and a half months.

The days passed. I listened to NPR, read books, and meditated. I had occasional visitors, and my mother came for a week to help out. She was sweet to me; it was one of my happiest times with her. It never occurred to me to engage in any deep conversations with her. I didn't even inquire how she was faring without her husband, gone about a year now. Neither did she share any feelings about him. Her presence alone comforted me.

My sister Judy visited on the weekends when she could. Rose and other friends occasionally brought us food and books to read. Jason did all the shopping, cooking, cleaning, and food prep—all after working a full day. When they finished their dinner downstairs, David and Jason would come up and visit with me.

"Hey David, come here and give me a hug." I'd open my arms.

"But I don't want to hurt the baby!" He'd hang back, although I knew he longed to jump onto the bed with me. Even at three-and-a-half, he was a sensitive soul.

"It's okay. You can climb up here slowly. Put your hand on my belly, right here. Can you feel your baby sister moving in there?"

His touch was gentle, and his eyes got big. He carefully put his head on my belly, listening for whatever his sister might have to say to him.

We played Uno and watched Disney movies over and over. I memorized every nanosecond of *Beauty and the Beast* and *The Little Mermaid*. Max came over with all his exuberance and cre-ativity, spinning stories about bad guys and heroes and acting out improvised plays with David at the foot of my bed—the cen-ter of my universe.

Max exuded *joie de vivre*. He lit up any room he entered with his delightful nature. He was easy to love, and I was privileged to be his stepmom. During bed rest, I was loved and cared for, and I also had my baby girl with me all the time, growing bigger and closer to term with each passing day.

During one of her visits, I asked Rose if she wanted to be present at the birth. "I'd so like you to be there. Knowing you're nearby will be comforting, and I want to share this with you."

"Are you sure? I am so touched. Don't you want just Jason there?"

"I definitely want Jason there, for sure. But I also want my best friend there. It would mean a lot to me."

"I can't tell you how honored I am. I will be there no matter what time of day or night. You call me, and I will drop every-thing." Rose's eyes teared.

"Good! Thank you." I smiled as I hugged her, leaning over my big belly.

When the time came, just after midnight one night, I nearly delivered our baby in the back seat of the car on the short ride to the hospital, barely making it to the delivery bed. My labor was so hard and fast that, before I knew what was happening, my midwife and a grouchy doctor had whisked my baby away. Then, to my distress, my entire body began shaking. I panicked, thinking I was having a seizure.

"What is this? What is happening? What's wrong?"

"It's just a normal reaction to a fast delivery. It's quite common," Amy reassured me. "You'll be okay in a few minutes."

"Why did no one mention this to me before now? I feel like I'm about to die!" I was terrified.

Eventually, the convulsive twitching stopped, and I was able to hold my baby girl in my arms for the first time. One look at that miraculous bundle of perfection convinced me her name was Savannah, a strong and unusual name that I immediately saw she had the presence to carry.

Savannah came out a free spirit with unquestionable command over life and us. She was a child who insisted on being part of everything and was fearless and undaunted by anything.

I like to think she is everything I could have been, had my early circumstances been different.

*twenty-three*

_____

# RETURN TO A DIFFERENT
# CHRISTIANITY

OVER THE FOLLOWING DECADE, JASON AND I UPGRADED OUR houses, grew in our careers, continued to wrestle with Max's mother, and gave all three of our kids fun and crazy home birthday parties. Jason was devoted to me, steadfast, loyal, and committed, and I was devoted to him. Still, we could not get beyond our stuck dynamic and get to the enchanted relationship we sought. I know Jason longed for the bright, open, self-confident, and sexy woman I seemed to be when he first met me. Instead, he found someone who was competent, loving, and highly functioning, yet was far entrenched behind an invisible and impenetrable wall, and whose sexuality had become a litany of constraints and limitations. Even through his frustration, he knew intuitively and with certainty that there was a deep well of soul and spirit in me, which he longed to see expressed.

Despite working with therapists, we continued to be two exhausted, deeply disappointed, baffled, and battered people who knew they loved each other with strength and tenacity and longed to be deeply connected, yet who consistently came up short. My wall of isolation didn't just separate my essential being from Jason, but from friends, family, co-workers, and myself—

nearly everyone in my life, except for my children, with whom I miraculously bonded freely and deeply.

Jason, by asking for more of me, led me to the depths of my personal hell. At the same time, by asking for more of me, he threw the lifeline that pulled me into the light.

In a few years, I would discover the Buddhist view that our deep anguish is a portal to wisdom and greater freedom, but we have to face what hurts and walk through it.

Through his abiding love and persistent belief that there was more to me than he or anyone was getting, Jason stayed with me and held up a mirror. For me, it was a mirror of pain. For so many dark and lonely years of our marriage, I looked in that mirror and saw only my shortcomings, melded with my shame and inadequacy. But eventually something changed. Instead of pain, I found freedom.

During those years, I turned to spirituality and God for guidance. The Christianity of my youth had let me down; God had turned out to be another absent father.

"You know, not all Christianity is like the kind you grew up with," Jason suggested.

"Don't be silly, of course it is. It is all the same. You have to believe that Jesus saved you, whatever that means, or you can't be a Christian." I knew better. No matter what Jason thought, I was the one who grew up in Christianity.

"The problem is, I don't know where to go to find a good spiritual community the kids can be part of. I'm not a real Christian and I'm not quite a Buddhist, either. I don't believe in the old-man-in-the-sky kind of God. I believe God is a benevolent divine presence within us, who created us, loves us, and somehow, in some unfathomable way, guides us and wishes us to live in joy and peace. Where can I find other people who believe like I do?"

"Maybe you should just check out different churches. Try the Unitarian church in town or the Episcopal church across the street. I think it's pretty liberal," Jason proposed.

I decided to visit the Unitarian Church; it seemed the most benign. The service I attended left me uninspired; something was missing, although I couldn't say what. Next, I tried the Episcopal church across the street, as Jason suggested.

The building was arts-and-craft styled red brick on the outside, a square bell tower, and inside, more brick, ornate wood, and stained-glass windows. I crept in and sat in the back, with infant Savannah and low expectations in tow. Parts of the service seemed familiar to me, and immediately my body tensed and my mind closed. But the priest did not deliver the fire and brimstone or the simplistic rhetoric I had expected. Instead, he gave a thought-provoking sermon, and he seemed like a man of substance and depth. The congregation was friendly— friendlier than I was, certainly.

On the way out, I saw a rack with the little pamphlets I consider church propaganda, and prepared to be dismayed, expecting to read the platitudes I assumed would be there. I picked up one. "The Bishop's Response to the AIDS Epidemic." *Okay, this is the litmus test*, I thought to myself. In that booklet, I was sure the bishop would tell me what my mother thought: People with AIDS brought it upon themselves by living an immoral lifestyle, and if only they were church-goers, this would not have happened to them. Instead, I scanned through a message of love, compassion, and inclusivity.

I went home and told Jason, "It was not too bad. The sermon was good."

"I told you so! Not every Christian church was like your father's. Are you going to go again?" he asked, only half-teasing.

"Maybe."

I did go again, and this time Jason and David came with Savannah and me. I was still hesitant and uncomfortable inside the church, but again, I was not disappointed by the sermon. Someone told me the church offered childcare, but I preferred to keep Savannah and David close by, as I confess to harboring some concern they'd get a solid brainwashing. We went a third time, and then later that week, I got the phone call.

When the friendly woman introduced herself as Joy, a volunteer on the Welcoming Committee from the Parish of the Epiphany, I sighed and braced myself for the hard sell and the proselytizing. I decided to be very upfront and tell her I wasn't a Christian, and I wasn't sure if I'd be coming back. But Joy did not proselytize.

"I'd love to know more about you. I'm curious about what brought you to Epiphany and what you are looking for?"

"I'm looking for a spiritual community for my family, but I don't have a clear vision of what that would be. I guess I want an open-minded place where people can have differing spiritual beliefs. I'm not sure that's a Christian church. I am not looking for the kind of strict Christian upbringing like in my father's Lutheran church. Honestly, I struggle with many of the prayers and rituals."

That would put her to the test, I was certain. I expected her to bring the conversation to a quick close. Again, she surprised me.

She said, "Many of our parishioners at Epiphany struggle

with various parts of the service. I'm not even sure all of them are Christian."

That was pretty heretical. "Is that okay?" I asked. "I mean, don't they get pressured into believing what everyone else believes, or in what the church thinks they ought to believe?"

"No, there isn't pressure. At least I don't think people feel pressure. I don't. Our priest, Rob, is very laid-back. He isn't pushy. He says all people are on a spiritual journey, and wherever they are in that journey is just fine. He says they are seeking a relationship with God."

"Well, that's unusual," I mumbled. And quickly amended, "I mean, I like that; I think that's a good way to think about it."

Joy told me some things she liked about Epiphany and encouraged me to take advantage of the childcare. My private thoughts about bodysnatching and brainwashing somewhat allayed, I told her maybe I'd come again sometime. After hearing my dark secret about not liking Christianity, she didn't chastise me, hang up, or promise to pray for my soul. We chatted for twenty minutes.

After a few more visits to Epiphany, I still wasn't sure I belonged there. The stained-glass windows and high altar rail stimulated my childhood sense of religious guilt. I still suspected God would discover my heresy, and the wrath of God might strike me down. Could someone who believed in reincarnation go to that church? I wanted to be upfront with this priest, so he'd know where I stood. If he was going to reject me, I wanted to establish that before going much further with this exploration.

Jason and I invited Rob to come over one evening, and I shared the whole grim story with him. Sitting in our living room, with cookies laid out on a plate, I told him about growing up as a Lutheran minister's daughter and my subsequent aversion to the Christian church, my years of meditation, and my interest in Eastern spirituality. He listened to it all without any visible flinching. When I asked him if it was still okay for me to come to his church, he laughed.

He said, "You'd be surprised how many people are unsure of what they think about Christianity and wrestle with aspects of the faith. I *am* a Christian, and I wrestle with aspects of the faith. In some ways, the struggle itself brings us closer to God."

Jason spoke up. "My son, Max, who is eight, is from my first marriage and is being raised Jewish. He attends a Jewish day school and is very observant. He's sometimes with us on Sundays, and we'd like to bring him to church with us. Would the other kids welcome him, do you think?"

"I certainly hope the kids at Epiphany would welcome him! But I can say that I definitely welcome him. I'd love to have Max with us anytime."

Then he said to me, "We have a small group that meets once a week to meditate together. You're most welcome to come. We use a method called Centering Prayer, but you can do whatever style of meditation you like. I lead the group, and you can just drop by anytime. It's an open group."

"Okay, thanks!" I said, inwardly curious about the group. "One last thing. I don't know what I should call you. Reverend O'Neill, Father Rob, Pastor? What do people call you?"

He laughed again and waved his hand. "Oh, *please* just call me Rob."

"Okay, Rob it is," I said, glad about his approachability. No one *ever* called my father by his first name, not even my mother. The only way I ever heard her address my father was "Honey" or "Daddy." His parishioners and friends called him Pastor.

We started going to Sunday services most weeks. I continued to struggle with the basics of the faith, like, What was sin really? Was the resurrection real or symbolic? How did Jesus's death redeem the world . . . whatever that meant? And why did the church think we needed to believe in all this? I was uncomfortable with what I didn't understand. Despite my inner questioning, people were friendly, and they had some thought-provoking guest speakers talk about social justice issues, which I enjoyed hearing.

Then one night, I decided to visit the centering meditation group Rob had mentioned. I wanted to meditate more frequently, so I thought joining the group might help.

Rob welcomed me when he saw me approach the room, already ringed with a circle of chairs and candles lit. He explained how the evening went, and soon I was sitting in that comfortable and familiar posture of deep silence. The half hour of meditation ended with a brief break for coffee and tea, and then we reconvened to explore a passage from the Bible.

*Oh, here it is, the Bible study.* I tensed up. But we did something unusual. Rob read the words very slowly and then asked us to pick a single word or phrase that struck us. After a third meditative reading, he asked us to say anything the words meant to us personally, now in our lives. I found this process—which I learned was called *Lectio Divina*—intriguing.

In that circle of quiet, members offered insights and reflections, often personal and inspiring. I didn't know Bible passages could stimulate profound thoughts, feelings, or realizations. In my experience, the Bible contained only platitudes, commands, and judgments.

I found this centering and Lectio practice moving and thought perhaps I had found a home within Epiphany. In time, I became a regular in this group and found it a safe place to explore, sometimes out loud and sometimes privately, my struggles with Christianity and my view of God and the universe. People did not find me weird and seemed to accept my delicately offered, esoteric perspectives. I discovered that, with a slight reframing, the underlying spiritual concepts I held were also present in the words of the Bible. The prevailing culture at this church promoted the idea of divine love and an open, yet questioning, heart. It was revelatory to me that this was within the traditions and structure of the Christian church.

When the assistant priest asked me to be a church school teacher, I laughed at how far I had come. *Me?* The heretic herself teaching their children? Jason got a laugh out of it, too. He liked that I was warming up to Christianity; he was becoming more involved, too, and it became something we shared.

Over about one year, I found myself a person who went to Sunday services and weekly centering prayer, taught children, and then joined the Adult Education Committee. I began a relationship with a spiritual director, Sarah. A spiritual director was trained to accompany someone on their spiritual journey.

Sarah was a kind and attentive listener, often asking me to reflect on where God was in my life. We met monthly, and she soon became an important guide as I tried to understand not just Christianity, but my broader view of God, the universe, and life in general. A pretty significant change in the life of an avowed anti-Christian!

Along with my struggles in my marriage, I also struggled to find value in my career and looked to spirituality for guidance. No longer fulfilled by working in technology, I had a growing desire to do more "meaningful" work with my life, but had no idea what that could be. I had piles of notebooks from writing my questions and uncertainty. I meditated every day. I took long walks and asked God to show me how to make my life worthwhile and help me understand why Jason and I were still struggling with barriers in our relationship we didn't understand. I asked God to help me find my center, find peace and confidence, and embrace life rather than forge my way through it in a daze—in a "trance of unworthiness," a term I learned years later from Buddhist teacher, Tara Brach.

Then, one afternoon, a woman I didn't know called me.

"I'm looking for Liz Kinchen," she said.

"Who is this calling?" I replied, of course, assuming it was a telemarketer.

"I am a friend of Joe Murphy," she continued. "Are you Liz?"

That got my attention. "Yes, I'm Liz."

"Your name is in his address book, and I am making my way through his contacts. Is this a good time to talk?"

*What?* "Sure, yes. What is it?"

"I am really sorry to be the bearer of sad news, but this morning Joe was out walking the dog and was hit by a car and killed. I'm trying to let his friends know."

## twenty-four

### A PIVOTAL EVENT

"HE GOT HIT BY A CAR AND WAS KILLED? OH MY GOD, HOW awful! I'm so sorry to hear!" I wanted to ask for more details, but some dim corner of my brain wondered if it might be a crank call, that someone had discovered our secret of old and was playing a mean trick on me.

"Are you sure?" I asked. *Stupid.*

"Yes, it's horrible. It's a shock. He died right away. That's really all the information I have right now. We just want to let people know. People who were close to him. Listen, I have a lot of other calls to make, so I need to go. I just wanted you to know. We'll have more information about what happens next in a while."

My stomach twisted in knots of horror—horror that Joe died and horror that someone called me. Did Suzanne know I was on this list? Did she tell this unknown woman to call me? Guilt flooded my system all over again, always my first impulse when I thought of Joe.

"Yes, of course. Thank you for telling me. Please do let me know what happens next," was all I could stammer out. She hung up. I didn't get her name or phone number, and there was no caller ID to help.

I was trembling. I paced around, trying to breathe. Could this be true? How could I verify it? I hesitated for a millisecond—since Joe was a sensitive subject—but I was too overwhelmed by the enormity of this news to stop myself from dialing Jason's work number.

"Hey, sweetie," he said. "What's up? How's your day?"

"I just got the weirdest phone call." The words tumbled out.

Jason was quick to respond. "Why, what was it? Are the kids okay?"

"The kids are okay. I'm not exactly okay."

"What is it? Tell me!"

"Someone just called and said that Joe Murphy was hit by a car today and killed."

"That's terrible! Who was it that called?"

"I don't know who it was, some friend of his. She said he went out this morning to walk their dog and was hit and died right away. I wasn't sure if it was a crank call or not. I still don't know, but it seems like it could be true. Maybe someone from those days who found out about us? What do you think?"

Silence for a beat. "Tell me exactly what she said."

I tried to recall and repeat what was said. I heard buzzing in my ears.

"Take a deep breath. Maybe sit down."

"I don't know what to do."

"If they're going down his list of friends, then maybe they called other people from our old office. I'll see what I can find out."

We hung up, and I continued pacing. What if it were true? Dead? Joe and I hadn't had any contact in years. Not since our ragged ending, not since we all moved on when the company we worked for went under. It had been years, so why was I so affected? This sudden insertion of Joe into my relatively calm, stable life was disorienting. I felt once again like an interloper, like I didn't belong anywhere near him, not even to receive word of his death. It didn't occur to me that I was upset because someone I used to love died unexpectedly. Some part of me still didn't believe I was allowed to have loved him.

I waited for Jason to call back. I paced from room to room; I had too much adrenaline to sit down. I wondered what those last moments were like for him. Did he feel pain? I replayed the day in the gazebo when he told Suzanne about us. My whole body and heart groaned at the memory. I wondered if I could go to his funeral. My stomach churned. Finally, the phone rang, and I jumped.

"Sorry to take so long. I called a few people, and, well, it's true," Jason said. "I am so sorry, sweetie."

"I just don't know what to think. Or feel." I was worried about Jason thinking I was feeling *too* much.

"Well, this is big news. It would be okay if you wanted to cry and be sad," Jason said gently.

"Really? I mean, I guess that's right. I just don't know . . . What about a service? How can I go to a service? I can't go."

"Let's cross that bridge when we get there. We don't know anything yet."

So many conflicting feelings coursed through me—sadness, guilt, shock, worry, loss.

"Do you want me to come home early? I could leave work now."

"No, no. Don't do that. You'll be home in a couple of hours anyway. We can talk more then. Thank you, though. Thank you for being so kind."

We hung up, and I continued my pacing. Dead? Gone? Now I'll never know what happened with us. I wasn't expecting us to ever talk again, but if he was alive, there was an irrational chance. Now there was nothing. There was so much from our relationship that remained unresolved because it was never adequately examined or processed.

In retrospect, I know I loved Joe in the bubble of secrecy and constraint we created; it fueled and inflated the emotions. Everyone was hurt by what we did—Suzanne, Joe, Jason, and me.

The follow-up phone call never came. Suzanne must have intervened with instructions to omit me from the list of service guests. Of course, even if mistakenly invited, I wouldn't go. Imagine the scorned adulteress showing up skulking in the back row. My presence would be an offense. Of course, I stayed away with my shame and guilt, and once again, was left wondering.

But there was a gift in this sudden loss. Jason stuck with me and encouraged me to grieve and process the death and the relationship. We both hoped this could finally close the door on the Joe chapter and allow more room for us. Again, Jason's unfailing love and tenderness shone brightly, and my heart opened even more.

Over time, this sad event symbolized a new beginning for us, which we so needed. We christened this "The New World" and naively moved forward together with renewed hope.

Sadly, my desire to transform was not enough. I had to take on the hard work of looking into all the denied and repressed wounds. This beautiful man, my angel on earth, held me and our marriage together for many years. Without him, I can't imagine where I would be or what my life would be like. I am not idealizing him. I know he is not perfect. In addition to my relational handicaps, I know Jason has his own as well, and they have always been at play in our relationship. How could they not? He had unexamined insecurities and self-worth is-sues buried deep within his attentiveness to me. But it took a long time before I understood this. I never considered he could be doing anything to contribute to our problems. Part of my handicap was assuming everything wrong was entirely my fault, and I allowed us both to operate that way. I was always the "identified patient," the one who needed to get past her wounds. Because I certainly had identifiable wounds, I accepted this dynamic.

One day early in 2001, I received a phone call from God. Actu-ally, the call was from our priest, Rob, but it seemed divinely inspired. It pulled the thread that began unraveling my uncon-scious and hurt self and the subsequent reconstruction of my life. Rob and I had worked together on several projects and committees at church and spent many hours in meditation and reflection together. He knew about my longing to do something different with my life, and my not knowing what it was. Of course, he didn't know what I should be doing, either, but he encouraged me to stay open.

On the call, Rob told me about a school and home in Honduras for children who lived in extreme poverty, so poor that all one's efforts went toward merely staying alive one more day. These children were often not in school but on the city streets, scraping their way in life. This grassroots school—*El Hogar de Amor y Esperanza*, the Home of Love and Hope—was at a crossroads and needed to become better organized and supported financially in the United States. Rob and some other supporters planned to establish a nonprofit organization in the United States to help this fledgling organization, and they needed a director. As Rob talked, I wore grooves in the carpet around my dining room table.

"The program began in 1979 with five street boys and has now grown to over two hundred students. The school invites these children from the streets, from lives of poverty, crime, and drug use, into a different future. El Hogar offers them education, food, shelter, and an employable trade. They graduate with self-respect and the ability to care for themselves and their families."

*Wow. This sounds intriguing!*

"So, does this sound interesting?"

"Yes, I'm interested! Tell me more."

My heart filled with intuitive certainty that this was the answer to my prayer for more meaningful work. But I had some concerns. Not surprisingly, they offered laughably low pay. I wondered if we could afford to decrease my contribution to the household income. I diplomatically mentioned this. He had an idea.

"Well, the El Hogar position is part-time. I also have an opening for a part-time person to support the church's programs and committees—a lay ministry director. If you'd be interested, we could explore combining these two different jobs to make a full-time salary. It still probably won't amount to what you earn now in software, but this is probably the best I can do."

Both roles sounded pretty vague, but I was eager to hear more. "Could you tell me a bit about the specifics of these two roles? What would I be responsible for?"

"I'm glad you want to know more. I'll write some job descriptions, and then we can talk again." Rob's voice was animated.

I could taste the excitement of possibility. I was ready to leave my current job, which seemed increasingly soulless with every passing day. Waiting while this hybrid plan slowly came together was torturous. It took months of meetings and conversations before everything was approved. Jason was fully supportive of the change.

Finally, I gave notice at work, and with relief, joy, and some naivety and trust, I stepped from a secure and lucrative professional career of twenty-one years into the unknown. This second season in my career life stretched and changed me forever. Professionally, I became an organizational leader, fundraiser, and public speaker. Personally, my eyes opened to the immense privilege I was born into and to the inequities of global systemic poverty. Emotionally, it brought me joy to know I was helping to care for hurting children.

However, this significant change to my life's work was not the pivotal event that brought about the deep emotional transformation I sought. A small detail required by my part-time position on Epiphany's staff triggered a devastating insight into my childhood relationship with Mark.

The Episcopal church mandated every leader learn how to avoid, recognize, and respond to various forms of abuse and harassment in the church community. When I began working with El Hogar and Epiphany, I dutifully attended Safe Church training. This day-long workshop taught us how to watch for signs of child abuse among church volunteers, and the legal requirements for staff members should we discover these situations. More than one adult must be in a classroom or an automobile with children and teens, office and classroom doors must have windows, and a young child must be escorted to the bathroom by two teachers.

During the workshop, we watched a video with vignettes depicting various kinds of abuse. A teenage boy stole money from his disabled grandmother's purse; a minister had an affair with one of his parishioners; a male priest interacted with a teenage boy who came to him for counseling. This last video showed the tall, handsome priest welcome a boy of fifteen into his office. The priest listened intently and sensitively to the boy's struggles and his sadness over recently losing his father. He was a shy but earnest teenager searching for guidance and a new role model. The priest invited the boy to come back for more conversation anytime he wanted.

After a few visits, the man moved to sit on the couch with the boy, talked to him about growing up, and encouraged him to relax and be more at ease. This man treated the vulnerable boy like a friend. The boy began to trust him and looked forward to their visits together.

All my senses were alert. My heart beat faster, and my mouth was dry. Something was happening in that movie. Something was happening in me. Something subtle yet unmistakably familiar. Tendrils of dread curled into my gut.

During one scene when the boy visited his office, the handsome priest produced a cold beer from his mini-fridge and poured them each a glass to enjoy while they chatted. He was friendly, and the conversation turned to the boy's concerns about his relationship with his girlfriend.

"I may have something to help you out in that area," the priest reassured. "It's natural for kids to be a little anxious about sex. Maybe all they need is to understand it a little more. Not many people want to talk to kids about sex. I think I can help."

With that, he reached into a desk drawer, pulled out a DVD, and popped it into his video player. Together, they watched porn, sitting there on the couch with their cold beers. With each flash of erotic scenes, my mind said, "That's probably not his job to do; he's gone too far now. The priest should not be speaking to this boy about sex. And probably not serving him beer." The smoky dread-tendrils moved up around my heart, and suddenly, I felt *recognition*. A network of neurons activated inside me and escalated to full voltage. This man was *seducing* the boy. He was not just showing him a video about sex, not just offering friendship. Now I saw the whole long cultivation process. He had been kind and gentle, and all along, he wanted sex. He had lured him in. He seemed so trustworthy, thoughtful, and sweet; he took care of the boy, paid attention to him, and made him feel special. *I* was lured in by him. I wanted to trust him. As I watched, part of me did trust him, and part of me felt punched in the gut.

The movie then cut to this boy, several years later, looking older and sadder. The boy described how eventually, bit by bit, over time, the kind priest began a sexual relationship with him, all the while being gentle, loving, and attentive to him.

"Eventually, I knew something was not right, but it took a really long time to find the strength to end things with him." The young man sounded despondent.

"He told me he loved me," he said, his eyes speaking directly to me.

As I watched this video, I re-experienced all the complex emotions from my years with Mark. I experienced *myself* in the movie. I recognized Mark; I *felt* Mark as I watched the man in the video. They called this abuse. Never, in all the years with Mark and after, had I ever considered our relationship abusive.

Yes, I knew it was unorthodox, but I never recognized the planning, manipulation, and slow cultivation of setting the trap, as I experienced while watching this little vignette. I saw it from an adult perspective, from the perspective of a parent. I experienced a sense of protection for this boy in the video that I had never experienced on my own behalf. Now I had outrage at the exploitation of his innocence and trust.

The young man continued. "I was so mixed up. I didn't understand what love meant or what to expect from a relationship. After it ended, I was confused about my sexuality. I felt worthless, and as I think back on it, used."

The more I sat with my visceral experience of watching this video, the more connections I made to the abusive nature of my "lucky" relationship with Mark. I thought about everything I had read and heard about the impact of child abuse and now began to reflect on my adult relationships, especially my marriage. I knew something big had just happened.

Once home, I told Jason about my reaction to the video, and he *immediately* understood its implications for me and for us. This epiphany opened the floodgate of a new understanding of myself and the forces that held me captive.

*twenty-five*

---

## DEEP THERAPY

I SOUGHT A THERAPIST WHO COULD HELP ME REVISIT MY childhood and remember my years with Mark, in order to unlock their secrets more clearly. I was ready to do whatever it took to plumb these memories. I thought I needed a hypnotherapist but instead I found a kind, gentle woman named Patricia, who specialized in abuse and trauma recovery.

At the time, a trend in our popular culture was to identify events and people from our childhood as abusive, and at first, I resisted the notion for myself. I never considered my relationship with Mark, or my family of origin, as having induced trauma. So many people had much worse experiences. I did not starve, no one locked me in a closet or extinguished cigarettes on my legs, I was not homeless, and my parents never even yelled at me. Yet it was an undeniable fact I had serious problems with relationships, and they must have come from somewhere. My emotional inaccessibility, feelings of paralysis, and bafflement ran my life and strained my marriage. It took me a long time to understand that benign neglect in childhood and inattention to emotional needs are also traumatic for a child and have lasting effects.

Together, Patricia and I began a long, slow walk toward remembering and recovery. The process was laborious. During the early months and years of therapy, I began writing my story to help me recall childhood details and uncover emotions quashed so long ago. I discovered writing helped open memories long forgotten and shook loose some of the stuck places.

The therapy process is so intricate, like gentle neurosurgery of the psyche and soul . . . a rewiring of old neurological pathways and replacing them with new, healthier ones. Patricia likened the effects of trauma to living in a trance state—not fully aware and alive, living out of old protective habits. I often left Patricia's office feeling oddly deconstructed and reconstructed internally.

An addict who feels the pull to fall, or who does fall, has a sponsor they can call who will understand them—not judge or reject them, but love them back onto the path. Like that sponsor, Patricia gently held a lamp of understanding, a broader and deeper vision than mine, and a belief in me that led me to my larger self.

Jason witnessed and supported my recovery, even as he held his own anger and disappointment. A note he wrote early on in my therapy reflects his struggle and his love:

> My anger has come and gone and come again, but my love for you has always been steadfast and deep, even through my anger and your neglect. My love for you remains steadfast now. I still consider you the most beautiful and graceful woman in the world. Despite all that I have done to assure you and make you safe, I have failed to make you less afraid of me.

It was true I was afraid, and therefore avoidant. I neglected Jason's needs, even though it was unintentional. I came to understand how my dynamic with Jason was fueled by a very young, hurt part of myself. The little girl living within me felt alone in the world. She didn't trust anyone to love her honestly; she believed she wasn't worthy of love and attention. This hidden little girl ran my life. She drove the doomed cycle with Jason of not feeling "good enough." Longing for love, she believed she had to earn it by doing what a man wanted. This girl did not know what *she* wanted, or thought, or had the right to do; she could not advocate for herself. What she did best was to comply, shut down, or dissociate.

Each week, I sat in my usual place on Patricia's couch, facing her as she sat in her chair across from me, surrounded by thriving plants, an airy room with light-filled windows. I sat with the familiar mix of apprehension of the unknown and comfort that I was in safe, loving hands.

"Close your eyes and take a few deep breaths. Can you see this little girl? Can you feel her in your body? How old is she?" Patricia gently coaxed me.

I saw a sad, bedraggled, little girl with a brown, pixie cut standing alone under a tree outside my childhood house.

"I see her," I whispered.

"Tell me about her. What does this girl need right now? If the adult Liz could tell her anything, what would she most want to hear?"

Tears stung behind my closed eyes. "She just wants to be loved. She wants me to talk to her, pay attention to her, be with her."

"What do you say to her?"

"Hey, little one. I'll be your friend. I'll look after you. I'll take care of you." To Patricia, I said, "I want to pull her onto my lap, wrap my arms around her, and hold her there forever."

"Go ahead and do that. Hold her in your arms the way you would hold young Savannah or David or Max. You know how to love a child well. You're doing great. You're a wonderful mother. This girl needs a mother."

I always left our sessions drained, elated, and sad. I had a ritual of leaving her office in the morning and stopping in the nearby Panera Bread to order a latte and peanut butter and banana sandwich to take with me to work. This small gesture of nurturing I gave myself was new for me. Now I knew the lack of attention I received from my parents was precisely how I treated myself. Pretending I had no needs and ignoring anything that hurt, I treated myself like I didn't matter. I couldn't change the past, but I could change how I treated myself moving forward. I began a slow crawl away from constantly betraying myself and toward loving, supporting, and nurturing myself into health and fullness of being.

For many years, Jason came with me to therapy and together we sat side by side on her couch and navigated the internal family systems work Patricia did with us. He learned about my inner parts, which protected me, and many of his own, which helped him see ways he contributed to our painful dynamic. He discovered more about his demons and began meeting with his own therapist to work with them. Patricia's gentle guidance and unfailing belief in me as a person, and in us as a couple, helped us explore the deeper layers of our struggle together, learn about them, and find our way through them. It wasn't just that Patricia was a skilled therapist; there was something more to her presence. She was generous with her time. She gave me books and articles to read. She was even generous financially when Jason lost his job for a while.

One day as I was leaving, I said, "You are very kind and generous with us—with me—in so many ways. Thank you."

"I do it out of love." Her voice was gentle. At first those

words surprised me, but I sensed what she meant, what kind of love she meant. She lived from her loving heart. In Buddhist terms, she is a bodhisattva, one who lives from love to relieve the suffering of others.

I can summarize the essence of what I learned and how I changed through therapy. Through our work together, it became clear both the isolation of my childhood, and then the betrayal of my trust in Mark, left the imprint of trauma on my nervous system. This combined trauma drove the numbness, emotional protectiveness, and my fundamental sense of unworthiness.

Science backs this up. Modern psychological attachment theory shows we need to have a loving, attentive relationship of trust with an early caregiver in order to bond with others later in life. Relational neuroscience suggests the impact of trauma is lessened if someone is there to support us before, during, and after an overwhelming experience.

The kind of benign emotional neglect I experienced as a child wired my nervous system such that I struggled with self-worth and closeness in relationships throughout my adult life. With Mark, the trade of sex in exchange for attention shut down my trust of sexual intimacy. All these factors allowed me to live in emotional isolation, engage in secret and constrained relationships, and keep my emotions behind a wall, believing this was all I deserved.

One of the most powerful techniques we used in therapy was EMDR (eye movement desensitization and reprocessing), which uses thought, emotion, and physical bilateral tapping to literally rewire the nervous system. This rewiring allowed me to slowly tolerate emotional states that I had a lifetime of fearing and ignoring. Patricia's loving presence in my life for over ten years was instrumental in restoring my true self. She helped me find and foster my "essence," as we called it—the part of me that was undamaged, strong, and connected to something much larger than my personal story.

So it really was God on the other end of the telephone that day many years ago. The call from Rob led me to the video, which unlocked a critical door, which led me to a long, hard journey into light, allowing me to relate to others in a full, open-hearted, and healthy way. I slowly came out from behind my protective wall and authentically connected with friends. I replaced my lifelong belief that relationship is about obligation and transactional love with the deep knowledge that real love comes freely and joyfully. The unbounded love I knew with my children was the kind of love possible for me. I saw that I have not only my husband, but others who want to know me and love me. Patricia saw me deeply, and I was also truly seen by my spiritual director, Sarah, who for many years listened without judgment to my struggles with Christianity and how to live a life that mattered. Patricia and Sarah, two key healers in my life, both walk the Buddhist path, which also became a vital source of healing in my life.

After years of living a dissociated and fearful life, in a long string of relationships chosen and driven by fear, emotional protection, and the embodied belief I was not good enough, I was finally waking up to the richness of living with an open heart.

## *twenty-six*

---

## OLD FAMILY SECRETS

AS OUR KIDS GREW, JASON AND I REVELED IN WATCHING THEIR baseball and soccer games, attending their school plays, and meeting their friends. I wanted to know every detail of their lives and every hurt their hearts endured. My unconditional enthusiasm and love for them came naturally. I couldn't turn it off if I wanted to. Being a mother woke me up. It was an antidote for the isolation I inherited from my childhood. Visiting my own mother often rekindled in me those feelings of being unseen, yet I wanted our kids to know their grandmother, and I wanted her to know them. We made a point of visiting two to three times a year, mostly for holidays.

When my parents had retired, back when I was in college, my mother underwent a significant transformation. They had moved to a cozy, sweet little house on a densely wooded cul-de-sac in a quiet corner of New Hampshire ski country. No longer burdened with work, church, kids, and a fast-paced environment, Mom went from a withdrawn, tense, somewhat depressed worker-soldier to a relaxed, happy, and chatty person.

My kids loved visiting my mom. Her house was a quintessential Grandma's house in the woods. Her house had many things in it foreign to our house: bird-chirping clocks, plate collections mounted on the walls, afghans, quilts, quaint sayings in picture frames, and embroidered dish towels. There was not a square inch of uncovered wall or floor space. Her house was snug and full—some might describe it as cluttered. My kids loved it all. These visits matched their image of a sweet and quirky Grandma's house, and it held a warm and comfy place in their hearts, which warmed my heart.

One of the mysteries of my mother's house was how, year after year, she produced from a tiny, crowded kitchen, with barely one inch of available counter space, huge meals that fed a dozen people. Two people could not be functional in her kitchen at the same time. Her dishwasher and her refrigerator doors could not both open at the same time without colliding. Finding things in her kitchen was challenging because things were everywhere, and once an item was located, for example, in the refrigerator, there was no place to set it down or do anything with it. Cleaning up after a big meal was a staggering task, there being no place to put a stack of twelve dirty plates, glasses, and a myriad of serving dishes. Of course, there was no place to put leftovers in the refrigerator, either. Only one person could effectively clean up while the rest of us hovered nearby, pretending to help. I often fought the desire to open a window and throw everything outside into the fresh open air and imagine it dematerializing, like Scotty beaming it all up.

After dinner, people would either wander off to some other corner of the small house, sit on the living room floor, or attempt to clean up the kitchen. My mother and the kitchen-hoverers would carry on short snippets of conversation, usually about local happenings in Mom's small town or the weather. Many topics never got broached, such as politics, religion, our childhoods, culture, society, philosophy, personal struggles, or substantive details from any of our lives. This ban on meaningful conversation wore me out; I missed this opportunity to get to know each other a little. But I was also complicit in the superficiality of our time together.

During these years, my mother and my sister, Pat, formed a close-knit relationship. Pat lived in Florida with her second husband, an aloof and condescending man, who allowed her one visit to New Hampshire per year. She and Mom played bridge nearly every day with my mother's widowed friends, often devising elaborate themes and decorations for their parties. We never understood Pat's marriage. She had tried to leave her husband several times. More than once, I put her up in my home, offering temporary refuge and few questions. She always went back to him.

A few years after my father passed away, my brother Peter moved in with my mom. He had trouble keeping a steady job, and we were happy he provided company for her. It seemed like a mutually beneficial arrangement. Peter had severe mood swings. For months he bought and hoarded guitars and began countless home improvement projects. Then he entered a depression and didn't leave the house for months. Because we weren't a family that talked about difficult subjects, his mood swings went unexamined and untreated.

Several years later, Judy and Pat discovered Peter was siphoning money from my mother's bank accounts. Mom lived modestly but comfortably, sustained by funds from social security and a small family inheritance. When they confronted him about it, he angrily deflected and defended, saying he was just consolidating bank accounts, and it was none of their business. Mom didn't notice the funds dwindling, or if she did, she chose to ignore it. When we explained his deception to her, she denied the possibility and defended Peter.

Andy also lived in New Hampshire, a couple of towns away from my mother's small village, where he held an unskilled job in a restaurant. We saw him only on holiday visits when someone drove over to pick him up. He had lost his license years ago for multiple DUIs. Andy was amiable but didn't talk much. Holiday gatherings often numbered around eighteen. It made for a full house.

During one visit, my mother roused Jason and me out of our comfort zones. We had finished dinner and settled into the three seats in the living room, likely preparing to watch a football game or snooze a little, when my mother asked us, "What do you two think about what's happening in the Episcopal Church right now?"

Jason and I exchanged a glance.

Jason stepped in to clarify. "Do you mean the consecration of the first openly gay bishop?"

"Yes. You are Episcopalian. Do you think this is a good thing?"

The tone of her voice made it clear to me there was only one correct perspective on the subject, and it was not the view we held. How should we answer? The last time I checked, Mom still believed AIDS was punishment for living a sinful life.

I began with a vague comment, "I think the most important thing to keep in mind is to let love guide our actions and decisions. Love is the highest value."

"Yes, love is very important. But the Bible clearly says this is not an approved behavior," she countered, with only a little sternness in her voice.

I left further response for Jason, who was much more literate with scripture and theology than I. He could match her verse for verse, concept for concept.

But a Bible verse war was not what happened. All three of us contributed thoughtfully to the conversation, as short as it was. We didn't want to upset her with our heretical, liberal views, yet it was so unexpected and gratifying to engage in conversation with her about something meaningful. I do think she was seeking a discussion and not a soapbox. It would never have happened with my pre-retirement mother, and I was happy to see this evidence of her more expansive life. It was one of the most substantive conversations I had with her. In it, I revealed to her a little bit of who I was at the time. She disapproved, of course, but at least she knew that tiny bit about me.

When our kids were young, my mother and some of my siblings came to our house for Easter. For these visits, I tried to arrange to serve as an LEM (lay Eucharistic minister, or chalice-bearer) at church because I knew it would make my mom happy. In 2005, the last year she was able to make the trip for Easter, after the service, she pulled me aside as we passed in my upstairs hallway.

She said, "I am so happy to see that you have found a spiritual home and are active in the life of the church. You know, when I was pregnant with you, there were some . . ." She hesitated. ". . . complications. We were very worried for a while."

"Really? What kind of complications?" This was the first I had heard of it.

"You were having some difficulties," she continued, as though that explained it fully, "and the doctors were quite concerned."

I listened intently, hoping she'd take the initiative and share something more specific. Was I hesitant to invade her privacy?

"I offered a prayer to the Lord at that moment, saying I

would dedicate your life to His service, if I could, if He would allow you to live. And now, I see that this has come to be. My prayer was answered then and is being answered now because He has received you as His servant. It makes me very happy. I wanted to share that with you."

All I could think to say in response was, "Wow. Thank you for telling me. I didn't know. I'm glad it worked out."

*I'm glad it worked out?* No. How about, *Sit down. Please tell me more. Please tell me how it was for you in that moment, when I lived, and when I was a little girl. What did you do to give me to God? Were you happy with the results back then? How was it for you when I stopped going to church? And please tell me more about the difficulties you had. Was it during my birth? Was I in an incubator? How long was the crisis? What was the nature of the problem? Was your life in danger, too? What was that like for you? Tell me about your concern. Or how about, thank you! Maybe you saved my life. Or at least you tried. Thank you for loving me that much.*

The moment passed, and we went our separate ways in the house. But a small voice from somewhere behind my heart said, *Why didn't I know about this a long time ago? Why now? If we hadn't happened to cross paths in the hallway at that moment, maybe she never would have told me. What else don't I know—about her, me, our family—about anything?*

As a testament to our relationship, neither of us spoke about it again.

We usually celebrated Mom's April birthday at our Easter family gathering. As we approached Mom's ninetieth birthday, my sister Pat called.

"I know you have things you do at your church for Easter, but this is one year your church will just have to do without you. We want to have a big celebration, and you need to be at this party, so plan accordingly. And if you want to help us plan, just let me know," she said as an afterthought.

"Of course," I said, containing my irritation at her bossiness, and her assumption that I didn't have enough judgment to make the right decision about whether to attend or whether I'd be willing to help with the planning. Pat and Judy were unhappy with my infrequent visits and phone calls to my mother. I often sensed their judgment seeping out.

I was uneasy about spending the weekend with my family of origin. This event was more complex than a simple holiday visit, where we drove up and back in a day; but I did everything I could to make the event special for my own family, too. David and Max got haircuts. We received special permission from Max's mother to have him for the whole weekend, which didn't completely turn out that way, but he was there for most of it. Savannah and I bought new dresses. Many planning and preparation emails went back and forth among us three sisters. Our brothers Peter and Andy were not capable of planning anything, and we didn't even try to include them. We'd be happy if they just showed up and stayed sober. We Kinchens participated fully. Max, the extrovert, now in high school, was the videographer, interviewing guests on camera, and David helped. Jason was the photographer, and I was the MC. Savannah, age eleven, went to the microphone and read a sweet message she had written to her grandma.

Ninety years, has it really been that long?
Ninety years, and you're still going strong.

Ninety years has passed us by,
And that's why we're celebrating, wearing a suit and tie.
Ninety years of feeding the birds,
Had so much fun that I can't express words.
Easter eggs hunts and warm turkey dinners,
I'm sure it made us all feel like winners.


It was rare for the entire Fink family, including our few remote cousins, to come together. I was anxious about being with my siblings, worried a sister might silently scold me for some unspoken infraction or for not doing enough, or a brother might pass out drunk or mysteriously disappear.

But when the day came, the family and many guests made toasts, brought gifts, ate, danced, drank, and cut the cake. It all went smoothly, in a contained kind of way. The ninety-year-old birthday girl was pleased, which made me happy. I survived the event, feeling bolstered by my beautiful children and husband, an oasis of joy in a desert of restrained connection.

It saddens me to think how little my mother and I knew about each other. We just never talked about ourselves. Perhaps with the brief exception of the gay bishop topic, I don't remember ever being asked questions, as a child or an adult, that could invite a deeper knowledge of me, and I admit I hadn't much offered it, either. I carried around a fear that whatever I might say would offend her. We were both too entrenched in our safe, familiar patterns to push very far into the world of being vulnerable, exposed, and known to each other.

My mom and I treated each other with gentleness, but there was so much lost potential. She was a purely good-hearted person, almost like we think of saints. She taught me patience and kindness and how to give to others. From my mother, I did not learn intimacy, security, or self-worth. I did not learn how to navigate the world, feel safe, believe in myself, or trust others. I discovered these things through being a mother myself.

The passionate love I had for my children was a life force I had never known before. It filled me, consumed me, and through it I experienced pure joy. Through them I learned intimacy, security, and self-worth, and my deepest desire was that they know these things too. With my children my heart opened, and all my emotions were set free.

In so many ways, being a mother saved me.

## twenty-seven

### SEEING CLEARLY

EVERY MINUTE OF DAVID'S SENIOR YEAR IN HIGH SCHOOL seemed to have heightened illumination for me. I knew this was the homestretch, and he was soon going to walk through that one-way door and into his life, where he would become an adult and no longer need me in the same way. He was going to live somewhere else, where I would no longer see him every day and smell his unique Davidness. I would not know when he was happy or sad or in trouble, or proud of himself. Although I had been gearing up for this his entire life, the nearness of the change overwhelmed me. Max had taken a gap year in Israel before college, and Jason and I, as well as Max, were better prepared for his college drop-off. He was ready to engage with the college chapter of his life, and was comfortable moving to New York City.

The college drop-off experience with David was agonizing. After settling him into his dorm room, David went off to an evening meeting, and Jason and I checked into our hotel room for the night. The next day we were to meet for lunch, then say our goodbyes. The minute I saw David walk across the shady green campus to meet us for lunch, the pit in my stomach grew to watermelon size. Just seeing him from across the distance of a football field, I knew all was not well with him. He greeted us and tried to smile. We hugged, slapped him on the back in an upbeat manner, and asked how things were.

He shrugged ever so slightly, almost wincing, and said, "I don't know. I don't know what to think."

With a little prodding, he added, "It wasn't so great last night. Everyone on our floor met, and we played this 'getting to know you' game. That was all right. I don't know. People here seem really different from me. I'm not sure this is the right place for me."

The watermelon gained twenty or thirty pounds. "In what ways are they different?" I asked.

"I don't know. It's hard to say exactly. I just didn't see anyone who was like my friends from home or like me. Can we go somewhere to eat lunch? Can we leave this campus?"

"I noticed a sandwich shop a few blocks away," Jason said, ever the resourceful one in moments like this.

David hardly ate. My stomach hurt.

Back on campus, we took our last photos, hugged our remaining goodbyes, and waved our final farewells. David looked so sad yet so brave; it broke my heart. Tears trickled from behind my lids. He slowly climbed up the steps, and just before going in the door, he gave us one last look and wave, and then he was gone.

This moment was the accumulation of eighteen years of loving this child, caretaking, guiding, worrying, praying, and holding him in my heart. No longer needing to appear strong, I buried my head in Jason's shoulder and started to weep. He wrapped his arms around me and murmured some sweet things I cannot remember now, but he was perfect, of course. Jason was born to comfort those he loves.

❧

David made it through college, struggled, and also thrived. So did I. I learned I could let go of raising him, but never of loving him with searing fierceness and an overflowing heart.

Friends with daughters told me raising girls was much more difficult than boys. This was not my experience; Savannah was friendly, sweet, smart, and charming. She and I were close her whole childhood. But somewhere in late middle school, things between us changed. Exactly as she was supposed to do, my beautiful daughter exchanged me for a new and improved model—her friends.

On cue, she directed her attention toward her growing independence and definition of who she was. Even though I understood, I missed her. I held the candle in the window for her, as I always will. Her face was outward-focused, and my job was to keep the rest of her world steady and be there when she needed me.

The candle I held in the window brought her home to me sooner than either of us expected. During her sophomore year of high school, her well-put-together life and sense of self unraveled. Conflict arose among Savannah's friends, and they put her in the middle to establish peace. School was an academic pressure-cooker and some friends started hurting themselves. One attempted suicide. They sought refuge in Savannah's steadiness and kindness. She worried constantly and held herself responsible for other people's safety and well-being.

This worrying ruled her life. She could not focus, study, or eat, and it left her weeping in pain and turmoil. She developed full-blown panic attacks, which scared her to the core. To her credit and my great relief, Savannah reached for me through all this. She wanted me nearby, so some days I worked from home so I could physically be in the same room with her.

Savannah worried about everything . . . about getting phone calls from one of the girls, about not getting phone calls, about what they said, about what they did not say, and about whether someone would hurt themselves. She worried about the next school year, the summer, being home, being away, whether she would know the right thing to say, and whether any of them would remain friends into the next day. She worried about losing Jason and me and about not being able to fix things. She worried most about all the worrying she was doing and who she had become.

Clearly, something had to be done. Savannah began seeing my therapist, Patricia, and in time, she gained perspective. She learned techniques to manage the panic. She learned she was growing, and although life would not always be the same, it would still be good in its differentness. Savannah was moving from the innocence of childhood into the complexity of her approaching adulthood. It was disorienting, yet she remained her beautiful, thoughtful, kind, open self through it all and listened, learned, and soaked in everything, eager to live life to its fullest, just as she had from the moment of her exuberant birth.

Savannah knew she did not have to do it alone. She felt loved and held by us, and she had a place to go to share her worries and get guidance. She was safe, with many resources, all pulling for her. Jason and I loved her and believed in her, and would walk with her to the exact degree she needed.

She redeemed me by including me in this part of her journey, giving me the chance to offer her everything I never received when I was her age. No matter what life brings, she will have a strong attachment to me, and I will always do everything I can to keep her safe, loved, known, and supported.

I have learned also to do this for the young girl who lives inside me. I cannot rewrite my inner child's history, but I can provide the care, attention, parenting, love, and safety net she didn't have back then. Because she lives in me still, my adult self can offer her all those things, so she no longer has to run my life out of her fear and isolation. What sweet redemption!

The first time Jason and I went to Sanibel Island on the Gulf Coast of Florida, it was back when we were recently married, and I was pregnant with David. Sanibel immediately enchanted me; it was green, colorful, warm, and peaceful—welcoming. The sun warmed my skin, and the beach was full of troves of small, perfectly shaped shells of pink, purple, rose, and white. I couldn't collect enough of them.

Since then, our family has returned to Sanibel Island almost every year, seeking rest and warmth from the relentless Massachusetts winters. Some years we had friends come with us. These were happy, deeply satisfying times together as a family.

Every one of us feels Sanibel is our home away from home and holds it in a treasured place in our hearts.

When the kids were little, they spent hours building sandcastles, roadways, and small villages by the shore. We rode bikes all over the island on its eleven miles of wide, kid-friendly trails. We started with baby carriers on the back of our bikes, then graduated to trail-a-bikes hitched to the back and pulled behind one of our bikes. Then each of the kids, one by one, moved to their own bikes, and we became a fleet of five, some of us a little shakier and wobblier along the path than others, and one mother taking up the rear, praying like mad.

When we eventually bought a condo there, in 2008, it sealed our Sanibel times together for years to come. In this condo of ours, I first realized on a physical level how far I had come in my work toward recovery and health. On one visit, Jason, Max, and Savannah left a few days before I did so I could spend some extra time in the sun and do some writing, a rare treat for me. We all woke up before dawn. I drove them to the airport and was back at the condo before 9:00 a.m. It was quiet and empty. I saw a shoebox from a pair of sandals we bought for David the last time he was with us in Sanibel, and I nearly wept at the sight because he was so far away from me at college.

These are my children, and I hold them so deep into my soul. And Jason is part of my very fiber.

They were gone, and I was alone. I was unexpectedly bereft. *Who would have thought I'd miss them so much?* I said to myself. *It is just a few days, and there is no harm involved in any way.* I appreciated how utterly happy I was to have Jason and our three children in my life, and how unreservedly empty it would be without them. For all the ways that I wasn't securely attached to my family of origin, I was wholly bonded to this family of mine, a connection I could see, feel, name, and adore. They were in my heart and mind and soul, unlike anything I had known before.

One winter night, I was at a sleepover at my friend Diane's, who was forever connecting people from her various circles and creating occasions for both deep conversation and a lot of laughter. I didn't know all the women. They were friends of Diane, and this was my first time attending one of her sleepovers. We spent the night each sharing an update from our lives—challenges and celebrations.

When my turn came around, it was late into the night, and we were already nestled in our sleeping bags. I introduced the story of my recent Lasik eye surgery, an action I finally took after years of living with my worry about the catastrophe that would separate me from my glasses and contact lenses, rendering me unable to navigate life—literally.

"I'm so curious about Lasik surgery. Tell us about it," a couple of women urged.

"I was really nervous about it," I said. "I knew it involved scalpels on the eyeballs. Of course, they never used these words. I'm paraphrasing. They assured me it was painless."

"That sounds so creepy! You were brave. I probably would have bolted," confessed one woman.

I loved telling this story because it is a story of triumph—not just braving squeamishness about the procedure but also taking agency for my own well-being.

I continued, "I shuffled off into the operating room and looked back at Jason one last time. Who knew how I'd come out of this? Maybe I'd be blind. I was pretty freaked out, but I just put one foot in front of the other. The doctor said, 'We're going to help keep your eyes open with this little brace, is that all right? I will be happier if you don't blink during the procedure. You won't feel a thing.' I told him I'd do anything he asked because I wanted him to be *really* happy. This doc was now my best friend, and I had to trust him!"

The ladies laughed.

"I braced myself and tried to go with the flow. I could hear a machine clicking while the drill was in my eye. The assistant counted: 5-4-3-2-1, then the doctor said, 'Okay, that's it.' I think it took about thirty seconds. But who knows for sure because I had Valium-brain. Then they did the same thing to the other eye. When he finished, they put some eye patches with slits in them, like slotted spoons, over my eyes and helped me sit up. Even through the slotted spoons, my vision was crystal clear!"

"Hurray!" one of the ladies said from her sleeping bag. "When you took off the slotted spoons, what was it like? Did it start to hurt?"

"When I took them off later that day, I could see everything clearly, but my eyes felt like they had sand in them. But it didn't hurt. About two days later, the sand was gone, and I could see perfectly! Now I can swim in the ocean and see everyone on the shore. I can drive and read the signs. I can see the alarm clock when I wake up in the morning and do everything that requires good distance vision. It's flawless. I no longer have to live in dread of some disaster where I lose my glasses and can't function. Now my chances of survival are much greater. On some existential level, after this surgery, I feel like I finally have a physical place in this world, and I'm free to move about my life."

One wise woman spoke out of the darkness, warm humor in her voice. "So you can see clearly now?"

"Yes. Yes, I can." I smiled at the metaphor for this new me, whom I had loved and birthed into a fuller, freer self who *could* see so much more clearly now.

## twenty-eight

### OLD FAMILY DYSFUNCTION

EVEN AS MY CHILDREN GOT OLDER, I WAS STILL WARY OF SPENDING time with my family of origin for fear of being dragged back into the dynamic of superficiality and non-connectedness that damaged me. The years I spent in deep therapy helped me see the effects my childhood isolation and absentee parenting had on my life. I rarely spoke with my siblings, and I didn't call my mother very often, except to arrange an infrequent visit. This lack of connection was my choice. My sister, Judy, let me know how I disappointed my mother (or *her*) by my distance, but it was what I believed I had to do for my health and emotional well-being. Now, I was seeing my whole family dynamic through clearer eyes.

Then a crisis occurred that pulled me back in. My "little" brother, Andy, broke his back in an alcoholic tumble down a flight of stairs. He lived one town over from my mother in a one room hovel and worked part-time in a restaurant. After taking this fall, he moved into my mother's house for weeks of recovery. They were struggling with his medical bills, so I offered to help him file Medicaid forms, and while up there, to take him to doctor's appointments. These tasks were something neither Andy, my mother, nor Peter, who still lived in my mother's house, could navigate. Since I lived one state away, I offered to help. Andy had detoxed in the hospital after the fall, and I used our car rides to doctor appointments as an opportunity to suggest this could be a new start for him. He agreed. I located nearby AA programs for him to join.

After Andy's summer of healing, Judy invited him to her house in Florida for a little vacation before he started back at work. Andy had never traveled outside of New Hampshire. Alone in her house while she went to work, Andy took up drinking again. When Judy confronted him, he told her he wanted to go back to his life of "being a bum." When he became verbally abusive and physically threatening, Judy decided he must return to New Hampshire immediately.

The problem was, once she put him on a plane to Boston, he had no way to get to his place in New Hampshire, a two-and-a-half-hour drive from the airport. Andy didn't have a license or credit card. He didn't know how to take a bus or navigate an airport on his own. Pat intervened and called me. It was two days before I was scheduled to fly to Honduras for work.

"Someone needs to pick Andy up at the airport and drive him to New Hampshire," she said matter-of-factly. "Since Judy and I are here in Florida, and you are there in Boston, it's on you to do this." Pat was not one for diplomacy. The disdain in her voice was palpable; I knew she judged me, the neglectful sister and daughter. The same sister, she failed to note, who made several trips over that summer to file insurance claims, drive to appointments, and research various support systems.

"He can take a bus. He's a grown man, I'm sure he can figure that out, or he can ask people to help him," I countered, restraining my anger.

"You know full well Andy can't navigate an airport or bus system. You will have to drive him."

"Pat, I can't do that. I'm about to leave the country. Besides, even if I were here, I wouldn't do it. I worked hard to help Andy get back on the road to health and recovery. But if he's going to start drinking again, I'm not going to help him."

Silence. "Well, get Jason to do it, then."

"No, I won't ask Jason to do it, either. I don't want to enable Andy to return to his old ways; he'll kill himself. If he wants to do that, it's his choice and I can't stop him, but I won't help him, either." It took all my resolve not to give in and try to find a solution.

"Oh. Well, never mind then. It's clear this family cannot depend on you for anything. Thanks a lot for what you did for Andy, but we will handle this, and everything from now on. Without you. Tell me this. What did Mother ever do to deserve a daughter like you? And don't bother to call back. Ever. I won't take your call."

She hung up. I sagged in my chair. Then I shot out of my office, went outside, and nearly race-walked around the block over and over, blood pumping, heart racing. I had never been spoken to by anybody like that—much less a sister. I walked until I was calm enough to speak, then slowly returned to my office. I called Jason.

"Are you kidding me?" he nearly shouted. "She has nerve. After all you did for Andy, she does this? You are right not to pick him up, and I support you one hundred percent. If he wants to go back to his alcoholic life, that's his choice, but you don't have to help him get there. I won't, either. That's just like your family to hide their heads and pretend nothing is wrong."

"I wonder if I'm being mean, though. Or too stubborn." I waffled.

"No, you have upset the system, and they have no idea

how to handle it. Good for you! Stay strong! I'm on your side."

The whole thing was excruciating. Challenging my family dynamic was highly uncomfortable, and my sister's words stabbed me. But Jason's support and his firmness reassured me. Jason and I each emailed Pat to explain our position in more detail. She never responded. I called Judy to find out if she, too, was banishing me.

"No, I'm just disappointed that you won't help because it means I have to take time off from work, fly up with him, and then drive Andy to his house myself. But it's okay. What time did this exchange take place? If it was late in the day, you know Pat probably had one too many herself, and you know how she can get. Give her a little time, then call her back. I'm sure she'll forgive you."

## *twenty-nine*

## DEATH OF MY MOTHER

PERHAPS EVERYONE HAS A COMPLICATED RELATIONSHIP WITH their mother. How could we not? Motherhood is one of the most significant universal influences we know. Whether our mothers were wonderful, wise, and nurturing, or whether they were mean, indifferent, or troubled, they have an enormous impact on us.

Over time, I softened my distancing stance from my family of origin. However, Pat still disowned me, and I rarely spoke with Pete or Andy, leaving Judy as my primary connection with the family. I tried to respond to Judy's request that I call Mom more. I cared about them both, so I set an alarm in my calendar to call every Sunday, but I only succeeded in making the call about once or twice a month. One Sunday, our conversation seemed more stilted than usual, and Mom's voice sounded just a little odd, a little slower, and almost a little . . . slurred? It was just a vague impression, so I let it go. Maybe she had had an extra amount of her daily scotch and water. Later that day, Judy called to talk about her Sunday call with Mom.

"Did you notice anything different about Mom when you talked to her? Did she sound okay to you?" I asked her.

"Actually, I was going to say something to you. Yes, she sounded kind of odd, like tired or tipsy. She wasn't really tracking our conversation well."

"Yes! Exactly the same thing happened to me."

"I'll call Pat and see if she's talked with Mom today," Judy said.

Pat reported a similar experience. That settled it. I called Mom back, wanting to hear her speak again, and to talk with Peter to see if he noticed anything. Nothing had changed. Peter still "ran" everything, and Mom allowed it.

Some man who was not my brother answered the phone.

"I'd like to speak with my mom. Could you put her on the phone?"

"She's not available," he said.

"Why not?" I had just spoken with her a couple of hours ago.

"Well, she's sleeping."

"Can I speak with Peter?"

"He's not here."

"And who are you? What are you doing there?"

"I'm a friend of Peter's, and I'm just staying here, you know, keeping an eye on your mom while he's out playing in a show."

"Well, I am a little worried about my mother. She didn't sound quite right when my sisters and I spoke with her earlier. Is she okay?"

"Oh, yeah, yeah. She's okay, just napping. You know."

"When will Peter be back?"

"Not until late."

Judy and I conferred about this odd situation and decided something was *not* right. Jason and I both took the day off from work and drove up to New Hampshire the next morning to check things out. We were very uneasy.

When we arrived, my mother was sitting at the dining room table, staring down at a plate of scrambled eggs.

"Hi, Mom! How are you feeling today?"

At that, she raised her head and said with little emotion, "Hello, dear. It's so nice to see you." For me to appear out of the blue was highly unusual, so her mild reply concerned me right away.

Peter jumped up, impatient, exasperation in his voice. "She's just not eating! She's not eating a damn thing. It's like she's a retarded person!"

This was not a way my family *ever* referred to someone, and I was stung by the word's offensiveness. I walked over to Mom and saw her right arm lying limp in her lap, her mouth drooping to one side. Jason saw the same thing.

We pulled Peter into the next room, and I practically hissed, "Peter, she's had a stroke!"

"No, no, she hasn't. She's just tired."

"Are you kidding? We need to get her to the doctor right away!"

"I don't think that's necessary. I'm telling you, she's just tired. But do what you want."

When I called her family doctor, Dr. Wolcott, he said to bring her down right away. Jason and I put her into our car, and Peter followed behind us in his car, which I thought was a little odd, but what the heck. *He is odd.*

We guided her into Dr. Wolcott's office. She was quiet and compliant. He was gentle with her and asked her some questions, which she answered without concern.

"Yes, I cannot move this arm very well today. I don't know why."

He spent about three minutes with Mom before pulling Jason and me out of the room. Peter had not arrived yet.

"She's had a mild stroke. We need to get her to the hospital now so we can examine her more thoroughly. It's good that you brought her in."

The gravity of the situation hit me, and Jason and I moved into efficient emergency mode. Peter finally arrived, just as we were getting ready to leave for the hospital, and we explained Dr. Wolcott's diagnosis. Peter muttered and shook his head, like he disagreed with the whole situation. Jason and I bundled her into our car and drove quickly but carefully to the hospital. Peter again followed behind in his car.

The doctors ran tests while Jason and I stayed in the waiting room. The results confirmed a mild heart attack and stroke. When we went in to see her, Mom was doing much better; she seemed much more aware of her surroundings and her situation. Peter still had not arrived.

"They tell me I've had a mild stroke. I had no idea. I'd like to go home now," Mom said when she saw us.

The doctors and nurses agreed to send her home, saying she would likely recover more and more each day and gradually resume her usual activities. Mom told us Peter had previously hired a caretaker named JoLene to help look after her and that by now, she'd be at the house to start her shift. We breathed a sigh of relief when we met her and were comfortable leaving Mom at home with someone kind and competent. We waited a while for Peter to appear, but he never did, so we left Mom with JoLene and drove home. Over the next few days, Mom seemed to be more herself.

A few weeks later, Judy called. "Mother's had another stroke, and she's in the hospital in a coma. I've been up here visiting the last few days, and earlier today she fainted, and I called the ambulance. I'm at the hospital now. Do you think you can come up here? I know it's short notice, but please come as soon as you can. I don't know what will happen. Peter is nowhere around." I heard Judy's fear and urgency, and shared it. I left work immediately and drove the two-and-a-half hours up to New Hampshire. Judy sat in the hospital's waiting room.

"Thank you for coming so quickly." Judy sounded okay, but the stress was in her face.

"I made good time. Is there any update? How are you doing?"

"I'm hanging in there. Still no sign of Peter, but I don't want to talk about that. Mother is in a coma. Dr. Wolcott doesn't know whether she'll come out of it on her own or not, but it's likely she may not. She is ninety-six, after all. I'll tell the nurse that you're here. Dr. Wolcott was waiting for us to be together before talking to me further."

"Can I see her?" I asked, hesitant to see her in such a fragile state.

"Yes, she is just inside. We need the nurse to let us in."

She was so fragile and tiny, lying in the thin hospital bed. Her eyes were closed, and her face looked stressed, not peaceful or even neutral. Maybe I was projecting. Her brown hair, usually coiffed and tidy, was in disarray around her head, the gray roots well established. She appeared like herself and yet not herself. Fear and tenderness flooded my heart.

Dr. Wolcott came over to the bed and said, "She's a trooper. Her vital signs are strong. Let's go into the room just over there, and we can talk."

As we attempted to settle into a small family conference room, which tried to convey a comfortable atmosphere but filled me with terror, Dr. Wolcott gave us the grave prognosis.

"As I said, her vital signs are strong at the moment, but she isn't responsive to any sounds or other simple attempts to wake her up. There is evidence that she's now had a series of strokes, so I am not confident that she will wake up on her own." He looked thoughtfully at us as we absorbed this news, then suggested, "We have a nice hospice room right here in the hospital. Your mom will receive around-the-clock care, she will be made comfortable, and there is room for the two of you to sleep near her if you'd like to. I think this is a much better option than trying to take her home. It would be difficult to keep her comfortable there." He slowly stood. "I'll let the two of you talk it over. You can stay right here until you're ready." Crossing the room, he gently closed the door behind him.

"Wow. I didn't expect this. Hospice?"

Judy looked stricken. "No, this is so sudden."

She muttered, "Peter is not here to make this decision with us. I don't know where he is. I've been up here for a week, and I haven't seen him at all. Pat's away on a cruise, and I don't know how to reach her. Andy is . . . can't help. This decision is up to the two of us."

I took a deep breath, feeling the gravity of the moment.

"I know Mom always said she wanted to die at home, but here they know how to take care of her better than we can at her house. We can stay in the hospice room with her. Let's just decide that." I wanted to ease Judy's palpable frustration with Peter and focus on what was next.

"I agree. That's best." She sighed.

Judy and I settled in together. We brought some things from Mom's house—plants, a blanket, familiar items from her bedside table—and set them up in the hospice room. JoLene came to visit, but Judy and I slept in the room. We planned to be there day and night, no matter how long.

Doctors and hospice nurses came and went from the hospice room to tend to Mom. They were lovely and kind and answered our questions with honest compassion. They rubbed down her body—oh my, how thin she was, her skin sagging on her skeleton. They were comforting to me, too. Judy and I took turns sitting on Mom's bed, holding her hands, and saying soft things. Judy did more of this than I did. I was beyond out of my comfort zone. I wondered whether Mom could tell we were there and whether some part of her heard our murmurings. I wondered whether she knew she was dying. I reflected on the recent unexpected death of Jason's father, Al. He had gone into the hospital for some routine pulmonary tests and died without warning. We Kinchens were still reeling from the shock of our loss. Now mortality seemed so close, so real.

During these hospice days and nights, Judy and I talked. We perused old photos of our childhood home and church and tried to remember things from those days. We talked about our kids. We must have eaten food, but I don't remember. Judy lent me some of the clothes from her suitcase. It was sweet, and it was challenging. Judy and I had not spent time together or felt close for a very long time.

In the hospice room, I was very disoriented. My mother was dying in front of me. I was thrust into the heart of my family of origin, a family where I never quite belonged, and in more recent years, didn't want to belong. It sounded so harsh, but that family harmed me—not intentionally, I know, but they were emotionally unsafe to me. My time with Judy was poignant. I couldn't fully embrace her or the situation, but I tried.

Judy sometimes laid on the bed next to Mom, held her

hand, and spoke softly in her ear. Sadly, I could not do the same. Lying next to my mother felt foreign; I didn't know how to connect with her. I never had.

The next day a friend of Andy's, whom we'd never met, brought him by to see Mom. Andy reeked of cigarettes, and was shaking more than he usually did, likely coming off another bender.

"Can I speak to her?" Andy looked to us for reassurance. We nodded, and he crept over to her bedside.

"Thanks for everything, Mom." He didn't touch her, but bent his head and stood quietly for a moment.

He left her bedside, whispering to us, "Do you think she heard me?"

So tender, so Andy. He lingered a few minutes with us in the room. Andy was a sweetheart caught in a sad and troubled body. He was so compromised, it was heartbreaking. I appreciated that he wanted to come and say goodbye, and I was moved by how emotionally difficult this was for him, but he did it anyway.

Peter was gone. No one saw him or heard from him, and no one knew where he was. He had not come to visit.

I sent an email to people I thought might want to know what was going on with me—friends, Jason's family, people from Epiphany, and El Hogar. I was shocked by the outpouring of love and support I received back. Receiving these responses was a moment of grace for me, to see people show their love and support when it was most needed. *My* people showed this to *me*. So unexpected. So lovely.

On the third day, at 3:00 a.m., the hospice nurse woke us up and said in the kindest voice possible, "Your mother has passed."

Such gentle words. *Your mother has passed.*

Judy and I went to her bedside and spent a moment in silence. Judy cried and stroked Mom's forehead. I put my hand on her arm. Judy called JoLene, who came right away. We three sat with her for a while as the muted early morning light kissed the room with softness.

Then, without warning, I longed to leave, go home, be with Jason, and be in my own home.

I returned to New Hampshire a couple of days before the funeral service. A large dinner was planned at a nearby restaurant for all the family members present. This gathering was the first contact I would have with Pat since she disowned me, and I was very apprehensive. I decided to take the classic Fink approach and act like the estrangement never happened, while still being prepared to confront it if it came up. Pat apparently decided the same thing. We found ourselves sitting next to each other at dinner. We chatted amiably and never mentioned it. I guess neither of us had the heart to face what was painful between us.

We sisters also had to decide about Peter, who had disappeared and never resurfaced since the day Mom went to the hospital that last time. We were worried about his mental stability. We never found any trace of the money he stole. Would he show up at the funeral service, crash through the doors in an agitated and potentially crazed state, and disrupt the entire observance? We just didn't know what he was capable of, so we hired a police detail to stand discreetly at the back of the church to be on the lookout. Peter did not appear, and we never saw him again.

Moments before the service began, I turned toward the back of the church to check that the police were in place, and I saw Thomas, the new priest at our church, walking toward me. I never expected him to drive two and a half hours to attend the service of a woman he'd never met. I was so surprised and moved by this gesture of love that I ran down the aisle to meet him and fell into his arms.

"Oh my God! I didn't expect you to come here today! You had a church service to lead this morning. You are so, so kind. And thoughtful. I can't thank you enough!" I babbled, overcome with emotion.

In true Thomas fashion, he said, "Of course, I was going to come to your mother's service. How could I not? I am going to sit right here, not far behind you."

I had just gathered myself from this embrace when I saw my El Hogar colleague and friend, Phillip. Another person I had no idea would take half his Sunday to make the journey from Boston. I recognized their gestures as love—for me. They came because they loved me. I never understood how much it might mean to someone who has lost a family member to have a friend show their love and support. How ironic that through the passing of my mother, to whom I was not attached, I experienced the attachment possible in adult friendships.

*thirty*

---

## DEATH OF MY SISTER AND BROTHER

PAT SEEMED PERFECTLY FINE TO US AT MOM'S FUNERAL. SHE gave a lovely eulogy, which revealed a truth about my mother few people knew, and I was proud to hear her words.

"My mother was a woman of strength, courage, and resilience. She did not have an easy life. She lost her only sibling when she was a young child, and then lost her mother to grief, depression, and illness. Just after marrying our father, her widowed father became seriously ill and moved in with my parents so Mother could care for him until he passed away. She gave up her dream of becoming a nurse and was a dutiful and faithful minister's wife. She bore five children and suffered five miscarriages, one between each of my siblings. She lived through the Depression, she lived with poverty, and through it all, she lived with kindness and dignity. She has been a role model in my life, and I wanted you all to know about this side of Eleanor Fink. Rest in peace, Mother!"

But Pat wasn't perfectly fine. No one knew at the time, not even she, that she had pancreatic cancer. We learned of it in the late spring of 2013, just a few months after we buried our mother.

Keeping with recent tradition, I learned about Pat's prognosis through a phone call from Judy.

"Hey Liz, sorry to bother you at work. Can you talk a minute?"

"Yes, of course. What's up?" I wanted to cut to the chase. Despite her casual words, I didn't think she was calling to chat, and I braced myself for bad news.

"It's about Pat. She has cancer. Pancreatic cancer."

"Oh my God," My mouth went instantly dry, and my heartbeat echoed in my ears. "Oh, Judy. This is terrible. I am so sorry to hear this. Tell me what you know, please."

"She was having stomach pains and losing weight, so she went to see her doctor. Some tests immediately showed the cancer and it was already advanced. Liz, she doesn't have long to live. Maybe two months."

During the years of our estrangement, Pat and I never spoke, didn't send Christmas cards, and I carried a rock in my heart. Then, when Mom died, and we simply pretended our rift never happened, the rock lightened a little. Just a few months later, this death sentence came. Estrangement, reconciliation, now death.

I knew I had to see her one last time. I also knew before I made that farewell trip (none of us, of course, named it as such, although we all knew what it was) I needed to say some things to my sister. Neither of us would be able to tolerate my saying them face to face, so I wrote her a letter with some memories and thoughts I might have said in a eulogy.

"I loved those weekends as a preteen when I was your mother's helper and babysat for Chris and Donna. Sharing your young family with me back then was an act of generosity to a lonely kid. I remember your kindness toward Judy when she needed a refuge and lived in your basement for a while and toward Pete when he was young and depressed. Your saying the right things at

Mom's funeral service, so everyone could know her more deeply, was a gift to us all. I'm sorry for the rift that kept us apart these recent years. How ironic that the brief and sad time we spent together just a few months ago provided the venue, unfortunate as the occasion was, to move past it. What kept us apart doesn't seem very relevant anymore. You deserve to know that you are loved and admired, and have made an enormous difference to the people in your life. You will be missed, and the world a less bright place for your absence."

I sent off the letter, and a couple of weeks later, Judy and I went to visit her. Other than the yellow tinge of her jaundiced skin, Pat looked pretty great. She wore a flamboyant, multi-colored muumuu and a wide-brimmed hat. Her nails were painted ruby red, and her hair was cut and styled, as always, makeup perfect around her yellow eyes. Pat didn't mention my letter all day. We three sisters went to the beach, waded in the water, and Pat had her club deliver lunch to our beach chairs. We talked and reminisced a little.

It was important to me that my thoughts, feelings, and words reach her, but when I finally brought it up, I tried to sound neutral, casual even. "Pat, did you receive a letter from me in the mail? I just want to be sure you got it."

"Yes, thank you. I did receive it, and it was lovely. Thank you. I shared it with Chris and Donna and Judy. I hope that is all right with you."

"Of course, it is," I said.

That was all we said about it. I took it as a compliment that Pat shared it with those closest to her. At later points in time, they each told me they appreciated my saying those things to her.

At the end of the afternoon, we hugged on her front doorstep, and Judy and I climbed into my rental car. As we backed out of her driveway, I saw Pat standing there in her colorful muumuu. She waved, and I waved back at her.

I knew it would be the last time I would see her.

On a late spring day two years after Pat's death, Judy, Andy, and I spread the ashes of my brother Peter into the Gale River in New Hampshire.

The day of the ashes began months prior, when Judy (again) shared with me the unexpected news that Peter had died in his sleep. We didn't know where he was living or what he was doing. We lost touch three years ago, after he disappeared when Mom died, never saying goodbye to the mother he lived with for most of his sixty-five years of life. Or to any of his siblings.

Because Peter and Andy shared some mutual connections, Andy received a call saying the police discovered Peter's body in his bed at a New Hampshire campground where he was living. We learned nothing about his life situation nor the circumstances of his death, other than there was no apparent cause of death, so they called it a heart attack. I never saw the toxicology report that was rumored to exist somewhere. At first, I wanted to see the report, for a sense of closure and a small view into who he might have been when he left this life. He was an alcoholic, and I knew he had been friends with drug users, so it would be no surprise if this led to his end. But over time, this curiosity lessened.

The local funeral parlor held Peter's ashes because he died

in the winter when the ground was frozen. We didn't plan a service because we didn't know anyone who might have come, other than Judy, Andy, and me. When spring came, the funeral parlor notified Judy it was time to claim his ashes.

Judy and I drove to New Hampshire together. We collected Peter from the funeral parlor in his square, cardboard box. We discussed where to scatter him. In the river behind Mom's house? On a nearby mountain? In a lake? We didn't know. When Judy and I picked up Andy at the restaurant where he worked for twenty years as a food preparer, we had the ashes but still no plan. We hoped Andy could suggest something, being more familiar with the area. But he had no ideas, either. We noticed a river ran through the woods at the back end of the tavern parking lot.

"Andy, what do you think of spreading his ashes in the river right over there? Would you mind? Would you be reminded of Peter every time you came to work? Would that bum you out?" Judy chuckled, as though making a small joke. Peter and Andy never got along well, so it was an honest question.

"Nah. That's fine with me. It's right here. Convenient, right?" He laughed a little. "It's okay."

Judy, Andy, and I found a spot a few paces away from the parking lot and climbed down the riverbank over some rocks and roots. Judy wrestled the plastic bag open with a pocketknife, and abruptly, Peter's ashes cascaded into the water and stayed there clumped on the riverbed just below where we perched.

Andy sounded concerned. "Are those ashes just going to stay there now?" Seeing them stuck to the riverbed as though cemented to the spot was a little alarming.

"No, the river will eventually wash them away with the current," I assured him, feeling his discomfort.

"Does anyone want to say something?" Judy questioned. There was a long, uncomfortable pause.

I simply said, "Go in peace."

Judy tried to add some lightness. "I hope you get to heaven before the devil catches you!"

"See-ya, bro," Andy said.

Afterward, at lunch, Andy impressed us with the four alcoholic beverages he downed in short order while eating no food. These drinks had odd local names, one of which was AMF, which Andy told us stood for, "adios, motherfucker." The implication was to just how intoxicated one might get from drinking it, or for Andy, maybe it reflected his attitude toward his brother.

Andy's whole life consisted of his job and his free time spent drinking in this small tourist town in northern New Hampshire. He did not travel, read, use the Internet, go to movies, or watch TV shows, and he lived alone. What, then, could we talk about? I asked him about his job.

"It's good." Andy shrugged. He was a man of few words, bedraggled and thin, with brown teeth. The smell of stale cigarette smoke and alcohol wafted across the table. But he was sociable.

During our short walk through the town on the way to lunch, I noticed several people said hello to him, and he introduced us to a friendly fellow on the street.

"It seems people in this town know you. That must be a nice part of living in a small town," I said.

"Yeah, it's a good thing and a bad thing. Depends on what you're doing. But, yeah, it's mostly good."

He didn't drive and couldn't manage to purchase a car or navigate the DMV, even if he could reinstate his license, so he walked everywhere. Twenty years of this, as well as having some drinking buddies, probably led to knowing people. Andy used the money he earned at the restaurant for his "recreational use" (his words) and Mom's small inheritance to pay his rent and other bills. Actually, Judy paid the bills for him out of an account set up for his inheritance money. She wrote the monthly checks herself and mailed them off.

After lunch, both liquid and solid, we parted ways.

"Thanks for including me," Andy said several times, "and for driving up here to deal with Peter."

We said goodbye and watched as he walked back to his restaurant. His workday was over, but not his drinking. A lump of sadness settled in my stomach, watching him disappear into the building, as I tried to imagine his life.

Of my original family of seven, two parents and five kids, three of us remain today—Judy, Andy, and myself. Each person, each story, could fill books. I know so little about the books of my family members. Most of them are mysteries to me and always will be. I can't begin to imagine my stoic mother's story, with her ten pregnancies and five miscarriages, or what demons must have lived inside my sweet-hearted alcoholic father, who barely knew my name, or so it seemed to me. Pat, rebellious and strong yet perplexingly committed to a man who seemed to have no love. My troubled and manipulative brother, Peter, who was both companion and thief to our widowed mother in her elder years. What went on inside him was unfathomable. And my two remaining siblings . . . Judy, full of energy and enabling protection of those she loves, and Andy, so simple and so lost, another life-long alcoholic.

The nature of family is that bonds run deep, and I found I have love for them all, especially Judy. Other families taught me real familial attachment, though. Judy Weil back in high school,

Adam's and Jason's parents, and primarily the family Jason and I created together. Our family—Jason, Max, David, Savannah, and me, too—stands in brilliant contrast to my family of origin.

Still, my lifelong struggle to find genuine love, home, and family continued to have peaks and valleys.

# thirty-one

## RAPE IS NOT LOVE

SANDWICHED AMONG THIS STRING OF DEATHS, JASON AND I took a short trip to Mexico to rest and give us time to tend to our relationship and create space for closeness. On this trip, another kind of death occurred when, on the last night, our old dynamic emerged in sweeping force. I had a clumsy response to his request for greater intimacy between us, which triggered his anger. His anger triggered in me my old reaction of withdrawal. It was so familiar and so wearying to me. To Jason, however, it was not wearying. It was infuriating.

We fought. We were not at our best. I was devastated, frightened, and lost. My body was so heavy, my shoulders sagged, and it was hard to breathe. *How can we go from all these lovely days together and end up like this? What about all that time in Patricia's office, coming to understand each other better? Was it for nothing?*

This event was a watershed for Jason. It nearly broke us. He saw it as his last failed attempt to reach out to me. Now, he was done. Once home, he was so sad, dejected, and withdrawn.

After several days of this, I rallied my courage and asked tentatively, "How are you? What can I do? What can we do to make this better?"

"I don't know. I'm out of ideas. I am out of willingness to

try to reach you anymore. I won't do it. If you want this relationship, you will have to come after me to get it. I am out of gas."

I was torn apart. I seemed incapable of getting this relationship right. I despaired about what to do.

We spent the next several tense and sad months in this atmosphere. For the first time, I began to wonder if we could survive this crisis. Without Jason pouring his energy and belief into the system, we floundered. I was floundering. We worked hard in Patricia's office. She suggested we see someone she knew who specialized in sex therapy and had great success working with women with trauma histories.

Sessions with Aline—who was direct, no-nonsense, and bold, a big difference from Patricia's gentle, quiet approach— were emotionally intense. Working so deeply with what was holding me back was often overwhelming. But we reached a significant turning point in her office.

During that year, Jason and I sat side by side on the couch in Aline's now-familiar therapy room. One day, she asked me to imagine a scene with Mark. She had me stand up and move to the middle of the room while I described the scene in as much detail as I could remember. I recounted that first night in little Mark's bed with the cowboy sheets and curtains.

"Can you see yourself there? Where exactly are you? Where is he?" Aline coaxed.

"I am lying in the twin bed, and he is on top of me." I almost whispered because the words caught in my throat. I was trembling.

"You're doing great. As you look at sixteen-year-old Liz lying there with him on top of her, what do you want to do? If you could do anything, what do you want to do?" She waited a beat. "You are lying there, and he is on top of you."

"It's hard to breathe. I want to push him off and run out of the room." I surprised myself with those words, because I had never imagined this scene to be any different than how it actually took place.

"Great! Go ahead. Push him off!"

I imagined this in my mind.

"Do it. Use your arms to push him away—literally. Push against the wall. Right here. Use your body." She raised her voice and pounded on the wall.

I braced my legs and pushed on the wall with both arms.

"Use your voice, too. Say words if you have them. Make sounds. Mark is raping you. Keep pushing!"

"Get out of here! Get away from me! Get off of me! STOP!" while I pushed harder against the wall.

"That's great. Keep it up." Then Aline asked, "What are you feeling right now?"

I was breathing hard. "On one hand, I feel silly, but I also feel relieved and angry." I started to cry. "I want to sit down now," I said, caught off-guard by the mix of emotions coursing through me.

"Angry, yes! Can you say the words, 'Mark raped me'?"

I stood there for a moment longer. "I never said that before, but yes, I can see that what Mark did was rape." I sank onto the couch and buried my head in my hands. Just saying that word out loud changed something in me. Initially, I felt deflated and empty, like all the air was gone from my body.

After some time, I sat up straighter and took a breath. I saw Aline, fully present with me.

"Mark raped me. What happened to me was not love; it was rape." Those words were frightening and empowering.

"Yes, you had no choice. You were sixteen years old then, and he had been working on you—grooming you—since you were fourteen. You were taken advantage of by someone bigger, stronger, older, and more powerful than you. You trusted him, and he took advantage of that. He coerced you into having sex with him. That's rape. You were a young, gullible girl. A child. It was not your fault."

I sat back on the couch, with my head in my hands.

Aline spoke softly now. "Look at Jason. See how he's looking at you. What do you see?"

I sat up straighter and saw his face radiating love and concern and complete presence.

"I see Jason's love and care," I said, drained. I let my tears flow.

"Do you want anything from him?" Aline asked.

"I would like him to hold me."

Jason immediately wrapped his long arms around me and whispered in my ear, "You are so strong. You are safe now. So safe." He held me there while I cried.

"You did great, Liz." Aline went on. "What happened to you back then became hard-wired into your body and nervous system, for all these years. This is what makes intimacy feel so threatening. But you can move past this. What you did today is the beginning of changing that wiring. You can begin to increase your window of tolerance for intimacy by slowly gaining a sense of trust and agency over your own body when you are triggered."

*Is there no end to the layers of this?* I wondered.

Slowly Jason and I returned to each other as I became able to allow more closeness. By the end of the year with Aline, Jason and I were exhausted, but we were also healthier. We wanted a break from all the therapy. We wanted to walk on our own and believed we could. Jason thought maybe I had gone as far as I could, at least for now, and he could better accept my limitations and need to move slowly. I was feeling stronger and more open. Things did get better. Not perfect, but easier.

When my high school held its fortieth reunion, I reconnected with Bonnie, Sophie, and Joan. We loved seeing each other and promised ourselves we would stay in touch. It took a few years to make it happen, but eventually we arranged a weekend together at Bonnie's house.

Shortly before this planned weekend, Savannah and I spent a week together in Sanibel. During one leisurely walk along the beach, she asked various questions about my past. Savannah knew the headline about my history with Mark—a teacher of mine in high school had a relationship with me. But that was all she knew. Savannah was an expert at gently eliciting stories, and now that she was older, I was comfortable sharing more with her. I told her the whole story—all of it.

After she heard it all, she stopped walking and hugged me

tightly. "I am so sorry those things happened to you." She reacted immediately and emotionally to just hearing about those events in my life, whereas it took me most of my life to reach such understanding and offer those words to myself. Sharing my story with Savannah opened a channel of raw emotion in her. She overflowed with all the outrage I could not access for myself for so many years.

I find I still cannot adequately access the rage this crucial piece of my history rightly deserves.

Coming from this emotional experience with Savannah, I felt vulnerable entering the mini-reunion with these three high-school friends. I wanted to talk with them about Mark and wasn't sure they had any interest in revisiting those events. I expected to be disappointed. Joan would arrive on Saturday, so Sophie, Bonnie, and I spent Friday together, starting with a laid-back lunch at a nice downtown seafood restaurant overlooking Boston harbor. The mood was upbeat and celebratory.

It took only thirty minutes into lunch before Bonnie said, "Can we talk about Mark Johnson?" She glanced at me. "Would that be all right with you, Liz?"

"Yes! I was hoping we could talk about him. I want to know more about your experience of those years, and what you make of what happened with him and the rest of us." I was relieved it came up so easily.

Sophie immediately replied, "Yes! We need to talk about those times."

Bonnie began. "I think Mark was going though some personal stuff back then. I think for him it was a coming-of-age time, and his relationships with us were innocent. I don't think he had any malicious intent."

Before I could respond to that, Bonnie continued. "First of

all, Liz, we need to acknowledge that your relationship with him was completely different than anything we had. He loved you. You were with him for so many years, for God's sake. Sophie, how many times did you sleep with him? For me, it was just a few."

Sophie said, "For me, it was just the one time, I am pretty certain. I haven't thought much about it since, or think there were any bad consequences for me."

I had to interrupt. "Wow. I'm a little surprised at how easily you brush aside what he did. He was our teacher and he slept with all of us. That is not okay! I'm glad you weren't hurt by it, but I was."

"Yes, it was wrong, I agree. I just don't think he meant to hurt you, Liz. And I am very, very sorry that you were hurt. Please know that." Bonnie assured me, and Sophie nodded.

"Yes, I totally agree, Liz. I can understand how you were more hurt—your relationship was much more intense, and you were so young when it began. I think he was just fooling around with us, but he really did love you. I am sure he slept with us after you two broke up. It was later that summer, but still that was wrong, just messed up. I'm sorry I was a part of it."

Bonnie sat upright. "Oh, I just remembered that strip club Mark took a bunch of us to once. You guys were there. I am pretty sure it was during our junior year. It was way before Sophie or I slept with him. I remember this because they had a two-drink minimum, and I ordered martinis. I guess I thought that was cool. This was all underage drinking, so I went all out. They brought two of them together, and I drank them down kind of fast."

"What was Mark even doing taking us to a strip club?" Sophie asked. "And letting us drink?"

"I am starting to remember this now," I said slowly, as

some tendrils of fog slipped away from my brain. "I can see us sitting around a table, although I'm not sure who all was there. I also don't clearly remember seeing women strip, but I can picture a stage, and it being dark."

Bonnie added, "Well, I remember getting sick to my stomach on the drive home. Mark had to pull over to the side of the road for me to open the car door and puke onto the road. That was really unpleasant! Sheesh."

"I guess it says something that he took a bunch of sixteen-year-old girls to a strip club. I wonder how he got us in. Maybe it was easier back then." Sophie shook her head.

Bonnie repeated, "Still, I firmly believe he was confused and trying to figure out his life. He didn't mean any harm to anyone. I know you were hurt by what happened, Liz, and that is bad—awful, terrible—but I know he didn't think he was hurting you."

Bonnie's defense of Mark hurt and disappointed me, but I didn't direct the testiness in what I said next to Bonnie, but to the no-longer-alive Mark.

"I can't imagine how he didn't know it was something that would hurt me. Real love would not allow a thirty-something-year-old married man with children to begin cultivating a five-year-long relationship with a student he first met when she was fourteen years old. That is not love, I am certain. It took most of my adult years to come to that awareness. He was in a position of power and authority, and he took advantage of my innocence and isolation as a teenager—really a child—in order to have sex with me. That's rape."

My voice tightened, so I took a breath. Because of my work with Aline, I could now say those words out loud. "And it burns me now that Mark went to his grave without hearing me tell him how much he harmed me. I wonder if he had relationships with other girls after us. That would make me so mad!" We had learned of Mark's death back at the fortieth reunion, but none of us knew the circumstances of his death.

"Yes, that would be wrong too, and I hope he didn't. I don't think he did, but what do I know? You could only do what you could do at that time. It wasn't your fault." Bonnie tried to reassure me.

"I know none of it was my fault." I sighed.

"I am so sorry for what happened with you. Regardless of how he might have felt about you, it was wrong," Sophie said.

It was such a relief to talk openly with these women. They are the only people who witnessed that part of my life, and it was validating—so validating—to talk about it with them. It made my past feel real to me. It made me real to myself.

The next day Joan arrived just before lunchtime. As we sat and passed platters of spinach salad and sandwich makings around the table, Joan smiled and said, "Can we please talk about the elephant in the room?" I was thankful; she spoke so little about her relationship with Mark, and I was eager to hear what she had to say.

Bonnie began, "Joan, you had a long relationship with Mark, right? In college? How long did it last? How did it start?"

"It was fine . . . for a while. He made me feel special. It was kind of a compliment that he would travel four hours each way just to see me. But by sophomore year, I wanted to have my own college experiences, and I told him not to visit anymore, which pretty much ended it. I think he knew it wasn't going to last forever. I don't think I saw him after that."

Joan looked at me. "But, Liz, it was you he really loved. He loved you a lot. There is no doubt. It was different with me.

Sure, maybe he loved me, too. But not like you. I think he wanted to marry you. Not to say a relationship that started with a four-teen-year-old girl wasn't all wrong. It was *definitely* wrong!"

"I still believe he didn't *know* it was wrong," Bonnie insisted. "But, it *was* wrong, no doubt about that."

I shook my head, dazed. These three women all said the same thing. For them, the wrongness of Mark's relationship with me was conceptual, not emotional or visceral, as it was for me. What they saw as love was missing the betrayal, hurt, and damage. They downplayed that he systematically preyed upon me, groomed me for years, took advantage of my trust, seduced me, and coerced me to have sex with him multiple times during my adolescence. Knowing I was lonely and vulnerable, he allowed the transaction of attention in exchange for sex to take place.

I wasn't angry with them for not understanding. There was no tension among us at all. Rather, the conversation was such a gift to me, rounding out some of the fuzzier corners of my memory. But more than information, it was the cleansing process of talking it through with those friends who were there during those years. Talking about Mark with them validated my experience as being real. Of course, I knew it was real, but now it existed outside of just my mind and memory. It took my past out of the cloak of secrecy and isolation that characterized it back then and shone a light on it. This hidden part of me was now seen.

If I am seen, I exist. I am forever grateful to these friends for their generosity and kindness in helping me close the circle of what had launched me into young adulthood so damaged, so confused.

The weekend together helped bring a kind of peace to my heart that only they could have done.

*thirty-two*

## SABBATICAL, BUDDHISM, AND REBIRTH

I KNEW I NEEDED A SABBATICAL FROM EL HOGAR LONG BEFORE I asked for one. Even though I loved and identified with my job, I was run down and desperately needed a break. My sabbatical goal was to reconstruct my life and myself through rest, exercise, time alone, writing, meditating, and reading. I wanted time to connect with my husband, nurture my family and friendships, and think about who I wanted to be for this next and last chapter of my life. Over the past fifteen years, I had unconsciously given away all these things to El Hogar, and I needed to restore them all.

The first of my sabbatical activities was a trip to Spain with Savannah to walk part of El Camino, the pilgrim trail across Spain. Shouldering our large packs, we walked along wooded trails, resting over lunch in sun-drenched cafés and, at the end of a twelve-mile day, soaking in a welcome warm bath. For me, those five days with Savannah were about as pure gold as one can experience. My beautiful daughter and I walked, talked, laughed, listened, and loved.

When I returned from Spain, I spent glorious time alone in Sanibel and dedicated myself to writing. Taking long walks, breathing in sunlight, air, and nature, I loved the freedom to do whatever I wanted with my time. Once back in Massachusetts, Rose introduced me to kayaking, and she and I traipsed off to lakes and rivers all over New England, paddling and talking.

During the sabbatical, I made an immeasurably important discovery: a book, *Running on Empty*, by psychologist Jonice Webb.

Focusing on the impact of emotional neglect in childhood, it is full of case studies of people who experienced *exactly* what I felt my whole life. I read about people who cannot make decisions, cannot feel emotions, don't know what they like or want, who withdraw or dissociate in the face of conflict, who have trouble with intimate relationships (like marriage). People who are not fully present. Me! The root of these behaviors stems from not being seen, not having enough emotional needs met during one's childhood—a condition termed Childhood Emotional Neglect (CEN) syndrome.

> Dr. Webb's website describes CEN: "It's a failure to notice, attend to, or respond appropriately to a child's feelings. Because it's an *act of omission*, it's not visible, noticeable or memorable. Emotional Neglect is the white space in the family picture; the background rather than the foreground. It is insidious and overlooked while it does its silent damage to people's lives . . . Children who are emotionally neglected then grow up to have a particular set of struggles. Because their emotions were not validated as children, they may have difficulty knowing and trusting their own emotions as adults. They may have difficulty understanding their own feelings, as well as others'. Because an important part of themselves (their emotional self) has been denied, they may find themselves feeling disconnected, unfulfilled or empty.

They may have difficulty trusting or relying upon others. Many describe feeling that they are different from other people; like something is wrong with them, but they're not sure what it is."

This book crystalized what many years of therapy taught me and put it into clear focus, with a name. It was liberating!

Another gift of my sabbatical was a deeper commitment to a formal sitting meditation practice. One day I returned from a multiday, silent Buddhist retreat, and Jason asked me how it was.

"I have found my spiritual home," I said through quiet tears.

I immersed myself in Buddhist readings, talks, retreats, and daily practice, and I joined a Buddhist practice group called a *sangha*, a word which means "community." The self-compassion aspect of mindfulness offered rich new territory for me to explore. I slowly softened a lifetime behavior of ignoring my needs, devaluing my worth, and ruminating and catastrophizing over events I cannot control.

As Buddhist practice and meditation became my anchor, I began to be more connected to myself, more embodied. I became more aware in real time of what I was experiencing. I developed a broader field of vision, reminding myself I am more than a specific thought, emotion, or belief. I understood that life has uncertainty, and life worked better when I didn't resist change. When life brought something difficult, I knew I could apply that non-intuitive yet powerful Buddhist principle of leaning into pain, rather than pushing it away. Listening, feeling empathy, compassion, and a connection with people all came more easily when I slowed down enough to be in the present moment. I became a better advocate for myself, knowing I deserve to have my opinions, emotions, and preferences and not to erase them before they even have life. I learned there is joy, always available, waiting for me to embrace it.

Ironically, Buddhist practice also helped me come to terms with Christianity. Buddhism helped me see past my disappointments in Christianity so I could relax more and see the similarities in these two traditions. The religion I was born into—Christianity—became more comfortable than in the past, even while I sat in the heart of Buddhist practice. God's loving presence in every moment became even more accessible and tangible to me.

Those days of sabbatical—and all the years of therapy leading up to them—were like emerging from a cryostasis chamber, where I had been slumbering in a state of numbness since I was a child. I climbed out and discovered the beauty around me, and I found love in my heart, strength in my body, and peace in my being.

I cry for that self of mine whose heart entered that chamber so many years ago. I cry, and I can now hold her in my arms and whisper in her ear, "It will be all right. I am here with you now. Now we are a pair, and I've got your back."

Two years after this sabbatical, I retired from El Hogar. One of the gifts of being "retired" is that I could spend longer stretches of time in Sanibel, escaping the Boston winter. Jason often visited on weekends.

We have been through a lot and our relationship still has stuck places, but it is light years from our dance of despair over too many soul-numbing years. All those years in therapy and hard-earned lessons in what we can and cannot change by sheer will, combined with what I consider a spiritual awakening, have fundamentally changed and healed me.

This change impacts all my relationships, but most importantly, my relationship with my husband. He stood by me through years of dissociation, distancing, confusion, and denial. He learned about his delusions, too, and the ways he contributed to our dance.

Today I can look him in the eye and drink him in. I can allow him his feelings and not take them on as my responsibility, and he can do the same. We can sit companionably on the beach, read our respective books, and not sit in tension and fear. Today I know what I want and am eager to assert my own desires. Since this is something Jason has wanted for so long, he is delighted to comply. We agonize less over how to express our love to each other. Today I am not afraid to tell him how much I miss him when we are apart. Today, I want to climb into his soul to be sure he sees and feels my love.

"Am I still 'the light of your life and the joy of your heart'?" I asked one day as we walked on the beach. He hadn't said this beautiful phrase to me in many years. There was a time he had said it nearly every day. Back then, I hadn't known how to understand or receive the feelings behind that sentiment, and as much as I loved it, it also made me anxious.

"Of course. Why do you ask such a thing?" Jason replied with a touch of concern.

"Because you never say it anymore."

"I stopped saying it because it scared you away." I sensed the sadness behind his words, yet I didn't take it as being my fault, and I didn't fall into an internal collapse of shame.

Instead, I faced him and held both his hands in mine. "I want you to know this. I'm not afraid anymore."

# afterword

I see how a human lifetime is a cycle of many small deaths and then rebirths, each followed eventually by another. I know the path to freedom is to face and befriend whatever life brings and pick myself up and begin again, each time stronger and wiser. I call this "waking up for life."

The crucial ingredient in this cycle is seeing and accepting the truth of *what is*. This has been so excruciatingly difficult for me, yet I know it is the key to it all, the essential piece to living a wholehearted and fulfilled life. My life was molded by secrets, lies, and deceptions, including deceiving myself. The work of my lifetime is to remember to put down the armor of delusion and to love myself enough to accept what is so and to accept who I am. When I forget, which I do with some great frequency, meditation invites me to remember again. Meditation, the key to cultivating awareness, is what uncovers the truth for me and brings the courage and compassion needed to face it directly.

Practicing this repeatedly is what sets us free. I am deeply grateful for the chance to be here, falling and rising, loving rather than judging, and knowing how to begin again. My gratitude compels me to bring others to the path of healing and freedom. After years of study and training, I now teach mindfulness meditation, and it brings me joy to practice, study, and offer to others this ancient path of wisdom, compassion, and liberation.

THE GUEST HOUSE

*This being human is a guest house.*
*Every morning a new arrival.*
*A joy, a depression, a meanness,*
*some momentary awareness comes*
*as an unexpected visitor.*
*Welcome and entertain them all!*
*Even if they are a crowd of sorrows,*
*who violently sweep your house*
*empty of its furniture,*
*still, treat each guest honorably.*
*He may be clearing you out*
*for some new delight.*
*The dark thought, the shame, the malice,*
*meet them at the door laughing and invite them in.*
*Be grateful for whatever comes,*
*because each has been sent*
*as a guide from beyond.*

—JELAL AL-DIN RUMI,
translation by Coleman Barks

1. The various factors that fed into Liz's sense of having no self-worth included her strict Christian upbringing, emotionally distant parents and siblings, few childhood friends, exploitation by a trusted adult, a disappointing first marriage, a relationship that ended unexpectedly, and a second marriage that asked for more than she had to give. What were the factors that restored her sense of self-worth?

2. What was the role of secrecy in Liz's story? How did it help? How did it hurt?

3. How might things have been different if Liz had confided in someone earlier in her relationship with Mark? What might people—the school, parents, siblings, and friends— have done at the time to help Liz see the potential dangers of her relationship with Mark? What can schools do today to raise awareness of the perils of unequal power dynamics in a relationship?

4. How do you think Liz really felt about Mark? Did she love him, or just that he made her feel special? Do you think Mark really loved Liz?

5. Liz portrays her childhood as lonely. How do you think the conditions that made her feel this way influenced her later years?

6. Do you think at age sixteen, and after two years of grooming, Liz was able to give consent? What does 'consent' mean to you?

7. Liz had many relationships as a young adult. How were they characterized?

8. What role does sex play in her wounding and her healing?

9. Liz says, "In more ways than I can count, being a mother saved me." What did she mean by this? What are some of these ways?

10. What is the role of religion and spirituality in Liz's story? How did it help and/or hurt her?

11. What were some of the other factors that led to Liz's healing? Do you think healing is ever complete?

# RESOURCES

———

To learn more about my meditation teaching, a list of mindfulness resources, and my blog, visit www.lizkinchen.com.

To learn more about CEN (childhood emotional neglect), visit
https://drjonicewebb.com/about-emotional-neglect.

# ACKNOWLEDGMENTS

———

In so many ways, this book has been a birthing experience. Like giving birth, there are ways it takes a village, and in some ways one does it alone. The earliest versions of this book began as a gentle suggestion from my deeply wise and compassionate therapist, Patricia, to use writing as a way to open doors to the past. Pat, you have helped me in more ways than I can say, not just to begin the process of creating this book, but to lead me on the path to birthing myself. Thank you. Similarly, thanks go to my therapist, Aline, who brought out my courage.

For all the spiritual friends and guides in my life: my karate sensei, Hidy Ochiai; priests Rob O'Neill and Thomas Brown; spiritual director Sarah Rossiter; my many Buddhist teachers, including Tara Brach, Jack Kornfield, Pema Chodron, Joseph Goldstein, Sharon Salzberg, my sangha teacher, Nina Carmel; and my beautiful sangha members. Thank you.

Thanks to my sister-in-law, Jennifer Bright, for connecting me with the perfect editor for those early drafts, Elizabeth Bartasius, who helped me wrangle way too many pages of words into the story that wanted to be told. She and her team guided and cheered me through later edits, as did Emma Peters.

My very first writing group, led by Elisabeth Carter, helped me see myself as a writer. Teachers and fellow writers from Grub St. Boston provided guidance and support, showing me the power of community for writers.

Thanks go to my circle of beta readers, for your time, perspective, and undying faith and support: Nancy Bain, Diane Cullen, Nancy Nies, Sarah Rossiter, and Rose Zimering.

Two of my most faithful supporters, who read multiple drafts and provided not only narrative help but, more importantly, the emotional support and affirmation I needed so many times over these years, were my beautiful and steady husband, Jason, and my insightful and infinitely kind daughter, Savannah Kinchen.

Of course, you wouldn't be reading this book now if it weren't for my publishing, marketing, and publicity team. Thank you, Brooke Warner, Samantha Strom, Lorraine White, and others at She Writes Press, for believing in me and giving my book the chance to meet the world. Dan Blank, at WeGrow-Media, you showed me how to think and talk about my story in ways people could access. There is little point in writing and publishing a book if no one will find it. You and my publicity team at Books Forward, especially Corinne Pritchett, provided immeasurable help in making those connections. Appreciation also to my re-found friend and colleague, Candy Coakley, who generously helped with the home stretch.

My village is not complete without the rest of my supportive extended family—I love you all!

Lastly, I am humbly grateful for my mindfulness practice, which continues to lead me to greater peace, joy, and freedom.

# ABOUT THE AUTHOR

Liz Kinchen is a writer, meditation teacher, and Buddhist practitioner. Her life is an interwoven tapestry of writing, healing from abuse, and spiritual journey. Her debut memoir, *Light in Bandaged Places*, portrays the creation of this tapestry, from childhood loneliness, young betrayal, and the journey to wholeness. With graduate degrees in computer science and counseling psychology, she worked in software development management for twenty-one years before moving into the nonprofit sector for seventeen years as executive director of a small organization working with underserved children and families in Honduras. Her passions are loving her family, meditating, teaching mindfulness, writing, talking with close friends, and walking in nature. She is a contributing author to the anthology, *Art in the Time of Unbearable Crisis*, published by She Writes Press in 2022. Liz lives in the greater Boston area with her husband of over thirty years, with whom she raised three beautiful children, and she happily spends significant time on Sanibel Island, Florida. Find her at www.lizkinchen.com/author and information about her teaching at www.lizkinchen.com.

## SELECTED TITLES FROM SHE WRITES PRESS

She Writes Press is an independent publishing company
founded to serve women writers everywhere.
Visit us at www.shewritespress.com.

*Baffled by Love: Stories of the Lasting Impact of Childhood Trauma Inflicted by Loved Ones* by Laurie Kahn. $16.95, 978-1-63152-226-0. For three decades, Laurie Kahn has treated clients who were abused as children—people who were injured by someone who professed to love them. Here, she shares stories from her own rocky childhood along with those of her clients, weaving a textured tale of the all-too-human search for the "good kind of love."

*Now I Can See The Moon: A Story of a Social Panic, False Memories, and a Life Cut Short* by Alice Tallmadge. $16.95, 978-1-63152-330-4. A first-person account from inside the bizarre and life-shattering social panic over child sex abuse that swept through the US in the 1980s—and affected Alice Tallmadge's family in a personal, devastating way.

*Say It Out Loud: Revealing and Healing the Scars of Sexual Abuse* by Roberta Dolan. $16.95, 978-1-938314-99-5. An in-depth guide to healing the wounds caused by sexual abuse, written by a survivor who's lived the process firsthand.

*Singing with the Sirens: Overcoming the Long-Term Effects of Childhood Sexual Exploitation* by Ellyn Bell and Stacey Bell. $16.95, 978-1-63152-936-8. With metaphors of sea creatures and the force of the ocean as a backdrop, this work addresses the problems of sexual abuse and exploitation of young girls, taking the reader on a poetic journey toward finding healing from within.

*Fourteen: A Daughter's Memoir of Adventure, Sailing, and Survival* by Leslie Johansen Nack. $16.95, 978-1-63152-941-2. A coming-of-age adventure story about a young girl who comes into her own power, fights back against abuse, becomes an accomplished sailor, and falls in love with the ocean and the natural world.

*No Rules: A Memoir* by Sharon Dukett. $16.95, 978-1-63152-856-9. At sixteen, Sharon leaves home to escape the limited life her Catholic parents have planned for her because she's a girl—and finds herself thrown into the 1970s counterculture, an adult world for which she is unprepared.